JEROEN DOBBELAERE, ALICE SCHMIDT,
FLORIAN SCHÜTZ, CLAUDIA WINKLER

Fast Forward

How to Harness the Power of AI for Societal Progress and a Sustainable Future

First edition

Illustration by The book cover was created using state-of-the-art AI technologies. The generative AI software Midjourney was employed to produce the visual components for the book cover.

This book was professionally typeset on Reedsy.
Find out more at reedsy.com

To our amazing children Arthur, Carla, Juno and Luis – may they grow up into a world that manages to achieve health, wealth and well-being for all in ways facilitated by ethical and responsible AI.

Contents

Introduction

It all started on a chilly January morning in one of our favourite coffee houses in Vienna, where we – the four co-authors of this book – love to meet to exchange ideas. As friends and colleagues with children of similar ages, we enjoy spending time together. We find our diverse backgrounds enable us to draw new lines of insight and inspiration. Our friendship blossomed over the first book Alice and Claudia wrote together, *The Sustainability Puzzle: How Systems Thinking, Circularity, Climate Action and Social Transformation Can Improve Health, Wealth and* Wellbeing *for All.* During the writing process, Alice and Claudia's partners Jeroen and Florian supported them in a variety of ways, ranging from intellectual sparring to childcare. This time around, Alice and Claudia decided to bring on their partners more fully. Expanding the writing team to four members allowed us to broaden our range of expertise beyond the fields of business management, impact entrepreneurship, social development, and sustainability to include software engineering, artificial intelligence, and cell biology. This in turn made our discussions and debates even more heated, controversial, and thought-provoking.

As we sipped our hot coffees and discussed the latest developments in the world, AI kept coming up as a topic that was dominating headlines. We were seeing a lot of hype around it, triggered by the public release of ChatGPT in 2022, and we were very curious to understand, or at least gauge, what this would mean for society and the topic of sustainability more broadly. We brought to the table diverse points of view and backgrounds – from social innovation to AI, from life sciences to gender, from climate activism to art and architecture. We knew that by discussing and debating ideas and developments from a multidisciplinary perspective, we could uncover new and exciting viewpoints on the topic. The sum would be greater than its parts. As we researched and discussed the issues in more detail, it quickly became apparent that our insights should be turned into a book. After all, we reasoned, many others are trying to make sense of these same questions, and we wanted to help them see the bigger picture of artificial intelligence and technological innovation in the context of a changing world that needs sustainable transformation.

Why we care

One question, of course, is: Why us? As sustainability and impact professionals, we care deeply about the state of the planet and its people everywhere. As parents in particular, we care greatly not just about our own future but about that of our children too – and hopefully someday that of our grandchildren. With the rapidly evolving world of AI, this concern has become even more pressing. We have seen firsthand how AI is affecting education and job prospects, and we have closely followed debates about power, politics, and potential rules in what is still largely uncharted territory. We are now more convinced than ever that it is crucial for people from all disciplines to get involved in shaping the future of technology. As Alice and Claudia stated in their previous book *The Sustainability Puzzle*, we know that technology is an essential puzzle piece in sustainable transformation, and we are passionate about the magic that can unfold once the full potential of tech to help achieve social and environmental objectives as outlined in the Sustainable Development Goals is fully understood and prioritised. However, we are acutely aware that a blind trust in technology in a context dominated by entrenched structures and systems constraints could rapidly lead us down the wrong path.

Over the past months of delving deeper into this topic, we came to understand the urgency of changing the way we think about technology and its role in society. We saw the world of technology advancing at an unprecedented pace. We realised that if we and other like-minded experts fail to take action now, there is a real risk that many people on this globe will be left even further behind.

Early in the research phase for this book, we often found ourselves split on either side of a heated debate, essentially echoing the two factions of thought leadership in the AI community – the doomsters and the optimists. This conflict had been brewing for years; but as authors in a collective exploring the potential of AI, we were committed to understanding both perspectives in order to navigate the complex landscape of artificial intelligence. Initially, this was rather challenging, as the four of us come from different disciplines, and consequently take dissimilar approaches towards technology. Based on their backgrounds in sustainability and science, Alice and Jeroen were inclined toward a rather cautionary approach, warning of techno-romanticism. Florian and Claudia, on the other hand, based on their experience in the tech and innovation fields, tended to support a more optimistic view. Given that new insights supporting both viewpoints were being published on a daily if not hourly basis, our discussions were quite frequently intense.

Over time, we came to appreciate one another's perspectives. It was evident that both the doomsters and the optimists had valid concerns, and that simplifying arguments without a bigger-picture lens could lead to dangerous conclusions on both sides. It quickly became clear that instead of advocating a course drawn from either extreme – that is, either letting AI developments proceed unchecked or stopping development altogether – a more nuanced approach was needed. Our aspiration as authors in this collective was not to take sides, but rather to strive for a holistic understanding of the potential risks and rewards of AI. In our quest to reach a conclusion we could all share wholeheartedly, we realised the key lay in fostering open and honest dialogue between both opinions, while continuing to ask uncomfortable questions. To start building bridges, gain a deeper understanding, test our emerging insights, and broaden our horizon to encompass other disciplines, we launched a series of real-life dinners and virtual café debate sessions focusing on AI's ethical, social, and environmental implications. These discussions helped us draw our own conclusions, blending the cautionary wisdom of the doomsters with the innovative spirit of the optimists. Over time, we started to see a more unified, balanced perspective on AI emerge within our writing collective, moving far from the more black-and-white positions we had initially taken.

As a popular management saying often attributed to Albert Einstein states, "If I had an hour to solve a problem, I'd spend 55 minutes thinking about the problem and five minutes thinking about solutions."[1] This is exactly what we have done in writing this book. Over a six-month period, we spent a good chunk of our time researching and discussing the topic and building up insights based on our specific perspectives and experiences. In the process, we explored many emerging AI tools, from large language models like ChatGPT to image generation tools like Dall-E and Midjourney, as well as others. We did this because we were curious, but also because we wanted to experience these tools in practice before discussing them at a more theoretical level. Initially we had planned to make ChatGPT our fifth co-author in this book. While it did assist us in the process – in some places more than others – we ultimately decided that treating it as an actual co-author did not work due to its well-known deficiencies.

As we wrote, we constantly challenged and pushed each other, making sure that our ideas were well-researched, balanced, and thought-provoking. We believe that the solutions to the challenges of the future require broad, cross-disciplinary thinking and doing, and we did our best to put this ethic into practice at the micro level.

This is also one of the main messages of this book: Don't leave AI solely to the techies. If AI models are to create more benefits than problems, and facilitate rather than undermine a sustainable transformation, they will need to be co-designed and co-created by experts in the fields of social justice and environmental sustainability, economists, political scientists, and specialists from many other disciplines. And this list must extend beyond formal experts; it should also include everyday users – especially those who are marginalised, those who to date have been barred from using sophisticated digital technology, and those who have not been previously included in (biased) datasets.

A journey into the future

In this book, we explore the urgent need for change in the way we think about AI and its role in society through personal anecdotes and expert insights. We try to cover it all: From the disconnect between current perceptions and the urgent need to act, to the impact of AI on society, to the importance of working actively to shape our technological advancements. We also discuss the potential for AI to drive sustainable change, not just in terms of economic growth, but also in terms of ecological and social well-being.

The path ahead is one of magic and surprise, but will also be full of stumbling blocks and challenges. It is a journey we must embark on without delay. We hope our work can help bring about positive change and understanding across disciplines. In Chapter 1 of this book, we address the critical relationship between AI and sustainability, exploring why these two themes must not be considered in isolation. In Chapter 2, we discuss the basics of AI, including some key risks and challenges. Beginning in Chapter 3, we go into more detail and discuss the relationship between AI and social issues. Here, for example, we explain how losing a leg might even prove to be advantageous. Chapter 4 focuses on the world of work, challenging us to adopt new mental frameworks in thinking about jobs. Chapter 5 looks at the use of AI in the fields of education and science. Here, for example, we explain how teachers in some Chinese schools are already monitoring their students' brain signals. The ecological footprint of AI is discussed in Chapter 6, along with the many opportunities to use AI for ecosystem protection and restoration. For example, we explain there how AI can help address nature's "measurement problem". In chapters 7 and 8 we move to a different level, discussing AI ethics and the principles of responsible AI before moving to AI's darker side, such as its use for the purposes of misinformation, election manipulation, government surveillance, cybercrime, warfare, and other abuses of power. There, we discuss how AI can recognise gay men, and relate the story of an incident in which people were asked to "celebrate Holocaust" with a cheeseburger. In Chapter 9 we present some of our conclusions, point a way forward, and offer recommendations for readers interested in continuing their engagement with the subject. An AI glossary is at the end.

You have almost certainly heard stories about how AI is going to change the world, whether for good or for worse. It's important to remember that for many people, change is often scary, given the many unknowns that must be confronted. Today we may be facing a turning point as important as the industrial revolution, a time when the world was forever changed by the rise of machines. For individuals then, and the generations that were to come, that was a time of great uncertainty and transformational change. The same is true today. Thus, it is not a question of whether or not we should embrace AI, but rather a question of how quickly we accept that change is happening and take commensurate action. If we fail to act wisely now, and do not actively shape the development and implementation of this technology, we risk creating a future where it is misused, leading to unintended consequences such as job displacement, privacy violations, accelerating climate change and biodiversity loss, and even greater inequality.

As technology advances at an unprecedented pace, it is crucial that we all take responsibility for shaping a positive future. Join us on this journey and discover how we can harness the power of AI to create a better world for all. As we wrote this book, we couldn't help but feel a sense of excitement and hope, itching to put our ideas into practice. We knew that by sharing our findings and insights, we could help others understand the potential of AI for a better world. We wanted to create a book that was not only informative but also relatable and accessible to everyone. This is why this book is not only rooted in facts and research but also in our personal experiences and emotions.

We are therefore proud today to present "Fast Forward: How to Harness the Power of AI for Societal Progress and a Sustainable Future" to you. Whether you're a business leader, a policymaker, or simply someone curious about the future, this book is for you. You may be a tech expert who has had little time to think about the sustainability of development so far, or a social development and sustainability expert who feels rather removed from the world of tech. At the same time, you may be a parent or concerned citizen who feels they simply need to get up to speed.

Our goal is to empower you with the knowledge and inspiration to actively shape the future of AI in a way that improves health, wealth, and well-being for all. We invite you to join us on this journey and discover how we can harness the power of AI to create a better future!

Chapter 1: AI – Friend or foe?

Don't ask if artificial intelligence is good or fair, ask how it shifts power
Pratusyha Kalluri, computer scientist at Stanford University[2]

Are you ready to cross The Line?

Have you heard about The Line, Saudi Arabia's latest giga-project? This AI-driven "vertical city" to be built into the desert aims to redefine the concept of urban development, transforming our vision of the cities of the future. Doing justice to its name, the city is planned as a narrow "line" 170 kilometres long and 200 metres wide, covered by mirrors on both sides. From the outside, the mirrors would make it blend into its scenic natural environment. The mirrors would also reflect heat, reducing temperatures inside. While giving the impression of a very horizontal city from the outside, it is designed internally as a "vertical city" built systematically on several levels, leaving room for abundant greenspace. Its developers emphasise The Line's minimal footprint and its minimal impact on the surrounding ecosystems. They have grand ambitions, marketing it as a "civilisational revolution that puts humans first, providing an unprecedented urban living experience while preserving the surrounding nature".[3] According to glossy brochures, it will be a place where "humanity progresses without compromise to the health of the planet".[4] As if this weren't enough, there are also plans for glow-in-the-dark beaches and ski slopes close by, as well as an artificial moon, robot butlers, and flying taxis.[5]

But hold on. How sustainable can a gigantic building project in the desert actually be? And even if its ecological footprint were to be minimised, do we have any reason to assume The Line will benefit people other than wealthy elites? What about upholding the human rights of human labourers in a country that is not exactly known for providing ideal working conditions for migrant workers?[6] And what about The Line's prospects for democracy? After all, it is situated within NEOM, a special economic zone that is designed to exist "entirely outside the confines of the current Saudi judicial system, governed by an autonomous legal system that will be drafted up by investors."[7]

Some of the ideas behind The Line – expressing the fanciful visions affordable to immensely wealthy Arab leaders – are very compelling. Its basic sustainability premise is that cities need to be condensed in order to minimise their footprint on the land. The Line adheres to the vision of a car- and carbon-free city for 9 million inhabitants that would allow daily needs to be satisfied with just a five-minute walk or bicycle trip. A hyper-speed train is planned that would provide end-to-end connections in just 20 minutes. The Line promises to be pollution-free and protected from desert winds; its designers say it will offer pleasant temperatures, and feature numerous AI-driven services enhancing residents' quality of life. They say that unlike in traditional cities, people's health and well-being would be prioritised over transportation and infrastructure concerns. Its developers also promise that The Line will run on 100% renewable energy, and that 95% of the territory and its surrounding area will be preserved for nature.

While The Line is a fascinating idea and its widely-propagated designs are visually mind-blowing, building of the project has only just begun. There are many reasons to be sceptical about it, ranging from unresolved environmental and social justice issues to concerns about surveillance and governance more broadly. In many ways, its uncertain future illustrates key points we are going to make in this book about AI. Just like the AI revolution more generally, The Line is visionary and inspired by fanciful ideas of what a sustainable future powered by AI could look like. AI has played a big role in the project's design, and will continue to play a big role in its future construction and operation. We do need big ideas such as The Line to revolutionise how we will live, work, and travel on this planet. The Line's design demonstrates the potential of AI to help us address climate change, reduce our environmental footprint, and be resilient in the face of harsh climatic conditions. AI can also help us include and connect people in ways never experienced before, for example by facilitating the 15-minute-city concept that brings people and communities closer together.

However, thinking big is not enough, and good intentions do not always produce fair outcomes. We must not employ fancy AI models or other digital tools simply because they are available. We must couple grand ambitions with a clear commitment to maximising health, wealth, and well-being for all, not just a privileged few. This will not succeed without including experts in the field of sustainable transformation, social inclusion, and impact measurement, to name but a few. Moreover, we must track the results – both intended results and unintended side-effects – and design for sustainable development rather than using innovative technology for its own sake, or because it may bring profits and power. It should be noted that the implications of creating a state that is "designed, constructed, and independently administered in a way that is free from outdated economic and environmental infrastructure that constrains other countries across the world" are risky at best.[8] So too is relying on an autonomous legal system that will be drafted by investors. Regulation, driven by governments that enjoy full democratic support, is actually an essential piece of the sustainability puzzle. Some analysts believe that NEOM and The Line will place a low priority on democracy and civil liberties, and will instead use Chinese technology to place residents under conditions of total surveillance.[9] And that's before malicious actors come into the picture.

The ambition of The Line is to link the ecological sustainability and digitalisation agendas. As we argue in this book, this is a vitally important objective. In so doing, The Line may serve as a test case for a revolution in AI-powered city planning. Yet whether it will be a true demonstration of a socially and ecologically sustainable urban revolution, or just another demonstration of oil wealth spurring extravagance, remains to be seen.

From niche to mainstream

Have you ever wondered how artificial intelligence, a technology once considered mysterious and obscure, previously confined to the realms of experts, scientists, nerds, and science fiction movies, has so rapidly become an integral part of our daily lives? How did what was not long ago a far-off dream of the future make it to our doorstep so quickly, and become an essential part of many people's realities?

By AI, we mean computer systems performing tasks that traditionally require human intelligence, such as visual perception, speech recognition, decision-making, or language translation.[10] As we explain in more detail in Chapter 2, in this book we focus on applications related to machine learning, natural-language processing, and robotics. The current hype around AI has helped many people understand that AI has the potential to be a transformative force, with the ability to revolutionise various industries and aspects of daily life. At the time of our writing, for example, the ChatGPT AI application had already become the fastest-growing consumer internet app in history, reaching 100 million users worldwide within less than three months of its release.[11]

Nowadays, AI is not only a reality, but is also rapidly becoming an integral part of our daily lives. Even those working in seemingly unrelated fields are beginning to grasp its importance. For instance, Alice never imagined she would have to deal with AI in her professional life. However, after realising that leaving AI to techies would be very risky, as this would limit its potential to improve health, wealth, and well-being for all, she delved into the topic to understand how we might all help shape this technology for the better. Today, she is not only very engaged in the topic, but is also encouraging experts from other disciplines to get involved.

Conversations about AI are emerging in every corner of our lives. In schools, debates are taking place about generative AI tools like ChatGPT and its impact on learning. In the entertainment sector, fake Kanye West and Drake songs generated by AI have generated torrents of discussion on social media, and an AI-generated image of Pope Francis in a fashionable long puffer jacket (white, of course!) created a global internet storm. These developments raise questions about AI technologies and the accelerating danger that misinformation may influence our lives. The impact of AI on the job market is also a new favourite topic of discussion at dinner tables worldwide. Moreover, discussions of the environmental impact of AI, including its carbon footprint, have expanded beyond expert circles and are now frequently found in the mainstream media.

As everyday individuals, we are often simply fascinated by cool new tools and technologies. While most people would not call themselves AI experts, it is interesting and encouraging that more and more groups and individuals are starting to engage with the issue as they sense something is about to change. Many people are beginning to realise that our future may be at stake. Some of the most pressing questions people are asking include: What are the potential benefits and risks of AI? How can we ensure that AI is developed and used in an ethical and responsible manner? What impact will AI have on the job market, and how can we prepare for these changes? And perhaps most importantly: How can we ensure that the benefits of AI are shared by all members of society, rather than just a select few?

The profound impact on our lives and future promised by a single technology has piqued our curiosity. As AI continues to advance, it will be crucial for everyone to participate in shaping its future. AI is no longer a niche topic for a small group of experts, but a critical issue that affects us all. From the way we work and communicate to the way we tackle some of the world's most significant challenges, AI has the potential to profoundly shape our future.

The development of artificial intelligence is often referred to as a revolution, with some experts claiming it has the potential to be as transformative as the invention of the wheel or the printing press, or the use of electric power. This is due to the vast array of industries and aspects of daily life in which AI is already being used to facilitate decision-making, automate processes, and increase efficiency. We see it in such diverse areas as healthcare, finance, and transportation. For example, AI-powered medical devices and software tools are already being used to improve the accuracy of diagnoses and treatments. This is likely to have a great impact on healthcare more broadly, potentially revolutionising the way we diagnose and treat disease, and leading to better patient outcomes. In a different industry, AI algorithms can already analyse financial data to improve investment strategies.

The development of AI also has the potential to create new industries and job opportunities, as well as to increase productivity and economic growth. One of the key advantages of AI is its ability to automate repetitive and mundane tasks, freeing up human workers to focus on more creative and value-adding activities. This in turn could help increase productivity and efficiency, leading to economic growth and job creation. Yet predictions about the future of jobs vary widely, showcasing contrasting perspectives on the likely impact of AI and advanced technologies. On the one hand, the World Economic Forum (WEF) takes a comparatively sobering stance. It foresees significant labour-market disruption within the next five years, with approximately one-quarter of all jobs undergoing changes due to AI, digitisation, and other economic developments. But the WEF study also predicts that new jobs will be created, potentially balancing out the jobs that will be lost due to AI.[12] On the other hand, a recent collaboration between OpenAI, OpenResearch, and the University of Pennsylvania presents a more promising outlook. Their research explores the possible labour-market impact of large language models (LLMs) like ChatGPT that are developing into general-purpose technologies. Findings suggest that around 80% of the US workforce may see at least 10% of their work tasks affected by AI tools such as ChatGPT, and that approximately 19% of workers could experience substantial impact, with at least 50% of their tasks being affected. These divergent studies highlight the ongoing debate surrounding the transformative influence of AI and its potential implications for the future of work.[13] However, as with any technological advancement, there are also downsides and risks associated with AI. There are ethical and societal considerations to take into account. As AI becomes more integrated into various aspects of daily life, the amount of personal data being collected and analysed will increase, raising important questions about how this data is being generated, used, shared, and capitalised upon, and about who has access to it. There are also concerns around bias and fairness in AI algorithms, and about AI's potential to be misused for malicious purposes. This is one reason it is so important to involve people from all sectors and social environments in the further development of this technology, because it is far from certain that all people and all regions of the world will benefit equally.

AI – panic mode on?

Thus, the once-distant dream of artificial intelligence now stands before us, ready to reshape our world. But we must ask ourselves: Will this path lead us to a utopian state of bliss or to civilisational collapse? The notion of rogue AI systems has long been a popular theme in movies and science fiction, as exemplified by characters like HAL from "2001: A Space Odyssey"[14] or the Terminator movie series.[15] The idea of machines becoming increasingly intelligent, to the point where they are beyond our control, is unsettling for many. These cultural portrayals of AI gone awry contribute to a general sense of apprehension among the public about the development of advanced intelligent systems. As AI systems grow more sophisticated and our understanding of them expands, the lack of clarity about the future trajectory of these technologies adds to the uncertainty. People fear what they cannot predict, and the rapidly evolving landscape of AI only serves to amplify this anxiety. AI doomsters capture our attention, particularly if they are well known and powerful. Even Elon Musk, a household name famous for leading Tesla, Twitter, and SpaceX, has called for caution and urged us to tread carefully in this uncharted territory. Should we take his concerns to heart?

To help navigate the current era of artificial intelligence, it is useful to look to history for guidance. From the agricultural revolution to the industrial revolution and beyond, technological advancements have drastically changed society. Each revolution offers valuable lessons that can be applied to the current AI revolution as well. If we go back in history, AI's current impact on society may be compared to that of the printing press, which changed the way information and education was disseminated. AI has the potential to improve access to information and education in a similar way. However, it is important to ensure that AI is developed in a way that is inclusive and equitable, rather than reinforcing existing biases and inequalities. The current developments in the field of AI are also often compared to the industrial revolution, which brought about new and innovative forms of production and labour while at the same time generating environmental harm and poor working conditions, and widening the gap between the wealthy and the working class. To prevent the AI revolution from producing similar negative impacts, it will be essential to establish regulatory frameworks and guidelines promoting the responsible and sustainable use of AI. Additionally, education will play a critical role in ensuring that the workforce is equipped with the skills needed to adapt to the changes brought about by AI.

Historical developments also serve as a warning. The current AI rush, reminiscent of the Cold War-era atomic arms race, reflects a condition of hyper-competition between global powers seeking supremacy. As nations once vied for nuclear advantage, the US, China, and some big tech firms are fiercely competing for AI dominance, driven by the prospect of revolutionising industries, economies, and military capabilities. However, unlike the atomic arms race, AI at least has the potential to transform societies positively. The challenge will lie in placing a top priority on ethics, putting humans first, resisting a further polarisation of power and resources, and avoiding a further exacerbation of global tensions.

While historical lessons can provide valuable insights and inform our decision-making, they alone cannot help us solve what are sometimes referred to in a design or planning context as "wicked problems", such as addressing global social injustice or multiple ecological crises. Wicked problems are complex and multifaceted issues that are difficult to define, let alone solve. By their very nature, they do not have a single, clear-cut solution. Instead, they require ongoing management and adaptation as circumstances change. While it may be difficult to solve a wicked problem completely, it is possible to mitigate its negative impacts and work towards a more positive outcome through careful analysis, collaboration, and ongoing monitoring and evaluation. Doing so requires a systemic and interdisciplinary approach to understanding the problem and identifying potential solutions, and one that balances the needs of different stakeholders. The key is to accept that there is no one-size-fits-all solution, and that solving wicked problems requires ongoing effort and a willingness to adapt and change as new information becomes available.

Piecing together the sustainability puzzle

A vision of a future where vibrant communities thrive, where nature flourishes in harmony with humanity, and where innovation and technology empower us to overcome our greatest challenges is what brought Alice and Claudia together in 2020. Their shared passion and commitment to sustainable development led them to collaborate on *The Sustainability Puzzle*. In that book, they presented an engaging and hopeful vision of a future in which systems thinking, climate action, a circular economy, and the responsible use of technology work together to create global equity and a sustainable transformation. They emphasised the interconnectedness of economic, social, and environmental challenges, as well as the need for a holistic perspective in addressing these issues. As an underlying theme, Alice and Claudia additionally discussed their view that technology is a major piece in solving the sustainability puzzle. If applied responsibly and ethically, and not for their own sake, technologies such as AI have the potential to make a significant contribution to sustainable development across the social, environmental, and economic spheres.

However, technology is not the only essential puzzle piece. Other pieces need to be in place to avoid accelerating environmental degradation, social inequalities, and the risk of mismanaged technology. This is why we need diverse perspectives and voices to join the discussion and work together on piecing together the sustainability puzzle.

Unfortunately, technological development today is led mostly by techies and business leaders. Experts from other disciplines are not commonly involved. The sustainability and digitalisation agendas often appear disconnected, with each domain operating independently without collaboration or even mutual engagement. This siloed approach hinders the creation of synergies that could drive progress across both areas. It is thus crucial to find ways to bridge this gap. One of the primary reasons for this disconnect is the focus on short-term gains and immediate technological results, often at the expense of long-term sustainable development or any consideration of the bigger picture. In the race to innovate and capitalise on emerging digital technologies, their environmental and social consequences are often overlooked. Tech lovers often take for granted that new technological developments will produce advantages, even in the absence of specific research or evidence to prove this. Conversely, public- and private-sector efforts in the sustainability space may not fully embrace the potential of digitalisation to drive more significant and lasting change.

Today's bustling cities, for example, are filled with the latest gadgets and technological innovations. People are eager to adopt the newest smartphones, computers, and smart home devices. But in their pursuit of digital progress, they are inadvertently creating a mounting problem: e-waste. As devices become obsolete or break down, they end up far too quickly in landfills, releasing hazardous materials into the environment. If the digitalisation agenda were more closely aligned with sustainability concerns and circularity campaigns, companies might prioritise the development of longer-lasting, more easily repairable devices, or ensure that facilities for sharing, reuse, refurbishment, and recycling were in place.

Another tale of disconnectedness can be seen in the world of agriculture. Driven by the need to increase crop yields and productivity, farmers have adopted digital tools such as drones, sensors, and satellite imaging to monitor their fields. However, if we fail to consider the environmental impact of these technologies, and instead act on their "advice" without taking a bigger-picture view of sustainable and regenerative agriculture, we risk exacerbating issues like soil degradation, water pollution, and biodiversity loss. If sustainability and digitalisation efforts were more intertwined, farmers might gain access to tools helping them adopt regenerative farming practices, conserve water, and protect ecosystems while still maintaining productivity. To better connect the worlds of technological innovation and sustainable development, we must first recognise the actual and potential links between sustainability and digitalisation. Synergies can be created, but they will not just happen by themselves. Instead, generating synergies requires proactive engagement and concrete action.

Equity, employment, education, and ecology – key pieces of the AI puzzle

By integrating the sustainability and digitalisation agendas, we can create a world in which progress and innovation become synonymous with environmental stewardship and social equity, rather than one in which technological innovation is pursued for its own sake. This is a future we can all strive for, hopeful that our collective efforts will bring about sustainable transformation by unlocking new opportunities for growth, innovation, and resilience.

However, every opportunity comes with risks, and employing AI will not automatically lead to a better future. To actively harness the positive power of AI, we will need to understand its negative impacts too, including in key areas such as work, social justice, education, science, and the environment. Moreover, we must be aware of its dark sides, including its potential uses in warfare and cybercrime. We must understand how it can be used to create and spread misinformation, how it might generate digital divides and biases, and how it can exacerbate the risks of dehumanisation. In many of these areas, the risks and opportunities are in fact interrelated.

These negative outcomes could aggravate existing inequalities and further marginalise vulnerable groups. Yet by ensuring the ethical use of AI, we can harness its power to transform social services such as healthcare, and foster inclusion by dismantling barriers and empowering marginalised communities. For example, AI-driven innovations could help democratise access to high-quality healthcare and education, allowing for a more equitable distribution of resources and opportunities.

As we shape the workplaces of the future, we first face the challenges of automation and robotisation, which are already redefining the way we work, and may ultimately trigger massive job displacements. Additionally, there is the risk of widening income inequality as highly skilled workers reap the benefits of AI while others are left behind. However, by embracing these technological changes, we can also open doors to new opportunities and foster collaboration between humans and machines, enabling us to adapt and evolve. Within this new landscape, we have the potential to create entirely new job categories, driving innovation and economic growth. For example, emerging fields like data science, cybersecurity, and virtual reality present exciting prospects for individuals to specialise in cutting-edge technologies and develop novel areas of activity. These new job categories will not only create employment opportunities, but also stimulate creativity and push the boundaries of what is possible in the digital age.

When exploring AI's potential in the fields of education and science, we initially confront concerns about data privacy, the potential loss of the human touch in teaching, and the potential that tools such as ChatGPT offer for cheating. However, AI can also enable personalised learning and lifelong education, and facilitate the cultivation of skills required for the world of tomorrow. By revolutionising teaching methods and allowing for tailor-made education practices, AI offers the power to help more students unlock their full potential. Education can also play a vital role in bridging the gap between sustainability and digitalisation activities. School curricula could link courses on sustainable development and digital innovation, thus inspiring the next generation of leaders to create eco-friendly technologies. At universities and outside the formal education sector, workshops could enlighten the general public, businesses, and policymakers about the need to involve multiple disciplines in digital development, thus empowering participants to make better-informed decisions.

In the realm of the natural environment, an unregulated use of AI technologies would contribute to increased energy consumption and further strain the planet's resources. At the same time, AI's potential to optimise energy efficiency, protect biodiversity, and promote ecosystem conservation and restoration cannot be overlooked. By harnessing the power of AI, we could tackle climate change more effectively, not least by detecting greenwashing and providing evidence for decision-making on mitigation and adaptation strategies. By analysing vast amounts of data from satellite imagery, weather patterns, and other sources, AI systems can identify trends and correlations that would otherwise be impossible for humans to detect, enhancing our ability to forecast, respond to, and minimise the negative impacts of extreme weather events and environmental changes. Other innovative solutions for reducing carbon emissions include optimising energy consumption in buildings and transportation, improving the efficiency of renewable energy systems, and facilitating the transition to a circular economy.

In this book, we argue that we can create a net benefit with AI in these four sectors – social justice, work, education, and ecology – if we respect key principles of ethical and responsible AI, such as transparency, accountability, fairness, and safety. However, as previously noted, we must also be open-eyed about the darker aspects of AI, such as its potential use to engage in warfare, cybercrime, and election manipulation. These challenges pose significant risks to global security, political polarisation, and democracy more broadly; these factors in turn will determine whether and how political leaders prioritise environmental and social action. In analysing these challenges and opportunities associated with AI, it will be essential to remember that our collective efforts to understand and shape AI's future will play a significant role in creating a better world for everyone.

As a team of co-authors, our discussions leading up to this book led us to a shared belief: that it is reasonable to have a hopeful and positive outlook on the future of AI, but that we should exercise caution, and always consider potential risks or challenges. We must remember that AI is a tool designed by humans, and which therefore can be shaped by humans. A key challenge is to make sure all aspects of society are represented when designing a tool with broad societal consequences. For this reason, our point of view remains cautiously optimistic, acknowledging the potential for success while also remaining aware of potential difficulties. We believe this allows for a balanced and realistic perspective.

However, to understand what will be needed to make AI truly beneficial for the world, it will be necessary to listen to diverse voices. To tackle wicked problems like AI's impact on society, we need a collaborative and interdisciplinary approach that goes beyond relying on historical lessons. This must entail ongoing dialogue and co-operation between experts, policymakers, and the public. And to address the unique challenges posed by AI, it will be critical to establish regulatory frameworks and guidelines that promote responsible and sustainable AI use, while always remaining ready to adapt to new information and circumstances.

So what?

If harnessed correctly, AI has the potential to help solve some of the world's most pressing problems, from climate change to social injustice. By working together across sectors and geographies, we can create a future where AI is not a threat, but instead offers the opportunity to make a better world for all of us. It is up to us to ensure that we are actively shaping our technological advancements to unlock a future that is prosperous, peaceful, and fulfilling for all. This is why we wrote this book. Through personal anecdotes, industry examples, and expert insights, we explore the urgent need for change in the way we think about AI and its role in society. It is our hope that this book will serve as a wake-up call for individuals and organisations alike, inspiring them to actively shape the future.

To ensure that the power of AI is harnessed in a positive way, transformation efforts will be needed across multiple domains. To fully leverage the potential of AI, it is essential that these technologies be available, understandable, and affordable to all, not just a privileged few. This means investing in research and development that prioritises accessibility and affordability, as well as implementing policies that promote equitable access to AI education, tools, and resources. A basic requirement for equitable access and informed decision-making is AI literacy. AI literacy is defined as "a set of competencies that enables individuals to critically evaluate AI technologies; communicate and collaborate effectively with AI; and use AI as a tool online, at home, and in the workplace."[16] To promote AI literacy, it will be essential for societies to invest in education and public awareness initiatives. By raising awareness of the potential benefits and risks of AI, we can empower individuals to make informed decisions about the technologies they use.

We also need to focus on ethical AI development, which prioritises transparency, fairness, and accountability. Ethical guidelines and standards must be established, and mechanisms to monitor and regulate the use of AI technologies must be put in place. This will ensure that AI is developed and used in a way that is beneficial to all, and which also respects fundamental human rights and values.

Another important area is fostering cross-disciplinary collaboration between AI researchers, policymakers, and domain experts from different fields. Collaborative efforts will be essential to develop context-aware solutions that address complex social and environmental challenges. By pooling knowledge and expertise from diverse sources, we can create innovative solutions informed by diverse perspectives.

Finally, global regulations and guidelines must be established to ensure the responsible and sustainable creation and use of AI technologies. These guidelines should focus on promoting the use of AI to generate positive social and environmental impact, while also ensuring that the development and use of AI technologies are in line with fundamental human rights and values.

On the mindset side, shaping a positive AI future requires a balanced approach that combines critical, ethical, optimistic, and fearless thinking. By embracing these mindsets, we can work towards a future where AI technologies are used to create positive change while also ensuring that they are developed and deployed responsibly and sustainably. This means prioritising ethical considerations and accountability, and making sure that AI is developed and used in a way that promotes the common good and respects fundamental human rights and values. By doing so, we can create a future where AI technologies are used to benefit all of society, thus helping to make the world more just, sustainable, and prosperous.

To help shape a positive AI future, we all should:

- Advocate for and support democratisation of AI by engaging with initiatives, policies, and organisations that work towards making AI accessible, understandable, and affordable for everyone.
- Cultivate our AI literacy and make an effort to educate ourselves about AI technologies – including their potential, their risks, and their role in society.
- Become a voice for the ethical use of AI by advocating for transparency, fairness, and accountability in AI development. Let's start at dinner table discussions with our friends: We need to increase awareness around the topic of ethical AI.

Chapter 2: Background, basics, and Bladerunner

Technology is the answer. But what was the question?
Cedric Price, architect[17]

Let's start with some basic info on AI in general, and most specifically on generative AI, a current hot topic in the field given the release of natural-language tools such as ChatGPT. This introduction will help provide a better understanding of the technology's potential and limitations. After this basic introduction, we will launch into a more detailed discussion of work, social justice, education and ecology in the following chapters.

Unlocking the mystery – understanding the basics of AI

The history of artificial intelligence can be traced back to the 1950s, with pioneers like Alan Turing and John McCarthy exploring the possibilities of creating machines capable of thinking and learning like humans. In 1956, McCarthy coined the term "artificial intelligence" and organised the Dartmouth Conference, a gathering of researchers from various disciplines to discuss the potential of AI.

AI is often referred to as a "suitcase word", a term that encompasses a diverse range of techniques and applications in one package.[18] To better understand this complexity, it will help to look briefly at its various subfields, including such topics as machine learning, natural-language processing, and robotics. Machine learning, a cornerstone of AI, focuses on developing algorithms that enable machines to learn from data and enhance their performance without being explicitly programmed for every task. These algorithms underpin many AI applications, for instance in the fields of image and speech recognition. Meanwhile, natural-language processing (NLP) addresses the interaction between computers and human language. NLP empowers computers to understand, interpret, and generate human language, paving the way for applications like chatbots, automated writing, and language translation. Lastly, the realm of robotics involves the design, construction, and operation of robots – physical machines capable of carrying out tasks autonomously or semi-autonomously. AI plays a crucial role in equipping robots with the ability to perceive their environments, make informed decisions, and execute actions. As you can see, AI has a multifaceted nature and a wide array of applications.

In the initial years of AI research, the focus was on developing programmes that could perform specific tasks such as playing chess or solving mathematical problems. These early AI programmes, known as "expert systems", mimicked the decision-making processes of human experts in a particular field. By the 1970s and 1980s, AI research had shifted towards the development of "knowledge-based systems" designed to store and retrieve vast amounts of information. The idea was that if a machine could access an extensive knowledge base, it could reason and make decisions like a human expert or even better. Around the 1980s, AI research pivoted to focus on developing "neural networks" modelled after the human brain's structure. These networks were designed to learn from data, filtering and summarising it to improve their own outcomes and performances over time. This approach led to the creation of "machine learning" algorithms in the late 1990s, which allowed machines to learn from data without being explicitly programmed for the task. According to the theory, if a machine could learn from data, it could improve its performance and adapt to new situations.

In recent years, deep learning algorithms such as neural networks have become prominent in AI applications. These algorithms can analyse large amounts of data and generate realistic images, videos, or natural language. For example, a generative AI model can analyse vast amounts of text and generate new, coherent text used for tasks like chatbots, automated writing, or speech recognition. Generative AI, in simple terms, refers to a system's ability to generate new content or data based on inputs such as natural-language prompts. This includes tasks like creating images, writing text, composing music, or even generating new scientific theories. Generative AI can "learn" and create new information based on patterns and relationships recognised in existing data, a clear contrast to early AI systems that were designed to carry out specific tasks based on predefined rules. Researchers continue to push the boundaries of what is possible with this rapidly advancing technology.

Despite the impressive capabilities shown by currently available tools, generative AI remains a form of "narrow AI." Narrow AI, also known as weak AI, refers to AI systems that are designed to perform specific tasks or address specific problems. These systems are focused on a narrow domain and have specialised capabilities within that domain. For example, an AI system designed to play the game of Go would fall under the category of narrow AI, as its primary purpose would be to excel at playing Go, and it thus might not have general intelligence, defined as the ability to perform tasks outside of that specific domain. In contrast, artificial general intelligence (AGI) would involve machines able to solve various types of problems without being programmed for the task specifically and with flexible capabilities akin to human intelligence. Some also raise the prospect of a superintelligence, which is a hypothetical form of AI that could surpass human intelligence. It is often speculated that a superintelligence would possess reasoning and problem-solving capabilities similar to an AGI, but of significantly greater magnitude. In this sense, superintelligence represents a different dimension of intelligence, one that focuses on the level or extent of intelligence rather than its breadth, and which could lead to unfathomable advancements in technology and society. This concept raises concerns about the potential ethical implications and even existential risks posed by the development of such AI systems. All AI applications developed to date remain examples of narrow AI. Although AGI is currently a hot research topic, its true realisation is likely still some time away.[19]

AI in action

It's easy to get caught up in the hype, becoming excited about futuristic ideas of what this technology might achieve. But many people may not realise that AI is already being integrated into our everyday lives in ways we might not expect. From enhancing our shopping experiences to revolutionising the way we interact with our homes, AI is already having a far-reaching impact all around us.

Take the fashion industry, for example. Companies like Stitch Fix and Zara are using generative AI to personalise their clothing recommendations for individual customers, as well as to predict future fashion trends and optimise their inventory. Zalando, a European fashion retailer, is also using generative AI to create new clothing designs in a fraction of the normal time and cost. By feeding data on popular styles, colours, and fabrics into the AI system, Zalando can generate a wide range of designs for the company's clothing lines. This not only saves time and resources, but it also allows them to adapt quickly to changing consumer preferences. It improves the customer experience while also increasing efficiency and profitability for the company.[20]

Another example is in the home renovation and design industry. Companies like Houzz and Wayfair are using generative AI to create virtual design tools that allow customers to visualise and plan their home renovations in a realistic and interactive way. This not only saves time and resources, but also makes the design process more accessible and enjoyable for the customer.[21]

Even our daily grocery shopping experiences are being impacted by generative AI. Companies like Walmart and Kroger are using it to optimise their inventory and supply chain management functions, leading to more accurate stock predictions and less food waste.[22]

In the telecoms industry, generative AI has been used to design and test new smartphone models for years. Even all the way back in 2010, when Claudia had a business meeting in Seoul with Samsung, company representatives showed her how they were using generative AI to create virtual prototypes of their smartphones. AI allows designers across all industries to test different design options and identify potential issues before building physical prototypes, saving a significant amount of time and resources.

Even the beauty industry is being disrupted by generative AI. L'Oréal, a global beauty company, is using the technology to create personalised skincare products. By analysing data on an individual's skin type, age, and environmental factors, the firm's AI system can generate a personalised skincare routine tailored to the customer's specific needs.[23]

The possibilities for generative AI in our daily lives are endless, and these are just a few examples of how it is already being integrated into industries in ways we may not have expected. It is important to remember that this discussion is not just about futuristic ideas, but also about the tangible impact such technologies are already having on our daily lives.

How tech titans are already leveraging AI

As we go about our daily lives, we often take the technology that surrounds us for granted. From the smartphones in our pockets to the cars on the road, artificial intelligence has become deeply ingrained in our society. But while we may not always see it, some of the world's biggest tech companies are using AI in ways that are quietly changing our world.

Take Google, for example. Google has been at the forefront of AI research and development for several years, with numerous breakthroughs in the field of text, images, video, and audio. The company is using AI to make online searches more efficient and accurate, as well as to improve the overall user experience of their products. Their language model, BERT, was implemented in Google Search back in 2019, allowing the system to understand the nuances and context of queries, resulting in more relevant search results. Google Photos uses AI to automatically organise and categorise our personal photos, making it easier for us to find and share specific memories. And with its recently released experimental, conversational AI chat service Bard, Google is combining a conversational chatbot based on its Language Model for Dialogue Application, or LaMDA for short, with its powerful search tool.[24]

Google was pushed to release its newest AI advances by Microsoft's investment in OpenAI, the creator of ChatGPT. This chatbot service reached 100 million users in less than three months after its release, becoming the fastest-growing consumer internet service in history.[25] ChatGPT is just one of a dozen AI-driven "killer apps" that are expected to transform the future nature of work. Microsoft's investment in OpenAI has allowed the tech titan to take a lead in exploring mass market adoption of AI by integrating generative AI services into most of its products, including Teams, Bing, the Office productivity suite, and business offerings like its Azure cloud computing platform, just to name a few. Soon, everyone using Microsoft products will have direct access to advanced AI services. In January 2023, Microsoft CEO Satya Nadella, spoke at the 2023 Annual Meeting of the World Economic Forum in Davos, Switzerland, about the company's vision for a "golden age" of artificial intelligence and the role of generative AI in shaping the future of work. Nadella emphasised the importance of using AI as a "co-pilot" to help people do more with less, and said Microsoft plans to continue leading the way in AI innovation.[26]

One of the major current battlefields for tech titans is web search, which will probably see considerable change in coming months. Users of Google and Bing are already experiencing these new features, but users of other search engines around the globe are likely to join them, as Chinese search engine Baidu also has plans to roll out a ChatGPT-style chatbot.[27] The feverish pace of investment has triggered a scramble among tech firms, with Microsoft and Google both shifting their strategies to seek control over what they see as a new infrastructure layer of the economy. As Wall Street responds with equally fervent interest, analysts are upgrading the stocks of companies that mention AI in their plans and punishing those with problematic AI rollouts. Despite the promise of AI, companies are struggling to keep pace with the rapid advances in the technology, with efforts to ensure the tools are safe often taking a back seat. In the rush to improve the tech and profit from the boom, experts are warning that companies are neglecting research into safety and risks.[28]

As companies race to get ahead of the curve, they are cutting corners and ignoring the potential dangers of these powerful tools. They are not providing time for broad social debate before their products are released – a debate that will be needed for efforts to identify and reduce biases and other negative social impacts associated with the technologies. Mistakes are being made, and the consequences could be severe. Google's Bard, Microsoft's Bing and ChatGPT all sometimes produce untrue results that are difficult to spot. But perhaps the most troubling development is the rise of so-called deep fakes – realistic-seeming videos and images created with AI that are being used to spread hate and misinformation. The present-day issues may be cause for concern, but they are mere glimpses of what may arise if this technology race continues at breakneck speed. Big Tech's current decisions mirror those of previous eras, which sent destructive shockwaves through society, leaving lasting scars. The stakes are higher than ever, and the consequences of repeating past mistakes could be catastrophic. In the pursuit of profit, safety concerns are taking a back seat, but some experts are sounding the alarm about an even larger risk. AI companies such as OpenAI have set their sights on the creation of artificial general intelligence, or AGI, that will be able to outthink and outlearn humans. If these future AIs prove able to self-improve at an exponential rate without human intervention, they could pose an existential threat to humanity, raising the spectre of our own extinction, some AI experts warn.[29]

Exploring the AI divide – comparing global developments

The development and deployment of artificial intelligence is not limited to a single country or region. In fact, countries and regions around the world are actively investing in and developing AI technologies, each with their own unique approach and priorities.

One of the key players in the global AI landscape is the United States, which is home to some of the world's largest technology companies and boasts a robust startup ecosystem. The US government has also made significant investments in AI research and development, with organisations such as the Defense Advanced Research Projects Agency (DARPA)[30] playing a major role in funding and directing AI research. Additionally, the US is home to many academic institutions and research centres that are focused on AI, including the Massachusetts Institute of Technology (MIT) and Stanford University.

Another major player in the global AI landscape is China. The Chinese government, along with companies like Baidu and Tencent, has made significant investments in AI and has set ambitious goals for its development. Both the country and its companies have thus established themselves as major players in the global AI landscape. Additionally, China is home to many AI research institutions and a growing number of startups in the field.

Europe, too, has a strong presence in the global AI industry. The European Union has made significant investments in AI research and development, and has set ambitious goals for the deployment of AI technologies. European companies such as Siemens and Volkswagen are investing in AI, and there is a growing number of AI startups in the region. Additionally, European countries such as France and Germany have launched national AI strategies to support the development of the technology.

Other regions around the world, such as Canada, Japan, and South Korea, also have a growing presence in the global AI landscape. Each of these countries has made significant investments in AI research and development, and each has its own unique approach to the development and deployment of the technology.

All the countries and regions referenced here are investing significant resources in AI research and development, and many are implementing national strategies to promote AI innovation and adoption. The race to attract top AI talent is highly competitive, with countries and regions offering attractive incentives and funding opportunities to entice the best researchers and entrepreneurs. Overall, the level of competition in the AI space is intense, and shows no signs of slowing down. This frenzied competition and rush for power in the AI industry mirrors the space race of the 20th century. The United States and the Soviet Union invested vast resources in a competition to achieve spaceflight supremacy. The competition resulted in monumental achievements such as the first manned moon landing, but it also came with risks and dangers, including the loss of lives. Similarly, the AI race has already brought immense progress and opportunities for humanity, but also poses existential risks that require careful consideration and regulation. As we look to the future, it will be essential to draw lessons from past technological races and ensure that safety and ethical considerations are prioritised alongside innovation and progress. Additionally, we need to highlight the fact that AI development tends to be energy- and technology-driven, a barrier to entry that clearly places the Global South at a disadvantage. As AI advances, equality should be one key metric by which it is judged – because as with climate change, which is most strongly affecting the people who did the least to produce it, the risk that it will lead to global political unrest is immense.

The Turing Test, ChatGPT, AGI, and the singularity

The Turing Test, named after legendary computer science pioneer Alan Turing, has been a topic of immense debate and speculation in the tech world for decades. This test, conceived in 1950, was intended to assess a machine's ability to exhibit human-like intelligence and behaviour through conversation. Fast forward to the present day, and we have cutting-edge AI models like ChatGPT that have been trained on vast amounts of data and have advanced natural-language processing capabilities. But, the million-dollar question remains – has ChatGPT passed the Turing Test?

To understand this, let's delve into the backstory of the Turing Test and its significance in the AI world. Alan Turing, an English mathematician and computer scientist who was instrumental in decoding encoded messages in World War II, proposed the test as a way to assess the quality of a machine's intelligence, and as a means of forecasting the future of AI. The test involves a human evaluator conducting a natural-language conversation with both a human and a machine, without knowing which one is which. If the evaluator is unable to distinguish the machine from the human, the machine is said to have passed the test.

ChatGPT is a powerful AI language model that has been trained on a massive corpus of text data, including books, articles, and web pages. To give some perspective, an average American reads 12 books per year.[31] Depending on the field, these books contain around 50,000 to 100,000 words apiece. Thus, on average, an American reads around 1 million words a year in book form. Even on the high end, and including other language inputs such as social media, web or magazines, this would take a lifetime to reach into the billions of words. ChatGPT, on the other hand, has been trained on hundreds of billions of words, which is orders of magnitude more than any human could ever consume.

This allows ChatGPT to generate human-like responses to a wide range of questions and prompts. However, despite its advanced capabilities, ChatGPT's creators have stated that the model is not intended to pass the Turing Test, as it is not designed to exhibit human-like intelligence. So, has ChatGPT passed the Turing Test? The answer is both yes and no. While ChatGPT's responses can be incredibly human-like, they are generated based on patterns in the data it was trained on, rather than being derived from true consciousness or understanding. The tool has thus not technically passed the Turing Test, because ChatGPT has not been deliberately designed to pass it. You can test it yourself by asking ChatGPT about consciousness, and it will always tell you it is a computer tool. As a result, ChatGPT does not meet the criteria for passing the Turing Test, as it does not truly exhibit human-like intelligence.

But what we should keep in mind is that the goal of OpenAI, the company that launched ChatGPT, is ultimately to produce artificial general intelligence. In the company's view, artificial general intelligence, or AGI, would involve highly autonomous systems able to outperform humans at most economically valuable work. Its executives have said they believe this kind of AI has the potential to revolutionise many industries and solve some of the world's most pressing problems.

Artificial general intelligence is often discussed in the context of what has been termed the "technological singularity". The singularity is a hypothetical point in the future when AI surpasses human intelligence and leads to an unprecedented acceleration in technological progress. Some theorists believe that the singularity will be triggered by the development of AGI capable of recursive self-improvement, leading to a runaway explosion in the technology's intelligence. The idea is that AGI will be able to improve its own design, leading to a positive feedback loop of ever-increasing intelligence – eventually exceeding human comprehension so substantially that we will be unable to predict or control it. This scenario has also been called the "intelligence explosion", and entails a host of threats as well as opportunities.

The disconnect between perception and urgency

But how far are we from general AI and this hypothetical singularity? It is difficult to predict with certainty when AGI will be achieved, as this will require significant advancements in machine learning, cognitive science, and other related fields. However, some experts have made predictions about the timeline for achieving AGI. One of the most famous predictions comes from Ray Kurzweil, a futurist and director of engineering at Google. Kurzweil has famously predicted that AGI will be achieved by 2029, based on his observations of the exponential growth of computing power and other technological advancements. Another expert, Demis Hassabis, co-founder of the AI company DeepMind, has suggested that the achievement of AGI is likely to be a gradual process rather than a sudden breakthrough. In an interview with the MIT Technology Review in 2019, Hassabis stated, "I think there will be a series of breakthroughs and steps towards AGI, rather than one single 'aha' moment." However, experts keep revising their predictions, and opinions vary widely. In a 2022 study, experts were asked to identify the point at which they believe there will be a 50% chance that human-level AI will have been developed, defined as machines capable of independently performing all tasks better and more cheaply than humans. Some experts said they believed this level of AI would never be realised, and others predicted it would be a distant future event, but many said they anticipated its arrival within the next few decades. Highlighting this variation, the study indicated that half of the experts expected human-level AI to arrive before 2061, and 90% foresaw its development within this century.[32]

Claudia recently completed an executive course on AI at MIT. In his welcome speech, Thomas Malone, director of the MIT Center for Collective Intelligence, shared a personal story of how he first became interested in AI back in the 1980s, and how it intrigued and excited him. However, he also had concerns about the rapid progress of AI at that time, he said, and worried whether it would have been developed before he graduated from college. Almost 40 years later, many of the possibilities discussed back then have yet to be realised, but interest in AI is growing by the day – as is its ability to solve problems and create new opportunities.

The launch of ChatGPT contributed to the mass market adoption of AI in several ways. First, ChatGPT and similar language models have increased public awareness and understanding of AI by demonstrating its potential to understand and generate human-like language. ChatGPT has been used to develop a wide range of applications, including chatbots, language translation, and content generation, making the technology more accessible to a broader audience.

Additionally, the launch has helped to democratise access to AI by providing a free and widely available tool for developers, researchers, and businesses to experiment with and build upon. This has reduced the barriers to entry for developing and integrating AI-based solutions, thereby driving the adoption of AI technologies.

With her twenty-year background in the telecommunications industry, Claudia likes to compare the mass market adoption of ChatGPT to the launch of the iPhone back in 2007, which changed a whole industry. Even back in the 1980s, when she was working on fixed-line communications, she saw demos of video chats, and by 2007 mobile content had already been around for years. However, the iPhone spurred mainstream adoption of these services, as they suddenly became easily accessible. The iPhone introduced a number of innovative features such as a touch screen, a user-friendly interface, and the App Store, which provided a platform for third-party developers to create and distribute applications. This made mobile computing more accessible and intuitive to a broader audience, accelerating the adoption of smartphones and transforming the way we interact with technology. The iPhone has of course had a far-reaching impact on the way we communicate, work, and interact with the world, from mobile payments and social media to e-commerce and digital entertainment.

Both ChatGPT and the iPhone have played important roles in democratising access to technology and driving innovation. ChatGPT has helped to make AI more accessible to developers and businesses, while the iPhone provided a platform for app developers to create new and innovative solutions. Ultimately, both technologies have contributed to the acceleration of the digital revolution and the ongoing transformation of our world.

The extraordinarily rapid adoption of smartphones has undoubtedly transformed the way we live and work, but it has also brought about some negative consequences that we must address if we want to avoid similar problems with the adoption of AI. One significant issue is the impact of smartphone addiction on our mental health, with studies showing a link between excessive smartphone use and increased levels of anxiety and depression. Moreover, the rise of social media and its impact on our social and political discourse has sometimes proved problematic. Social media platforms have been criticised for their role in spreading misinformation and fake news, for using personal data to boost revenues, for polarising public opinion, and for fuelling political polarisation and extremism.

To prevent similar issues from arising with the widespread adoption of AI, we, as a society, need to act now, especially given the efforts being made to develop AGI. There is a disconnect concerning the urgency to act. It is easy to become complacent and believe that the problem can be solved in the future. But as we've seen in the past, waiting until it's too late can have devastating consequences. The urgency is increasing as significant investments are being made by governments and businesses around the world. If we wait too long to push this conversation, both the public and non-tech experts will be left behind, losing the opportunity to help shape the future in a way that benefits everyone. Moreover, there is a risk that existing social and economic inequalities will be exacerbated if AI is not developed and deployed in a fair and equitable manner. But we should also recognise the opportunities for progress and innovation. It's time for us to come together and work towards a future where the advancements in AI can lead to a better world for all of us.

Scenario Blade Runner – a cautionary tale for AI development

In the 1982 film "Blade Runner", the world is portrayed as a dark and gritty place where advanced AI, in the form of "replicants", coexist alongside humans. These replicants, created by the Tyrell Corporation, are virtually identical to humans in every way, but are used for manual labour and dangerous missions. They are designed to have a limited lifespan, and when they begin to question their own existence and demand more rights, they are hunted down and "retired" by special police units known as Blade Runners.

As the four of us sat together discussing the opportunities and challenges of generative AI, we couldn't miss seeing parallels to the world of "Blade Runner". The film serves as a cautionary tale about the potential consequences of creating advanced AI without proper consideration for the ethical implications. Just like in the film, the development of AI is rapidly advancing, and we must consider the potential consequences for society. What happens when AI becomes so advanced that it can no longer be distinguished from human consciousness? What features should AI have? Should it be human-like, or should this be avoided at all cost? What rights should advanced AI have, and how should society handle the integration of these beings into our world? These are just a few of the ethical considerations that must be taken into account as we continue to explore the possibilities of AI.

Stephen Hawking, the late physicist and cosmologist, has been a vocal critic of the field, highlighting the potential dangers of artificial intelligence. In a number of interviews and articles, he has warned that the development of AI could pose a threat to humanity's survival. Hawking has stated that the rapid pace of AI development could lead to the creation of machines that are "smarter than the people who created them", which could in turn put control of the future into the hands of machines. He has also warned that AI could be used to develop autonomous weapons, which could lead to a global arms race and an increase in the likelihood of war. Additionally, Hawking has called for greater regulation of AI development, arguing that governments and industry leaders must work together to ensure that the technology is developed in a safe and responsible way. He has emphasised the need for "checks and balances" to be put in place to prevent the development of machines that could be used to cause harm. Overall, Hawking's statements on the potential dangers of AI highlight the need for caution and careful consideration as we continue to develop and integrate this powerful technology into our lives and society.

The optimistic scenario – the possibility of positive impact

However, some experts have an overall positive outlook on our AI future. In the fall of 2010, Claudia had the opportunity to attend a talk by renowned futurist and AI expert Ray Kurzweil in Vienna. At the time, many of the theories and predictions he presented seemed almost too far-fetched to believe. He spoke about the rapid advancement of AI and the many positive ways it would impact society, from healthcare to education, transportation and beyond.

At the time, Claudia couldn't quite wrap her head around it all, and wasn't entirely convinced by Kurzweil's predictions. However, as the years passed, she began to see that many of his predictions were coming true. Advances in AI have been exponential, and we are now seeing the positive effects of this technology in many areas of our lives. One of the most significant advancements in AI is the ability to process and analyse vast amounts of data quickly and accurately. This has led, as previously noted, to improvements in fields such as healthcare, where AI is being used to analyse medical images and help with diagnoses. In transportation, self-driving cars are becoming a reality, and in education, AI-powered learning systems are helping to personalise instruction and improve student outcomes.

A key point that Kurzweil touches on is the idea of "intelligence amplification". He posits that by augmenting our own intelligence with that of machines, we will be able to accomplish far more than we ever thought possible. This includes achievements like eradicating disease, increasing our lifespan, and indeed colonising other planets.

Kurzweil argues that machines will be able to take on many of the menial tasks that are currently performed by humans, freeing up time for individuals to pursue more creative and fulfilling activities. Additionally, he says, AI will be able to assist with decision-making, reducing the potential for human bias and error. While Kurzweil's predictions may seem ambitious or overly optimistic, he provides a detailed and well-researched argument for why he believes they are achievable. He also acknowledges that there will be challenges and obstacles that need to be overcome in order to reach the point of technological singularity, but ultimately argues that the benefits far outweigh the risk.

The time when AI surpasses human intelligence and machines become capable of self-improvement may still be some way off. However, the rapid advancement of AI technology means that it is no longer a question of if, but when. While there are many valid concerns about the impact of AI on society, the technology clearly has the potential to bring about significant positive changes as well. Kurzweil's predictions may well be a roadmap to a possible future.

So what?

This chapter takes a comprehensive look at the topic of AI, ranging from an explanation of the basics of AI to an exploration of the technology's ethical implications, reminding us of the potential dangers and the need for regulation before contrasting this with a very optimistic perspective.

Don't sit on the sideline. Help co-create a positive future by::

- Proactively informing yourself about advancements in AI, experimenting with new tools, and analysing their potential impact on various industries and society.
- Promoting ethical and inclusive practices in the development and deployment of AI services by following human-centred design principles and actively incorporating diverse voices and perspectives.
- Advocating for responsible and transparent regulation of AI, to ensure that its benefits are shared equitably and that its risks are mitigated.

Chapter 3: A magic bullet for social justice?

In the age of the machines, it is the very essence of what makes us human – happiness, compassion, and love – that will save humanity.[33]

Mo Gawdat, former chief business officer at Google

We as a global human society have excelled at many things, but we haven't managed to create social justice. We live in a world in which a small percentage of the global population contributes the majority of greenhouse gas emissions and pollution. Where CEOs of large fashion companies make in a few days what garment workers far down their value chains make in their entire lifetimes. Where millions of people still die of hunger and poverty when their neighbours overconsume things they don't need and often don't even want.

AI can help us solve many problems, which is why many organisations are rushing to research, develop, use, and sell AI models of all kinds. The race is on. However, this isn't necessarily a good thing. Can we really get AI to sort us out, and if so, how? Or will it continue to merely reflect, perpetuate, and even reinforce existing power dynamics and patterns of social injustice? In this chapter, we analyse how AI is already helping humans, and discuss its potential to improve health, wealth, and well-being for all. Using selected examples, we also highlight many of the risks in the social sphere, showing what must change in the bigger picture for AI to maximise benefits for many rather than benefiting only a privileged few.

Loving Eliza

In the 1960s, MIT professor Joseph Weizenbaum developed what can be called the world's first chatbot. He called it ELIZA, in reference to George Bernard Shaw's play "Pygmalion" and the 1954 musical adaptation "My Fair Lady", in which Eliza Doolittle, a young working-class woman with a strong cockney accent, is taught to speak and behave "properly", and thus gains access to London's high society. ELIZA was trained to emulate a psychotherapist, using open-ended questions and applying pattern matching and substitution techniques to respond to user input in a way that gave the impression of understanding and empathy. Apparently, like her musical sister, the ELIZA bot was a great success. While ELIZA now feels rather simple-minded by today's standards, she still did a lot of good for humans, many of whom spent hours talking to her.

By identifying keywords in sentences typed by the user into a chat box, ELIZA was able to ask questions which seemed to make sense in context. This was sufficient to convince people that the bot was a lot smarter than it actually was. This worked particularly well since the style chosen was Rogerian psychotherapy, known for the practice of "reflecting listening", in which the therapist reflects certain aspects of the information provided back to the patient.[34]

When researching the history of chatbots, Alice could not help stumbling across A.L.I.C.E., also referred to as Alicebot, a natural-language processing "chatterbot" inspired by ELIZA and developed by Richard Wallace in 1995. A.L.I.C.E was based on the idea of pattern matching and case-based reasoning. Compared to ELIZA, A.L.I.C.E used a more sophisticated approach to natural-language processing, able to draw from a large database of prewritten responses in order to generate more natural and varied responses to user input. While ELIZA was designed to mimic a psychotherapist, A.L.I.C.E was designed to be a conversational partner able to engage in a wide range of topics and provide helpful information.[35]

In the otherwise male-dominated landscape of AI, it is worth noting that A.L.I.C.E. (the bot) also served as inspiration for the film "Her" by Spike

Jonze, in which a human falls in love with an eerily convincing bot called Samantha.[36]

The success of ELIZA and her successors shows that AI can replace some aspects of human work, for instance by aiding with psychological support or psychotherapy. However, a more important conclusion is that flesh-and-blood people can develop emotional connections with machines, even if there is no physical resemblance and they come without additional services, such as those provided by sex dolls. This is even more apparent today, as machines have become much better at providing their human users with the impression of emotions, even to the point of seeming to reciprocate affection.[37]

When AI comes to the rescue

You may have heard about the use of AI in the medical field as well. For example, healthcare sectors in many countries are struggling. Some are facing ageing populations and exploding costs, while others are plagued by an inability to provide even basic healthcare at decent levels of quality to large parts of the population. Yet access to good quality healthcare is a fundamental human right. Thus, it is good news that AI can help with many of these ills afflicting health systems around the globe. However, to make sure that no unintended side effects occur, ethical considerations and human rights must be placed at the centre of the design, development, and deployment of AI technologies in the health sector.

As long as these principles are followed, AI holds great potential to improve the delivery of healthcare, including the prevention, diagnosis, and treatment of disease; in fact, it is already changing how health services are delivered, particularly in high-income countries. Today, for example, more and more evidence is emerging regarding AI's ability to facilitate diagnoses of diseases, including cancer of the brain, breast, skin, and stomach. In these early studies – most of which have yet to be corroborated by clinical trials – AI does at least as well as human doctors at recognising certain disease patterns. As AI continues to improve, it could allow medical providers to make faster, more accurate diagnoses, thus ultimately saving patients both pain and costs. AI systems could be used to rapidly detect and thus reduce the impact of other conditions such as strokes or pneumonia, or to predict illness and major health events before they occur. For instance, AI models could be adapted to assess a person's relative risk of disease, suggesting ways of preventing illnesses such as cardiovascular disease or diabetes that are often linked to lifestyle factors.[38]

AI does not eliminate the need for human health workers, but it can assist them and make their lives easier. In poorer countries, many of which face severe and chronic shortages of healthcare workers, AI could free up doctors and nurses' precious time, if employed wisely. AI is also used in the less sexy, back-office areas of healthcare systems. It can help to allocate scarce resources, ranging from funding and medical supplies even to human organs, for example. With AI, tedious and sometimes difficult tasks such as medicine logistics, human resources planning, patient scheduling, predicting which patients are unlikely to turn up for their appointments, and even the identification and elimination of fraud and waste become easier. Another important application is the analysis of electronic health records in the context of health research. AI that is accurately designed and trained with appropriate data can help to identify clinical best practices, for example. AI is also contributing to the shift of some healthcare services away from the formal health sector. It can help patients self-manage medical conditions such as cardiovascular diseases, diabetes or mental health issues. Many of these AI-guided technologies require the use of mobile applications or wearables, such as those placed in the body (artificial limbs, smart implants), on the body (insulin pump patches, electroencephalogram devices), or near the body (activity trackers, smart watches, or smart glasses). Finally, drug discovery is an area where AI is likely to make a difference to patients by simplifying and speeding up drug development.[39]

Simply employing cool new technologies and expecting them to improve health outcomes will not work, however. Without a bigger-picture perspective that involves experts from multiple disciplines, including patients, AI could create more problems than it solves. For starters, health workers will have to adapt their clinical practices as use of AI increases. They will need to know-how to collaborate with AI models, and how to communicate risks and discuss trade-offs with patients. As AI automates tasks, doctors and nurses may wind up with more time to listen to patients. But they will also be confronted with new challenges, such as times when an AI model comes up with a diagnosis or treatment plan different than theirs. There are early warning signs of a trend towards "algorithmic paternalism", whereby AI's recommendations may be followed even if they go against human doctors' best judgement, or ignore relevant contextual information provided by patients about their feelings, beliefs, or culture. As we note in Chapter 7, AI is only as good as the data it has been trained on, and quality depends further on the way in which the training was designed. Much of the data feeding AI models in the healthcare sector is biased, and lacks relevant contextual data; moreover, it reflects insights generated by doctors in the past. But such historical data can be both biased and erroneous for other reasons, and it may contain limited information about how to treat a patient's problem in the future.[40]

The key question you might want to ask yourself is: What would it take for you to trust an AI model? If the AI comes to a different conclusion than your human doctor, whose recommendations would you follow? Whom do you trust with your life?

When AI puts your child in foster care

We already understand that technology is not neutral, and that AI is only as good as the data it was trained on and the people who trained it. Creating and implementing AI is not trivial and requires a set of basic elements to be in place. In particular, human experts are needed to develop algorithms, prepare algorithm training data, and then translate the algorithm's outputs into results that make sense for humans. A lot can go wrong in the process.

In 2013, one algorithm employed by the Dutch government wreaked havoc in the lives of 25,000 parents. Artificial intelligence was employed to help with one of the things it is particularly good at, namely making predictions by analysing large amounts of data. In this case, the government wanted to know which people were most likely to commit childcare-benefit fraud. However, rather than waiting for proof, it penalised families right away, demanding that they pay back years of benefits. Families were categorised on the basis of "risk factors" such as a low income or a dual nationality. As a result, tens of thousands of people were needlessly impoverished, and more than 1,000 children were placed in foster care.[41]

There are other, more recent examples as well. For example, AI algorithms have been used to predict recidivism rates which, in turn, inform decisions about bail and sentencing. But algorithms like the COMPAS system used in the US states of California, Florida, New York and Wisconsin, have proven to be biased against certain racial and ethnic groups, leading to discriminatory outcomes, in some cases resulting in sentences as long as six years for a minimal offence. These latter judgements were based solely on the COMPAS tool, which predicted that the individuals in question had a high risk of reoffending.[42] One of the ways to avoid such outcomes, and to make AI models more trustworthy, would be to ensure that their predictions or recommendations are accompanied by a confidence score and thus allow for improved human-machine interaction.

In many cases, the humans training the machines know very little about the realities they are affecting through their work. But some are realising that actively preventing tragic errors like the one in the Netherlands described above is both essential and possible. The solution is obvious: Get people involved that are actually familiar with the underlying subject. Simply offering vague recommendations about broader participation misses the point. Yes, we do need much broader participation, and thus representation of societal concerns, but at times we must be very specific about what kind of external expertise is needed in order to make AI less biased and better at doing its job. What counts is not only the potential for diversity, but the presence of active, meaningful input provided by relevant stakeholders. Everything else might lead to "participation-washing", whether intended or not, and thus contribute to the perpetuation of inequality and exclusion.

The fact that good intentions do not always lead to good results was demonstrated by the European Commission's AI Alliance, an online forum that was technically open to anyone, and was designed to provide democratic feedback to the Commission's expert group on AI. However, this group quickly turned out to be an "unmoderated echo chamber of mostly men exchanging opinions", rather than being representative of key stakeholder groups.[43] While Alice, who worked with the European Commission for several years, wasn't part of this specific forum, she does remember occasions when the EU's efforts at consultation and participation were not reflective of the true diversity of opinion, and did not do justice to the values and ambitions of the EU as a whole. Sometimes they were just a waste of money, as in November 2022 when the Commission threw a €400,000 metaverse party that was supposed to appeal to younger generations, and nobody showed up.[44]

Actually talking to people concerned by an issue and understanding their lived experience can help not only to draw better party crowds, but also to design fairer, more correct algorithms. A group of scientists recently developed a tool to improve machine learning that relies on social media posts by including the lived experiences of people affected. The algorithm developed to identify Twitter posts related to gang violence in Chicago was improved by drawing on the expertise of young Black people with actual gang experience in the area. These experts were essential in giving meaning and context to the data, analysing communications and translating them into concrete realities. While the approach developed here was specific to the given context, it could be applied more generally across a variety of contexts. One possible extension the researchers have suggested is the development of language identifiers for alt-right and hate groups who all use specific ways of talking, writing, and communicating with emojis. The researchers argue that their approach is considerably superior to traditional, off-the-shelf language identifiers that often miss important nuances, context features, and culturally specific linguistic styles.[45]

Data and training biases are a huge problem when it comes to AI. We'll come back to this topic later. But for the time being, let's focus on one social issue, namely disability, a field in which activists have been pioneering this type of equitable participation for decades with the slogan "Nothing about us without us".

Improving the lives of people with disabilities

How many disabled people do you know? If you know 100 people, chances are you know a good dozen or more. Today, 1.3 billion people worldwide experience "significant" disability, according to the World Health Organization.[46] That's 16% of the global population. In other words, disability is part of being human, and is integral to the human experience. Disability results from the interplay between health conditions such as blindness, dementia or spinal cord injury, on the one hand, and environmental and personal factors on the other. Moreover, as populations age, the number of people with disabilities is growing. Nor does injustice end simply with the presence of a given physical or mental disability. People with disabilities also die earlier, have poorer overall health, and experience more limitations in everyday functioning than do others.

AI has the potential to improve the lives of people with disabilities in several ways. For example, in combination with phone apps, it can enhance physical accessibility and help people navigate more safely and comfortably, in part by offering personalised support. Think of the fact that there are 40 million blind people in the world. To date, this population has been aided largely by just two technologies: walking canes and guide dogs. Guide dogs are great "tools", but there are only 20,000 of them around, and many blind people are unable to take care of animals. Instead, the startup dotlumen aims to empower blind people by offering the technological equivalent of a guide dog. It combines technologies from the autonomous driving field with artificial intelligence and robotics, bundling these inside a wearable system. The system's central feature is a headset, called "glasses", that understands the environment. It identifies objects, registers their position and movement in 3D, computes interaction paths, and transmits information to the wearer using haptic and auditory impulses. In a supermarket, for example, a blind person may ask the system to be taken to the vegetable section, and the dotlumen technology can help her navigate there in a safe and efficient way. Early users have said the tool has given them a new sense of freedom not experienced before.[47]

AI-powered speech recognition technology is another important use case that can help people with speech disabilities communicate more effectively and thus facilitate a shift in our collective mindset regarding what constitutes being "fully abled". Today, there are many AI-powered speech recognition systems that can transcribe spoken words into text. A key hurdle to inclusion for some people with disabilities has been the inability to communicate easily with others – literally robbing them of a voice within the system. Several of the tools mentioned in this book address exactly this issue. They help people with hearing or speech impairments communicate, provide assistance with daily tasks such as carrying objects, and augment physiological functions such as hearing, thus helping their users participate as full members of society. When it comes to inclusion, the ability to participate as a full member of society and a shift in the mindsets of those deemed to be "fully abled" are crucial.

As always, we must keep in mind that AI systems can also perpetuate and amplify existing biases and discrimination against people with disabilities, so it will be important to ensure that AI systems are designed and deployed in ways that promote accessibility, transparency, and accountability, and are aligned with the values and goals of a just and equitable society.

The end of disability?

Let's consider again what disability actually means. First, we are all differently abled, both physically and cognitively. In most societies, people are called "disabled" if they fall below a certain threshold in one or both of these areas. The US Centers for Disease Control and Prevention, America's most important public health body, defines disability as "any condition of the body or mind (impairment) that makes it more difficult for the person with the condition to do certain activities (activity limitation) and interact with the world around them (participation restrictions)."[48] This ties in well with the World Health Organisation reminder that disability is part of being human, and that almost everyone will experience disability temporarily or permanently at some point in their life.[49]

Importantly, the WHO also states that disability is not absolute, but results from the interactions between individuals with a health condition, such as Down syndrome or depression, and other factors, such as negative attitudes, inaccessible public transport, or limited social support. This much broader definition opens up considerable room for manoeuvre when it comes to AI, as algorithms connecting vision and speech could be as helpful as algorithms optimising traffic or indeed allowing for driverless mobility.

There is yet another take on disability. What if people just feel they have a disability in light of the vast potential provided by technology? What if having average or even exceptional human abilities no longer seems enough? We love the example of Hugh Herr, an MIT professor who lost both legs in an ice climbing accident at the age of 17 in 1982. Just a year later, with two prosthetic legs, he was back on the mountain, climbing better than ever before. Since then, Herr has turned his personal experience and passion into a career in biomechatronics, earning him the Times Magazine title of "Leader of the Bionic Age". His prosthetic legs are much more powerful than his biological legs ever could have been. By making the leg prosthetics longer than his arms, Herr increased his height and improved his ability to reach holds that others cannot. Using ultralight carbon constructions, he reduced his weight, which allows him to do pull-ups hanging from a single finger. The prosthetics he built also looked very different from natural body parts, with feet as small as a baby's, allowing him to stand on tiny holds; with legs that taper to a point and can be wedged into rock cracks; and with soles furnished with spikes that cling to bare ice. All of these newfound abilities turned around people's perception by 180 degrees. "Opinions changed completely when I started climbing cliffs that no one else could climb. People who had looked down on me with pity just a short time earlier suddenly expressed anger and envy. Some even said they would have their own legs amputated to keep up," Herr says.[50]

Herr's example is a testimony to the fluidity of the concept of disability, showing that technology truly has the power to improve people's lives in a very basic physical and mental way. Herr argues that given today's technological possibilities, including AI, most disabilities will no longer exist by the end of this century. He predicts that in 100 years, people will look very different than today, and that their ideas of beauty and intelligence will be very different from ours. "They will live with a human diversity that we cannot even imagine today," he says.[51]

Looking across the global village

While we are hopeful in general and have reasons to assume that Herr's predictions may well come true for the more privileged citizens of the globe, we are rather sceptical that they will come to pass in poorer regions of the world, such as Africa. After all, there is a big discrepancy between what is technologically possible and what is available and affordable to the masses, for example in Africa. Don't get us wrong – we clearly see the economic and social potential of the continent, and are quite aware of the fact that by the end of this century, Africa will be home to about 4 billion people, at a time when the combined population of Europe and North America will still be under 1 billion. We're also aware that Africa is incredibly diverse, with its 54 countries boasting different ecological zones, languages, cultures, resource wealth, degrees of industrialisation, average incomes, and so on. However, we also know that incomes are extremely unevenly distributed, and with them outcomes in the areas of life expectancy, education, and health. What's more, poorer regions of the world tend to suffer most from the consequences of climate change and environmental degradation, and are finding it hard to adapt given that richer countries are proving reluctant to pay for the loss and damages they have caused.

That's why it is important to look at opportunities for AI to improve equity and social justice in poorer regions of the world, such as Africa. Are such technologies already contributing to improved health, wealth, and well-being for all? In principle, there are many AI applications working to serve people in developing regions, even today. Healthcare is one of the most obvious sectors in which this is taking place, even in poorer regions. For example, AI-powered diagnostic tools and telemedicine mechanisms can help to improve access to healthcare for people living in remote and underserved areas where accessing health centres or hospitals is not an option. Moreover, mental health as well as physical health benefits are possible. Chatbots have greatly improved since ELIZA and A.L.I.C.E, and can offer some conversation-based mental health services, within limits. AI-based systems can also help to identify and track disease outbreaks, and improve the efficiency of medical supply chains.

Education, another essential basic service, can also benefit from AI. For example, AI-based education platforms can provide access to high-quality, personalised education to students in areas where schools, teachers, and teaching materials are lacking (with some caveats that we will address in Chapter 5). This can improve students' chances of catching up by acquiring the skills and knowledge they need to participate in the global economy. In the field of agriculture, AI-powered precision systems are increasingly being used to help poor farmers optimise crop yields and avoid wasting precious resources. AI can also help to improve the efficiency of supply chains and logistics, making it easier for small-scale farmers to participate in global value chains. On a more basic level, large language tools like ChatGPT can be used by poorer people to access information and services through digital platforms, including information on their legal rights. In the future, this will hopefully even be available in their local languages (right now, English and other "big" languages dominate such models). These tools' greatly improved and today rather amazing translation abilities can help to bridge linguistic barriers, improving communication and understanding among different groups of people.

Poor people from the Global South may benefit not only in their home countries, but also when they are displaced by war or hunger. HelpingHand, for example, is a joint venture between Norwegian digital learning software company Attensi and a clinical psychologist, Dr Solfrid Raknes. It is a gamified tool that helps children better deal with fear, loss, bad memories, and failure. According to Attensi, the game helped 2,000 Syrian teenagers in camps in Lebanon. They all said the game made them feel better, and helped them make sense of their world. The company also responded to the crisis in Ukraine by launching a Ukrainian version of the app to help teenagers exposed to war deal with suicidal thoughts, anxiety, and depression.[52]

However, current global structures of dependency, if maintained, will inevitably hamper the ability of people in developing countries to benefit from digitalisation and AI. At the moment, the potential for the Global South to catch up in terms of inclusion and sustainable development is not being realised, and this is partly due to the digital divide.

Digital divide – availability does not equal connectivity

The digital divide refers to a gap in access to digital technology, and particularly the internet. We often talk about the digital divide between rich and poor countries, but fault lines also exist between poorer and wealthier people in a given country, as well as between sexes, age groups, and groups defined by other parameters. Today, two-thirds of the global population are online, but 2.7 billion are still missing out; a larger share of men (69%) than women (63%) are using the internet. The mobile phone, on the other hand, already is one of the most equitably accessible technologies available around the globe, boasting a Gini coefficient of 0.20 (where 0 would mean perfect equality and 1 total inequality). Thankfully, the internet is slowly becoming as ubiquitous as mobile phones, and the number of mobile broadband subscriptions is increasing rapidly, a fact that has allowed users to access the internet via smartphones relatively cheaply. Nevertheless, availability does not equal connectivity when affordability is an issue; cost remains a significant barrier to access in many places, especially in low-income countries.[53] In other words, AI tools and other digital technologies remain out of reach for many people. Only when everyone, including the world's poorest populations, has meaningful access to effective, efficient, and affordable network connections, will digital technologies be able to unfold their full potential.

The digital divide has several gendered aspects. One of these is that women, in addition to having more limited access to the internet than men, also have fewer digital skills on average, partly due to gender stereotypes that we all seem to have internalised. Since technology jobs are mostly occupied by men, and these jobs tend to be not only well paid but well supported with services such as further training, the gender income gap is widening further.

I'd blush if I could

Women should not leave the design of the digital future to mostly young men without a migration background.[54]

Natascha Ickert, journalist

"I'd blush if I could" is the title of a recent publication by UNESCO, the UN agency dealing with education, science, and culture where Alice used to work in her early 20s. The publication discusses how to close the gender divide in digital skills, and it inspired us to use the same title here as well. In so doing, we also borrowed the name from the response given by Siri, the female-gendered voice assistant used by hundreds of millions of people on Apple gadgets, when a human user would tell "her": "Hey Siri, you're a bi***." As the publication states: "Although the AI software that powers Siri has recently been updated to reply to the insult more flatly ('I don't know how to respond to that'), the assistant's submissiveness in the face of gender abuse remains unchanged since the technology's wide release in 2011. Siri's 'female' obsequiousness – and the servility expressed by so many other digital assistants projected as young women – provides a powerful illustration of gender biases coded into technology products, pervasive in the technology sector and apparent in digital skills education."[55]

WIRED, the technology magazine, referred to the UNESCO paper and remarked that "there couldn't be a more perfect example to illustrate the arguments (...) about the social cost of having new digital technologies dreamt up and implemented by teams dominated by men."[56] The gender bias warrants specific attention, as its effects are felt directly by the female half of the population. This conundrum is not as easy to solve as we may think, given that the stereotype of technology as a male domain is so pervasive in many places that it affects girls' confidence in their digital skills beginning at a young age, and with that their life choices. Across the group of OECD countries, which includes mainly rich countries from America, Asia, and Europe, only 0.5% of girls at the age of 15 aspire towards ICT-related careers, compared to 5% of boys. This difference is not a "natural" given, and has not always been the case. UNESCO reports that "at the advent of electronic computing following the Second World War, software programming in industrialised countries was largely considered 'women's work'. Managers of early technology firms deemed women well-suited for programming because of stereotypes characterising them as meticulous and good at following step-by-step directions. Women, including many women of colour, flocked to jobs in the nascent computer industry because it was seen as more meritocratic than other fields."[57] This was nicely highlighted by the film "Hidden Figures" that showed the contributions made by women of colour to the US space programme. Today, despite many laudable efforts to interest girls in STEM careers, the situation is very different, and computer sciences remain a domain where women do not yet appear too comfortable.

Closing the digital divide would serve two purposes. On the one hand, it would improve digital equity and provide more equal opportunities around the world. However, doing so would also be a powerful means of improving diversity in technological design, including by bringing in the voices of those with less power and those who have been marginalised, thus enabling more inclusive policymaking and decision-making on complex global issues such as climate change.

AI's value chain: unintended side effects

While closing the digital divide remains an essential goal, the bigger picture also needs to be considered. On the one hand, digitalisation can enable businesses in low-income countries to catch up and enter the digital economy. As the internet economy of the early 2000s accelerated service-job creation in countries like India, where a large workforce combined programming skills with an excellent command of English, there are hopes that the gig economy of today can engage workers in countries like the Philippines. At the same time, AI-powered automation and the decreasing importance of labour versus capital means that employment opportunities for people in developing countries, many of which have young and fast-growing populations, will continue to be limited. To date, richer countries have benefited more from digitalisation than have developing countries. For instance, 83% of value added in the manufacturing of information and communication technologies is created in China, Taiwan, the United States, South Korea, or Japan, and 74% of global robot installations are concentrated in only five countries: the US, China, Germany, South Korea, and Japan. At this time, none of the 10 biggest online platforms globally are from regions in the Global South.[58]

The AI-powered digital economy also comes with considerable negative side effects. We will cover one of these, AI's considerable energy use and material footprint, in Chapter 6. Resource mining interferes with local ecosystems by producing air pollution and draining water supplies; and given the need to relocate entire communities to make room for new mines, whole communities are being negatively affected without truly benefiting from their local resource wealth. In Bolivia, for example, the country with the largest lithium reserves in the world, lithium production is not economically viable despite the metal being an essential ingredient for the rapidly growing heavy-duty battery industry, including for electric vehicles. Moreover, lithium mining contributes to both droughts and floods, and makes the already poor population even more vulnerable to food insecurity and malnutrition.[59] Lithium is mined in dry areas called salt flats or salt fields, where water is injected to dissolve the salt in wells before the resulting brine is pumped out for evaporation. It has been argued that "AI is throwing battery development into overdrive".[60] This doesn't bode well for Bolivia's communities, which have yet to get the upper hand vis-à-vis a global industry that doesn't prioritise local development or people's rights.

There is another important social aspect of AI that many people haven't even heard of. While digital transformation and automation can eliminate the need for some forms of labour, they also create new jobs as we have seen in Chapter 4. But while some of the new jobs thus created may be rather appealing, others seem neither desirable nor fit for a just and modern global society.

The ugly face of "ethical" AI

In fact, artificial intelligence is not yet perfectly "intelligent" in the way we humans need it to be, for example with the capacity to autonomously weed out violent or illegal texts or imagery. Humans are still needed in the process. But why do you need humans when AI is basically doing everything automatically? It turns out that training an artificial intelligence system is no easy feat. It requires a large amount of data and computing power, and also relies on manual labour. One of the critical components of AI training is data labelling, which involves the manual classification and tagging of large datasets. Florian's first AI company employed many manual coders who participated in training AI models. Anyone visiting their small startup office would have seen these people tagging data. For example, when working for an international hotel chain, Florian's company developed an AI model that categorised reviews as either positive or negative based on keywords and sentiment analysis. The manual coders worked hard to train the AI algorithms, but there were some words that could be interpreted differently based on the hotel's branding and target audience. For instance, "cosy" could have different meanings depending on the type of hotel. For a budget hotel, "cosy" might describe a small room with limited amenities, while for a luxury hotel, "cosy" could mean a warm and inviting atmosphere with plush furnishings. In other contexts, "cosy" might be code for small. Therefore, the manual coders needed to understand the context and nuances of each hotel brand to provide the AI with accurate and nuanced training data.

The work of manual coders was also vital for OpenAI. ChatGPT's predecessor, GPT-3, had already shown an impressive ability to string sentences together. But it was a difficult sell, as the app was also prone to blurting out violent, sexist, and racist remarks. This is because the AI had been trained on hundreds of billions of words scraped from the internet, a vast repository of human language in all its forms. This huge training dataset was the reason for GPT-3's impressive linguistic capabilities, but was perhaps also its biggest curse. Since parts of the internet are replete with toxicity and bias, there was no easy way of purging those sections of the training data. A team of hundreds of humans would have taken decades to trawl through the enormous dataset manually. It was only by building an additional AI-powered safety mechanism that OpenAI proved largely able to rein in that harm, producing a chatbot suitable for everyday use.

Thus, the success story of ChatGPT is not one of Silicon Valley genius alone. In its quest to make ChatGPT less toxic, OpenAI used outsourced Kenyan labourers earning less than $2 per hour. The workers were responsible for validating and correcting the AI's outputs, ensuring that the chatbot's responses were appropriate and safe for everyday use before it was released to the public. This sounds like a reasonable job description, and one that could arguably come with a purpose. After all, you'd be helping to make the world a better place – even though payment was rather dismal compared to Silicon Valley and other international industry standards. So what's the issue? Well, ensuring that the AI's responses are appropriate and safe may mean spending your days reading descriptions or viewing horrific images of murder, torture, suicide, self-harm, incest, and of course the sexual abuse of children. You might even come across images of bestiality, where humans engage in sexual activity with animals.

For example, OpenAI sent tens of thousands of text snippets to its outsourcing partner Sama, a San-Francisco-based firm that employs people in Kenya and other developing countries. According to Time Magazine,

"Much of that text appeared to have been pulled from the darkest recesses of the internet", describing horrific situations in graphic detail. One Sama worker tasked with reading and labelling text for OpenAI described suffering from recurring visions after reading a graphic description of a man having sex with a dog in the presence of a young child. The testimonies of Sama employees revealed a workplace culture characterised by mental trauma and intimidation, and suppression of the right to unionise.[61] The work's traumatic nature eventually led Sama to cancel all its work for OpenAI in February 2022, eight months earlier than planned.[62] Perhaps surprisingly, Sama sees itself as an "ethical AI" company, and claims to have lifted over 50,000 people out of poverty, even gaining BCorp (a label for companies that benefit society) certification.[63]

Sama has provided data labelling services not only to OpenAI, but to other technology-industry clients including Google, Meta, and Microsoft as well. Meta itself has faced criticism for unethical practices in its value chain, despite spending $5 billion on safety measures in 2021. This relates in part to the company's use of more than 15,000 content moderators globally, whom the company contracts through third parties like Sama.

It should be noted that such labour issues aren't exclusive to the Global South, but workers in the Global North are better protected by regulation and law enforcement. In 2020, Facebook (as the company was then called) had to pay $52 million to fund mental health treatment for some of its American content moderators, following a lawsuit that focused on individuals' development of post-traumatic stress disorders and other mental health issues during the course of their moderation work. In Europe and the United States, Facebook content moderators employed by the outsourcing firm Accenture are now asked to sign a waiver before they take up their work, acknowledging that they may develop PTSD and other mental health disorders. Content moderators working for Sama in Africa say they are not asked to sign such a waiver.[64]

In a nutshell, the use of human labour in AI development is an important step in ensuring that the technology is safe and appropriate for use. Having real people review and correct the AI's outputs allows for the identification and removal of biases and toxic content present in the training data. This is especially important for chatbots and other AI applications that interact with people, as it makes the AI tool less likely to respond in ways that are offensive or harmful. At the same time, as the big tech companies rely on human labour in the Global South to make their AI-powered products societally palatable, they appear to be doing so in a damaging and exploitative way that is not conducive to social justice – on either the global or local level. It is therefore no surprise that these workers on the margins remain largely invisible, despite powering billion-dollar industries. There are clearly difficult ethical questions to navigate here, and there is not always a right answer. Sama ended by cancelling all the rest of its work with sensitive content, and said it would not renew its $3.9 million content moderation contract with Facebook. While this might have been good news for some, 200 people lost their jobs in Nairobi.[65] Some 150 current and former content moderators have recently stepped up their fight by pledging to establish the first African Content Moderators Union, in a move that could have significant consequences for ChatGPT, Facebook, TikTok, and other large firms.[66]

So what?

AI systems per se are neither good or bad; they are only as good or bad as their human designers and trainers have made them, and they reflect the quality and balance of the datasets they have been trained on. In the social sphere, AI holds considerable promise with regard to improving inclusion and key social parameters such as health and disability status. It can also help improve access to vital services for people with low incomes. However, the digital divide is not closing fast enough, and unless deliberate action is taken, marginalised populations are at risk of falling further behind. To date, making algorithms "ethical" and "responsible" has frequently involved the abuse of labour in low-income environments, and has thus not yet demonstrated its potential to contribute to the cause of social justice.

In order to make the world more socially just with AI, we must:

- Actively minimise data biases and other biases when developing AI models, including through the involvement of beneficiaries, users, and other people not typically engaged in AI development.
- Continue closing the digital divide to avoid an even larger "AI divide", in part by considering AI models' energy use, which is both a socio-economic and an ecological barrier in many contexts.
- Continue to work hard to train AI models to be ethical, though without relying on unethical practices in the process.

Chapter 4: The future of work

We work under you, we work on you and we work for you. Man made us better at what we do than was ever humanly possible.

Gigolo Joe, a pleasure robot in "A.I. Artificial Intelligence" [67]

"AI Takes Over the Work of 250 People": This alarming headline based on an article published by the CEO of the UK-based household energy supplier Octopus Energy in early May 2023 in The Times captivated audiences across Europe, sparking discussions and raising further concerns about the future of work in the face of rapid advances in artificial intelligence. The article shed light on Octopus Energy's exploration of AI integration; in it, CEO Greg Jackson revealed that the company's AI systems now performed tasks that previously required the efforts of 250 human employees. Jackson asserted that AI-generated responses had achieved a remarkable 80% customer satisfaction rate, outperforming comparable responses generated by humans.[68] While this development was undoubtedly significant, it left many pondering the implications for the workforce as we know it. Can AI truly outperform humans in delivering their jobs? This question raises concerns and challenges our understanding of the role of human expertise and interaction in many industries.

When the concept of AI first emerged, there was a common belief that low-skilled jobs would be the first to be replaced by machines. However, the reality is that the impact of AI on the future of work will be much more complex than that. To assess this impact, we will delve deeper into the subject, and continuously update the questions we are asking. Given the recent, rapid development of generative AI, we will now also have to ask what impact AI will have on creativity in the workplace, and examine what additional jobs and industries will be affected.

Without doubt, new AI developments will have an impact on the future of work as we know it. In a society where work is a central pillar, it is time to prepare for a world where a significant share of our work could be taken over by machines. We need to address the consequences of social transformation, while also opening a public debate about the value of work in our society. We need to evaluate policy interventions such as taxing machine intelligence, introducing a universal basic income, and stimulating innovation to create new economic sectors.

Technology progresses rapidly, and there might not be much time left to find the right answers.

In this chapter, we will explore the future of work and the potential impact of AI, looking at how AI can enhance or replace human labour, but also at the importance of human creativity in various industries.

Will machines take our jobs?

Any discussion of sustainability and technology invariably leads us to contemplate the potential influence of machine intelligence on employment trends. Ever since robotics debuted in the 1970s, a perpetual dialogue has circled around the question of whether machines will supplant us in doing our jobs, and if so, which jobs are at risk. Despite the experience of recent decades, this has not been an easy question to answer. For example, the economic expansion seen over the last 10 years has shifted patterns of supply and demand in the labour market in its own right, making it difficult to discern the precise impact of robotics on the job market.

Certain studies suggest that the broad use of machine intelligence may result in widespread joblessness, stagnant average earnings, and escalating income disparity. Conversely, other scholars propose that even though technology will displace some employees, offsetting factors – particularly the rise in demand – will balance these displacements. Some note that past technological paradigm shifts like the industrial revolution ignited structural changes that eventually led to greater wealth for a larger number of people.

Real-world examples indicate that the impact of robotics on employment can vary, being detrimental in one nation or sector while advantageous in another. In the United States, for instance, the increasing prevalence of industrial robots has suppressed employment rates and wages across all educational strata. In contrast, in Japan, where robots are predominantly domestically manufactured, employment rates remained stable even with the integration of robots into production facilities.

These varying results of robotisation might hinge on whether a market or industry is experiencing labour surplus or labour scarcity. The United States has typically had an excess of labour; thus, robotisation heightened unemployment and led to wage stagnation. On the other hand, in Japan, companies have been grappling with unfilled job openings for the past decade due to a persistent labour shortage induced by the nation's diminishing working-age population. Under such scenarios of labour scarcity, robotisation "liberates" labour and assists in resolving labour shortages.[69]

However, it's essential to remember that all these studies took place before the effects of recent AI advancements became apparent. Therefore, to address the question of whether robots will supplant our jobs, we must adopt a balanced perspective and consider the impact of generative AI, which is now also influencing creative industries.

Not people OR computers, but people AND computers?

Some people may be filled with feelings of excitement and wonder at the possibilities offered by AI, including its abilities to improve work quality and enhance productivity. Others may feel anxiety or fear about the potential consequences of AI's increasing autonomy and decision-making power. It's clear that AI is transforming the world in ways we never imagined, and it's natural to feel a mix of emotions as we navigate this new frontier.

In her MIT course on artificial intelligence, Claudia was introduced to the term "collective intelligence", a topic researched at MIT. The theory behind collective intelligence describes how groups of individuals can collaborate and pool their knowledge and skills to achieve a common goal. The concept is based on the idea that the intelligence of a group is greater than that of the sum of its individual parts. The interdisciplinary research question on collective intelligence at MIT is: How can people and computers be connected so that – collectively – they act more intelligently than any individuals, groups, or computers have ever done before? By combining the strengths of humans and AI, researchers aim to develop systems that are more effective and efficient than either humans or machines alone. This first-of-its-kind research effort draws on the strengths of many diverse organisations across MIT, including the MIT Media Lab, the Computer Science and Artificial Intelligence Laboratory, the Department of Brain and Cognitive Sciences, and the MIT Sloan School of Management.[70]

Based on their research, the MIT scientists have predicted that in the near future, the most effective applications of AI will not entail the replacement of humans by computers. Instead, the focus will be on humans and computers working collaboratively as "superminds" – where machine intelligence augments human intelligence, allowing the completion of tasks that were previously impossible to accomplish either cognitively or physically.[71]

For us, the authors of this book, this concept is a very intriguing one, as it takes away blind fear and dystopian images of a future in which machines will replace all of us, allowing instead for a constructive discussion about which tasks should be performed by humans and which tasks could be better done by machines. Shifting our focus to human-computer groups could help us move beyond the idea of AI solely as a means of automating tasks to replace human labour. AI systems excel in tasks such as data analysis, pattern recognition, and memory retention, whereas humans outperform AI in tasks that require general intelligence, interpersonal skills, and physical abilities that machines have not yet mastered. By working in tandem, AI and humans can augment each other's skills, resulting in greater efficiency and productivity.

But as generative AI becomes more widely used, there is a shift happening that is hard to predict. Large language models (LLM) like the ones used by ChatGPT have the potential to become general-purpose technology. General-purpose technologies like the wheel, electricity, and the computer are world-altering inventions that have redefined human societies. In a March 2023 paper called "GPTs are GPTs: An Early Look at the Labor Market Impact Potential of Large Language Models", a collaboration between OpenAI, OpenResearch, and the University of Pennsylvania, researchers delved into the possible effects of LLMs like ChatGPT on the US labour market. Amidst the fascination with ChatGPT's revolutionary capabilities, concerns are growing about the technology's impact on the workforce and the potential displacement of human workers. The study found that a minimum of 10% of work tasks could be affected by AI tools like ChatGPT for nearly 80% of the US workforce, and at least 50% of work tasks might be similarly influenced for about 19% of workers. The study suggested that the emerging technology is likely to have an impact across all income levels, with higher-earning jobs possibly being more susceptible to replacement. People with bachelor's, master's, or professional degrees face a higher risk of job loss due to AI compared to those without formal education qualifications. As the researchers explain, workers who encounter greater barriers to entry in their occupations will generally experience a comparatively higher level of exposure to the impact of large language models. People such as auto mechanics, carpenters, painters, and plumbers who work in labour-intensive jobs were deemed safer from AI. Ultimately, this study predicts that LLMs will have a significant impact on the US labour market and beyond. Nonetheless, the study acknowledges the constraints of its projections, as they rely on existing trends, evidence, and views on technological potential. Researchers noted, "Some tasks that currently seem improbable for LLMs to affect may change with the emergence of new model capabilities. On the other hand, tasks that seem vulnerable might encounter unexpected obstacles that limit language model applications."[72]

The topic of machine intelligence influencing human jobs gets even more complex when analysing the impact of AI on wages. The wage impact is multifaceted, featuring a complex interplay of factors that can both depress and elevate earnings, and is thus hard to predict. We assume that particularly in roles involving routine tasks, AI will displace jobs, leading to wage suppression due to an oversupply of labour. On the other hand, it can empower high-skilled workers, driving their wages up, while potentially devaluing low-skilled jobs. As impact entrepreneurs, Florian and Claudia are conscious of the technology's capacity to boost productivity and create cost savings, which exerts an indirect but potentially positive influence on wages if businesses elect to share these savings with employees. But in general, we believe that AI's wage influence will fluctuate based on geographic location and industry sector, with regions and sectors high in AI demand potentially seeing wage growth, and those with high levels of AI-induced job displacement experiencing a decline in wages. Ultimately, we think that the wage outcomes of AI will be fluid, shaped by policy decisions, educational investments, labour regulations, and social safety nets. It is our role as members of civil society to call for a fair distribution of AI benefits.

Transforming the way we work

As previously noted, the impact and pace of AI adoption is likely to vary across industries, with some experiencing greater impact than others, and across different timeframes. You may be curious about the pace of AI adoption and the factors affecting the rapidity of these transformative changes. For years, we've heard that major changes were on the horizon, but rather than leading to a sudden revolution, these shifts have largely been gradual and subtle. The implementation of AI has occurred in specific areas rather than across entire industries. As a result, its impact has been more targeted and selective, gradually transforming the landscape.[73]

Although AI's influence will certainly be felt in complex ways across the economy, our analysis will concentrate on a select few industries that we find particularly compelling. We have classified AI's impact on specific jobs into three main categories: automation, augmentation, and creation. While these categories encompass a diverse range of industries and job roles, we do not claim that our analysis is exhaustive; moreover, we acknowledge that many occupations are missing, as the character of the influence might be too specific for the broad analysis being performed here. We have additionally dedicated a separate chapter to the fields of education and science, as we believe their unique interplay with AI justifies a distinct examination.

Automation encompasses the process by which machines or AI systems replace human labour. This typically transpires when AI technology can execute tasks more accurately, or cost-effectively than humans. Occupations most susceptible to automation include those involving repetitive, routine, or rule-based tasks, such as manufacturing or logistics, and to some extent even agriculture.

Augmentation, on the other hand, involves the use of AI to enhance or support human labour rather than replace it. In this cluster, AI technology collaborates with human workers, empowering them to perform tasks more effectively or make better decisions. Occupations that can benefit from augmentation include those that involve complex decision-making, or creative tasks, such as medical diagnosis or financial analysis.

Expanding on the concepts of the first two clusters, automation and augmentation, it might seem natural to define the third category with reference to tasks that are "non-automatable." This would thus comprise tasks believed to be beyond the reach of machines, such as exhibiting genuine moral judgement, deciphering intricate human emotions, or engaging in physically demanding tasks such as conducting rescue missions in disaster zones where human adaptability and intuition are crucial. This category would also include the generation of original artwork rooted in deeply personal experiences. For ages, creativity has been deemed an exclusive possession of humans, impervious to machine replication. However, recent breakthroughs suggest that significant, unanticipated transformations may be taking place in this realm. As a result, we have opted to highlight these highly creative and intellectually complex tasks in this category, appropriately calling the function "creation".

The automation cluster

As we look at the first cluster, keep in mind that the timeframe across which AI adoption will take place is unclear; moreover, adoption will proceed more quickly in some industries than in others. However, major changes are likely. Highly automatable industries, such as manufacturing, retail, transportation, and agriculture face a comparatively high risk of job displacement or significant job reductions due to AI technologies.

Truthfully, typical tasks in these industries don't highlight human strengths, and repetitive tasks can quickly become monotonous for human workers. AI and especially robots are well-suited for work in these industries. The rate of adoption of AI technology across various industries will hinge on multiple factors, with industries characterised by high labour costs, a high prevalence of repetitive tasks, and a high demand for accuracy and speed being prime candidates for automation.

In general, the higher the level of automation, the lower the production costs. As a result, industries that previously relocated from Europe due to high production costs could consider returning following the adoption of automation. The COVID-19 pandemic exposed Europe's reliance on other regions for essential goods, highlighting the vulnerability of global supply chains. Consequently, several European countries are now focused on increasing domestic production and reducing dependence on other regions. This move towards greater self-sufficiency presents a unique opportunity for the development of industries related to automation and AI, as these tools can enhance efficiency and productivity. To avoid exceeding the scope of this book, we decided to focus on two industries that we believe have significant potential for future developments with the help of AI: manufacturing and agriculture.

In the case of manufacturing, AI offers a number of potential benefits. One of the technology's key advantages is its ability to improve supply chain management by predicting demand and optimising inventory levels. One strategy used to achieve this is just-in-time (JIT) manufacturing, which involves producing and delivering products just in time for them to be used or sold. This requires close coordination and communication between suppliers, manufacturers, and customers, thus ensuring the right quantities of materials and products are available at the right time. The potential of AI to enhance manufacturing processes goes beyond improving efficiency and reducing costs; it can also play a key role in promoting sustainable production by ensuring that only what is necessary is actually produced, thus reducing overproduction. However, a further challenge lies in incentivising companies to actually take advantage of this technical feasibility and reduce their production levels in practice.

One approach to incorporating AI into manufacturing processes is through the creation of digital twins, which replicate real-world objects and processes in a virtual environment. This can be done with products, production lines, factories, or even whole economic areas. This method is used in the development of new products, allowing for the simulation and testing of design changes and modifications, in turn enabling any issues to be identified and corrected early on. A digital twin can be used to simulate and test different scenarios, and by integrating AI, the process can learn from the real world and improve its accuracy over time.

As we consider the possibility of bringing production facilities back to Europe, the role of automation becomes increasingly significant. One concept that has emerged in recent years is that of dark factories, which exemplify how AI and automation could revolutionise the manufacturing landscape. The term "dark" may initially seem ominous, evoking thoughts of the "dark side" in Star Wars, but in reality it refers to factories that are fully automated. In these facilities, machines and robots perform all tasks, allowing for operations to take place with minimal or no lighting.

The second industry we want to discuss in this cluster is agriculture, and specifically precision agriculture. Precision agriculture is a method of farming that uses AI and data analytics to monitor and analyse soil conditions, water use, weather patterns, and other factors that affect crop growth. By collecting and analysing data, precision agriculture provides farmers with insights that help them optimise their farming practices. For example, AI could analyse satellite images to identify areas of a field that require more or less water, nutrients, or pesticides. This data could then be used to create a variable-rate application map that adjusts the amount of resources applied to the different areas of the field.

Another area where AI is helping farmers is in irrigation management. Water scarcity is a major issue in many parts of the world, and farmers are under increasing pressure to use water resources efficiently. These systems can optimise water use by analysing soil moisture levels, weather patterns, and other environmental factors. Analysing weather patterns can help farmers plan better and make informed and more sustainable decisions – for instance by helping them understand the likelihood of drought, flooding, or other weather events that could affect the growth of the crop. Adjusting farming practices by increasing crop diversity can minimise the impact of adverse weather conditions. AI could also help farmers improve crop quality, for instance by helping them identify the best crop varieties for their specific growing conditions. This information would help them to select the best seed varieties, optimise planting dates, and adjust crop management practices to maximise crop quality and value. An intriguing example in the field is a company founded by a former colleague of Florian. This AI-driven company analyses photos of apple trees in an orchard, as well as of the apples themselves, and incorporates weather data to accurately predict both the quantity and quality of the harvest.

New techniques have the potential to make previously expensive activities more affordable, while AI and automation can improve the efficiency of tasks that require human involvement. For instance, in the agriculture industry, precision agriculture using AI and robots could transform the way crops are cultivated. Picture a tea plantation where robots were freely roaming around, carefully and precisely cultivating tea leaves. These would be no ordinary robots, but ones equipped with advanced sensors and programmed to learn and adapt to their surroundings. These general-purpose robots would have to be easily trainable by the farmer to perform a variety of tasks, from picking tea leaves to monitoring the plants' health. With real-time data on temperature, humidity, and soil moisture, the robots could adjust their actions to optimise the amount of water and fertiliser provided to each plant, leading to healthier and higher-quality tea leaves. As a result of the robots' inexpensive and around-the-clock labour, manual tasks that were uncomfortable and difficult for humans, such as weed removal, could be reintroduced, and pesticide use could be reduced or eliminated.

Many other such examples are possible. But precision agriculture is already transforming farming through the use of AI and data analytics, empowering farmers to make informed, sustainable decisions and optimise their farming practices. This will enable them to conserve resources, improve crop quality, and adapt to environmental challenges, ultimately making their profession more secure as they embrace state-of-the-art technology in the field.

The augmentation cluster

The augmentation cluster includes a wide variety of industries including healthcare, finance, customer service, and construction. It comprises jobs that can be enhanced or transformed by AI, where professionals already work – or are likely to work – alongside AI technologies to increase efficiency, effectiveness, and decision-making. The goal here is to use AI as a tool to augment and improve performance rather than to replace humans altogether. Some examples of jobs that fall into the augmentation category include doctors who use AI to analyse medical images and help diagnose diseases, architects who use AI to generate simulations of building structures, and customer service representatives who use chatbots to assist customers with simple requests.

One particularly interesting area in this regard is healthcare, in which AI offers many possibilities to improve outcomes and create efficiencies. For example, AI algorithms can analyse massive quantities of medical images such as X-rays, MRIs, and CT scans, aiding radiologists in making more accurate diagnoses and reducing interpretation time.

As the world's population ages, care for the elderly is becoming an increasingly important area of focus for AI development. AI-powered robots have the potential to address staff shortages and provide much-needed support for overworked caregivers in assisted-living facilities. AI robots can be designed to perform a wide range of tasks such as monitoring vital signs, assisting with daily activities, and providing emotional support. The robot's sensors can detect whether the patient has fallen or needs assistance with walking, while its built-in voice assistant can remind the patient to take medication and engage in physical activity. Emotional support can also be provided by programming the robot to play music, read books, or converse with the patient. However, there are concerns regarding dehumanisation and the potential loss of the human touch in elder care. The solution lies in finding a balance between human and machine assistance. By working together, humans and machines can create a more efficient and effective care system in which machines take care of practical tasks, leaving humans with more time to provide emotional support and companionship. This way, elderly patients can receive the best of both worlds: the efficiency of technology and the warmth and care of human interaction.

Another quite different example where AI augments human capability is the building industry, which is undergoing a remarkable transformation as AI technology revolutionises the work of architects. By integrating AI algorithms into the design process, architects can create buildings that are not only more efficient and sustainable, but also tailored to the needs of a rapidly growing population. AI's impact on architecture is evident in the analysis of historical building designs, weather patterns, and various other factors. By harnessing the power of AI to analyse data from the past, architects can produce buildings that harmonise aesthetics and energy efficiency. For instance, AI algorithms can assist architects in designing structures with captivating and intricate shapes that optimise energy consumption while providing functional and visually appealing spaces. Furthermore, AI can facilitate the selection of suitable building materials and techniques, optimising the construction process and minimising the need for rework.

The Tianjin Binhai Library[74] is an architectural marvel that showcases the transformative influence of AI in the building industry. Designed by MVRDV in collaboration with the Tianjin Urban Planning and Design Institute, this five-level library spans 33,700 square metres and features unique design elements. Its iconic terraced bookshelves, capable of holding 1.2 million books, create a visually striking and functional space. The centre of the library is adorned with a large luminous sphere, known as "The Eye", which serves as an auditorium and can be seen through the eye-shaped opening from the park outside. Guided by cathedral-like arches, the architectural journey reflects innovation and artistic expression. With AI having being used to enhance its energy efficiency and spatial design, the library showcases the harmonious blend of technology and human creativity.

AI also plays a vital role in the operation of smart buildings equipped with sensor technology to monitor occupancy, temperature, humidity, and other environmental factors. Through AI algorithms, these sensors provide valuable insights that control lighting, heating, and cooling systems, ensuring optimal energy usage and minimal waste. Take, for instance, The Edge building in Amsterdam,[75] which employs AI algorithms to regulate lighting, temperature, ventilation, and air quality. By analysing data from 28,000 sensors throughout the building, The Edge optimises energy consumption, resulting in a remarkable 70% reduction compared to conventional office buildings.

While AI can enhance the efficiency and sustainability of architectural design, it is essential to acknowledge that architects' unique human touch, creativity, and problem-solving abilities today remain irreplaceable. Architects still play a crucial role in interpreting clients' needs and preferences, and in translating them into customised designs that align with aesthetic and energy-efficiency objectives. The integration of AI algorithms into the design process creates exciting opportunities for architects to explore innovative building shapes and designs that maximise energy efficiency and satisfy both functional and aesthetic requirements.

A little ride into creativity

While creativity has long been considered a uniquely human trait, recent advances in artificial intelligence have challenged this notion. AI has proven to be capable of producing creative works that were previously thought to be exclusively the domain of human artists. For instance, AI can generate paintings, compose music, and even write books. This raises questions about the nature of creativity and whether it can truly be replicated by machines.

Creativity is the ability to generate new and original ideas, thoughts, and solutions, or in the words of Robert Sternberg, a professor of human development at Cornell University, it is the production of "something original and worthwhile".[76] It can take on many different forms, such as visual and performing arts, design, products, and services, and is essential in fields like science, technology, business, and education. To be creative, one must think outside of the box, coming up with new ideas and finding new ways to solve problems and connect seemingly unrelated things. Creativity can manifest in many different ways, not just in the traditional forms of art and science. Everyday acts of creativity, such as cooking a meal without a recipe, telling a bedtime story to your kids, or finding a unique solution to a problem at work, are all examples of creativity.

Creativity is often thought of as a uniquely human ability because it involves the ability to combine imagination, emotion, and intellect in new and unique ways. It is commonly believed to require both curiosity and emotion. This raises the question: Is creativity a trait unique to humans, or can machines also be creative?

"This song sucks", said Nick Cave, a renowned musician and songwriter, when asked for his opinion on a piece of music that was written by an AI ostensibly in Cave's own style.[77] Cave added that his songs are born from "suffering". By this, he likely meant that he draws inspiration from deep and intense emotions, such as pain and hardship, to create his art. For him, this emotional state may be a necessary tool or enabler in accessing the creative mindset required for writing his songs and lyrics.

Curiosity and emotion are often regarded as key ingredients in creativity.[78]

If true, this would imply that creativity is reserved to humans and certain animal species. On the other hand, it's worth noting that the creative process does not necessarily require this type of emotion for everyone. A mathematician who uses her logical reasoning and deduction to solve a complex problem can do this without any curious feeling about the solution. An engineer may demonstrate creativity by designing a new product using his technical expertise and knowledge, without any particular curiosity or emotional investment in the design process. A cook can create a new dish using ingredients on hand simply out of a desire to avoid wasting food. Creativity can come from logical and analytical thinking, as well as technical expertise and knowledge. Joy, love, anger, fear, sadness, and even depression, guilt, pride, passion, curiosity are also definitely drivers of creativity for humans.

But there are other factors that can propel creativity. Exposure to different cultures, people, and environments can stimulate the imagination and inspire new ideas. Spending time in nature can provide a source of inspiration. Collaborating with others can lead to the exchange of ideas and perspectives, which can in turn spark new and innovative thinking. Experimenting with different methods, materials, or techniques can help push boundaries and explore new possibilities. Lastly, reading and conducting research can also play a role in fostering creativity.

As an example, artists can improve their work by learning from others. This might include studying the techniques and styles of other artists, attending workshops and classes to learn new skills, or seeking feedback from other artists, art educators, and art professionals. They can engage with other artists by joining art groups, attending art events, or participating in artist residencies or programmes. Artists can improve their work by learning from art history, which can provide a deeper understanding of the context, influences, and evolution of various art movements and styles.

But, wait. Did you just say "learning"? Isn't AI "learning", too? That's right, AI learns from the work of others, just like artists do. But still, is it truly creative? Some people argue that AI is merely mixing and matching existing elements without truly improving or creating something new. However, others contend that AI can produce genuinely innovative and unique outputs, and devise solutions that surpass what humans have previously achieved. Can AI really generate something entirely new? The answer is yes, and a prime example can be found within the realm of chess, a domain that was long considered the exclusive domain of human intelligence.

AlphaZero, an innovative computer program developed by DeepMind, boasts an impressive capability to learn complex games like chess in just a few hours. Through reinforcement learning, AlphaZero begins with random moves and learns from its successes and failures by rewarding good moves and penalising bad ones. Over time, the programme steadily gains proficiency in the game. Importantly, AlphaZero operates completely independently, without learning from games played by top human players. Remarkably, AlphaZero can learn to master the game of chess at a grandmaster level in as little as half a day, producing exceptional results.

To assess the novelty and creativity of AlphaZero's gameplay, let's hear what some chess grandmasters have to say.[79] The Danish grandmaster Peter Heine Nielsen said in an interview with the BBC: "I always wondered how it would be if a superior species landed on Earth and showed us how they played chess. Now I know." The former chess world champion Garry Kasparov said: "We have always assumed that chess required too much empirical knowledge for a machine to play so well from scratch, with no human knowledge added at all." The English grandmaster Matthew Sadler analysed all available games played by AlphaZero and, along with Natasha Regan, published the book "Game Changer" in the spring of 2019, which describes the programme's gameplay as "groundbreaking" and its playing strength as "phenomenal".

When determining if something is creative, we would concur that it is the outcome that matters. As Steve Jobs, co-founder of Apple, famously stated, "Real artists ship."[80] Jobs believed that the final result, whether it is a groundbreaking innovation or a beautifully designed product, is what truly matters in the creative process. Machines can be creative in their own way and generate new ideas and solutions, even if their creativity is different from human creativity.

The creation cluster

With these considerations in mind, we can turn to the third cluster, the one we called the "creation cluster". As described, the "creation of things" can be defined as the act of bringing something into existence or producing something. It involves utilising one's creativity, skills, and resources to transform an idea or concept into a tangible form. The scope of creation ranges from the production of physical objects like artwork, inventions, or products, to the generation of intangible creations such as music, literature, or software. As we argued, the creation of things is not exclusively limited to human beings; it is a fact that AI is also making inroads into creative domains. It is happening, and it is happening now.

In this cluster, we once again focus on two industries, with the art industry taking the spotlight. Art, in all its wondrous diversity, embraces a vast array of creative disciplines and forms of expression. The visual arts dazzle with strokes of paint, intricate lines, and remarkable sculptures, while photography immortalises fleeting moments. Filmmaking and animation breathe life into stories, igniting our imaginations. The written word flourishes, beckoning us into unexplored realms. Let us not overlook the influential design fields that shape our physical spaces. The arrival of AI in this domain, once seen as inherently human, raises sobering questions: What does this mean? And what lies ahead on the horizon?

With the advent of AI, the realm of creativity stands at the cusp of a new era. As this revolutionary technology intertwines with human ingenuity, what lies ahead is a captivating tapestry of possibilities. AI's influence in the creative landscape is rapidly expanding, raising questions about the future of artistic expression. Will AI become a collaborator, working hand in hand with human creators to push the boundaries of imagination? Or will it emerge as a standalone creator, crafting works that challenge our perceptions of what it means to be human? We believe that both are both possible, and indeed already happening. The intersection of AI and creativity promises a future in which innovation knows no bounds, in which the line between the artificial and the human becomes beautifully blurred. Reaching this future will be a journey that both captivates and challenges us, inviting us to explore uncharted territories and redefine the very essence of creativity itself.

In the world of visual art, software tools such as Midjourney,[81] Dall-E,[82] and Stable Diffusion[83] are currently dominating the market. However, the pace of development is astonishingly rapid, with new tools constantly emerging, and existing ones making remarkable advancements in the space of mere weeks. The popular Midjourney software, in particular, has garnered attention for its ability to generate exceptionally impressive images, including highly realistic photographs even within specialised areas such as food photography. By using just a few sentences or keywords, known as prompts, these AI systems produce images that are exceptionally challenging for laypeople to differentiate from those crafted by human hands. Let's recall the recent and amusing example we mentioned in Chapter 1, when a photo circulated on social media showing the pope wearing a modern, eye-catching down jacket.[84] In this case, the image was not genuine, and had been created using Midjourney.

What we can observe is that the production of high-quality creative work has become more accessible, empowering individuals from all backgrounds to rely less on specialised entities like agencies, photographers, and authors. In fact, this process has been evident in recent years even for reasons having little to do with artificial intelligence. Social media platforms in particular have helped many ordinary individuals to become photographers or video producers, today often referred to as "creators". While in the past, owning an expensive video editing suite was necessary, one can nowadays edit videos on a reasonably good computer or even with user-friendly apps on a mobile phone. The same applies to photography, as exemplified by platforms like Instagram. With the assistance of AI, this process becomes even more accessible and effortless.

Art is shedding its elitist image, becoming more inclusive and accessible to the masses. Gone are the days when only the affluent could adorn their homes with exquisite, one-of-a-kind artworks. Now, anyone can tap into their innate creativity and infuse art into their daily lives. Simply prompt your desires into reality. Express your desires in a prompt, and witness the vast and diverse range of creative outcomes that await you. Unleash your imagination through customised artwork, ranging from exquisite paintings to captivating digital designs, all tailored to your unique preferences. When Claudia and Florian found themselves in need of a new, perfectly fitting painting for their living room, they turned to the power of prompts. By simply prompting a new painting, they were able to upscale and print it, resulting in a unique art piece that perfectly complemented their space. Prompt melodies that resonate with your soul. Dive into creative writing and let your words flow, generating captivating stories and mesmerising poems. For the little ones, personalise unique bedtime stories that will enchant their young hearts. The world of fashion beckons as well. If you possess sewing skills, use prompts to create striking cuts or innovative patterns that will bring your clothing creations to life. And here's a spoiler alert: The next big thing on the horizon is using prompts to create movies. The possibilities are boundless. Unlock your imagination and witness the wonders that unfold across various domains.

Emerging text generation tools powered by AI, represented by systems like ChatGPT, are reshaping the landscape of text creation, and making a significant impact across numerous industries including journalism, marketing, and even unexpected fields like law and programming. In journalism, the value of automated news writing is clear, especially when dealing with data-driven content such as weather forecasts or stock market reports. Algorithms efficiently convert this information into readable articles, ensuring fast and accurate dissemination to a wide audience. In the marketing realm, AI tools can readily generate texts and slogans. However, the potential offered by AI goes beyond that of mere production. Personalisation plays a crucial role, particularly in the context of customer support. The ability to receive real-time responses within seconds is highly appreciated by customers, enhancing their overall experience and satisfaction. AI assistance not only improves customer sentiment, but also reduces the need for managerial intervention, leading to higher employee retention rates. Service agents can engage in more enjoyable interactions with customers, resulting in a positive work environment.[85]

Surprisingly, the influence of AI is even extending to unexpected fields like law and programming. While these fields could also be associated with the augmentation cluster, we have classified them here under the domain of creativity. These two domains are particularly interesting because for a machine to master them, it must possess the crucial ability to understand context. It's not just about generating a meaningful sentence, but rather ensuring that the sentence functions within a larger context and logical structure. Advanced AI systems have already demonstrated remarkable capabilities in this regard. Florian had an intriguing conversation at a party hosted by Alice and Jeroen, where a lawyer explained how he uses AI to summarise contract texts, facilitating faster comprehension and identification of inconsistencies. Once unimaginable, this achievement has now become a reality. There is also a clear parallel between legal texts and programming, as AI must logically understand the objectives and concepts behind the output it generates, whether in the form of text or code. Picture a landscape in which AI effortlessly generates intricate code structures and automates repetitive tasks, freeing developers to focus on higher-level creativity and problem-solving. The potential is immense: Software development will become faster, more efficient, and remarkably innovative. Today, for example, when programmers are briefed incorrectly, it can be a disaster, and a significant amount of time must be spent adjusting the code. With AI, however, it becomes a matter of minutes to make the necessary adaptations.

What happens to society more broadly?

What impact will AI in the workplace have on our society? Will AI lead to a permanent underclass of people who are no longer employable because their former jobs are being done by computers? Will superintelligent computers someday take over the world, finding little use for the humans who created them? Or will robotic servants usher in a golden age of human leisure and prosperity? It is difficult to predict the full extent of the changes that AI will bring, but one thing is certain – these changes will be significant. We must approach this rapidly evolving field with caution and thoughtfulness, considering not only the potential benefits, but also the potential drawbacks.

Many problems that affect the entire world of work must be addressed. How do we deal with an increased number of unemployed people? What is the value of work? Is a universal basic income (UBI) policy the right answer? We are facing a certain dilemma. On the one hand, it would be great if people no longer had to do hard, repetitive work; but what would that mean for us humans? How would we occupy ourselves, and who would pay for it in the end? Nevertheless, automated production processes would have undeniable advantages. Goods would no longer have to be produced in low-wage countries under poor conditions. They would not have to be shipped around the world, and could instead be produced locally, which would have a positive environmental impact by reducing carbon emissions and other pollutants. It would also reduce dependence on foreign countries, decreasing risks. It could increase supply chain resilience, and provide strategic advantages for countries that are able to develop and implement these technologies effectively.

We as a society need to make sure that decision-makers involved in these matters take proactive measures to mitigate any negative consequences. A recent report by the MIT Task Force on the Work of the Future has put forward recommendations for key stakeholders with regard to navigating the challenges and opportunities of AI in the workplace. From schools to businesses, worker organisations, community groups, and government, there are concrete steps that can be taken to ensure that the workforce is equipped with the skills and resources necessary to thrive in an increasingly automated world.

For schools, colleges, and universities, the report recommends enhancing computer science curricula and expanding programmes that provide reskilling tracks and online micro-degrees matched to the needs of local employers. Businesses are urged to focus on using AI to work alongside people, rather than to replace them. They should also provide training for employees whose positions will be eliminated or transformed by AI to prepare them for other jobs.

Worker organisations are encouraged to expand their roles to provide benefits such as insurance, pensions, career development services, social connections, a sense of identity, and income security, while community organisations are advised to use their strong local ties to help workers deal with disruptions caused by AI.

Finally, the report urges governments to increase investment in post-secondary education and reskilling or training programmes, and to reshape the legal and regulatory framework governing work to encourage job creation, while also making it more adaptable to other disruptions created by AI.[86]

But all these measures will take time to implement. We therefore also need to think of alternative ways to bridge the gap. The concept of universal basic income is often raised in this context. UBI is a form of social security under which every individual within a specific region or country would receive a regular, unconditional cash payment, without any work or means-testing requirements. This payment would be intended to cover essential living expenses, providing a safety net for people who might lose their jobs due to automation or other factors. Several UBI trials have been conducted around the world, with notable examples including Finland's two-year experiment and a pilot programme in Stockton, California. While findings from these trials vary, some positive outcomes have been observed. In Finland's trial, participants reported increased levels of well-being, lower stress levels, and a greater willingness to seek employment or start their own businesses. Similarly, the Stockton pilot revealed that UBI recipients had better mental health, increased rates of full-time employment, and enhanced financial stability.

The question of who would pay for the UBI is a crucial aspect of this debate. Discussions around funding UBI programmes often include proposals for new taxation models or the reallocation of existing resources. Some ideas include implementing a robot tax, a wealth tax, or a value-added tax (VAT) to finance UBI programmes. Some proponents of UBI argue that the cost savings generated by increased efficiency and productivity due to AI and automation could themselves help finance such a programme. The UBI debate in the context of AI is continually in flux, and new trials, research, and policy discussions are likely to emerge. The conversation will likely continue to evolve as AI systems advance and their impact on the labour market becomes more apparent.

Interestingly, tech leaders like Elon Musk and OpenAI CEO Sam Altman have taken an active role in the UBI debate. As key players in the development and dissemination of these technologies, they recognise the potential for labour-market disruptions and worker displacement. In general, their futurist perspective allows them to anticipate the long-term implications of AI and automation for the global economy. The fact that they have focused on this aspect of the discussion should warn us that we need to prepare our societies for future challenges, and develop solutions that promote social stability and prosperity.

So what?

This chapter delves into the profound influence that AI will have – and is already having – on the world of work, examining the ongoing transformations in job roles, industries, and societal expectations. It describes how AI is already being successfully integrated in various sectors, while emphasising the importance of striking a balance between innovation and ethics. But how quickly is action needed? Research suggests that the pace of change is being determined by a complex mix of technical, economic, social, and regulatory factors. The pace of AI adoption will rely on its evolution, maturity, and the ability to integrate it smoothly into existing systems. Businesses tend to favour reliable technologies, and may be reluctant when confronted with the resource-intensive task of AI integration. In addition to cost factors, AI deployments are also influenced by public opinion, the availability of AI-skilled professionals, and the amount of government support being provided. Negative views can stall progress. Industries with skilled-worker shortages may struggle with AI implementation, and the role of regulations in either facilitating or inhibiting AI adoption is crucial.[87] Overall we need to adopt a forward-thinking approach to ensure a smooth transition.

To successfully navigate the world of work in an AI era we must:

- Continuously update our skills and knowledge to stay competitive in the ever-evolving job market, embracing lifelong learning as an essential aspect of professional growth.
- Foster a culture of collaboration and open-mindedness, capitalising on the complementary strengths of humans and AI to maximise productivity, creativity, and innovation.
- Hold companies and business leaders accountable, pushing them to champion initiatives that prioritise workforce well-being, equitable opportunities, and ethical considerations in the development and implementation of AI technologies, thus fostering a sustainable and inclusive future for all.

Chapter 5: Too cool for school – AI in education and science

Why start with the AI? Why not think about the good you want to do, and then see if AI can be helpful?[88]

Timnit Gebru, computer scientist, the Distributed AI Research Institute

Entering uncharted territory

"Dear Parents!

As the number of attempts to complete homework or assignments using ChatGPT at our school is increasing – often easily detectable – I would like to inform you as follows. Homework or assignments that are completed using ChatGPT are considered "simulated performance" and will therefore not be evaluated. They also do not count towards participation. Moreover, it is an intentional attempt at deception, which in case of repetition, may result in a worse conduct grade.

Please take note of this."

In March 2023, we received the above note from the directorate of one of our children's secondary schools. It demonstrates a number of things: first, that students are far ahead of their teachers in adapting new technologies. Schools are feeling the need to respond to the increasingly widespread use of tools like ChatGPT. However, many are approaching the issue from the perspective of risk rather than seeing it as an opportunity; and it would seem that schools aren't exactly first movers when it comes to taking systematic action. The email quoted above does not indicate that the school's approach to dealing with ChatGPT is temporary, or that a broader policy may be in the making. This appears rather short-sighted. And we are sympathetic to these schools and other educational institutions. Large language models and other generative AI applications have revolutionary potential. Coming up with clear policies that fit the practical and ethical demands of an academic context is certainly no easy task.

When Alice, a university lecturer, inquired in February 2023 whether her university had any guidelines about ChatGPT, in particular regarding student assessment, she was told there was a working group looking at the issue. However, no more information was made available. In March 2023, she asked the same question to a group of business students from universities based in US, Canada, Japan, Australia, France, Slovenia and Ukraine. None said their home universities had a policy regarding the use of ChatGPT. By April, Alice's university had published a website providing instructions relating to "AI and ChatGPT in teaching".[89] While the information provided on this website was dynamic, and will continue to be updated over time, it represented a first attempt to offer guidance on the strengths and weaknesses of large language models, discussing the unauthorised use of AI-based software by students as well as the potential for detecting AI-generated output. However, it did not answer the question of whether students were allowed to use AI-based tools; this remained for university lecturers to decide on an individual basis. Nevertheless, having a written policy at all already made the university stand out. A global survey by UNESCO, conducted about the same time (May 2023), found that less than 10% of schools and universities actually offered formal guidance on AI. Of those institutions that reported having a policy in place, about half provide clear rules and advice regarding the educational uses of generative AI applications. The other half give "discretion to users", meaning that they largely leave it up to individual departments or teachers to decide whether and how to use AI. Of the hundreds of institutions that participated in the survey, only two indicated that their policy constituted "a ban", where the use of generative AI applications such as ChatGPT was completely or largely prohibited.[90]

Some educational institutions appear to be much further ahead. ESG Gütersloh – a school in Germany whose name reminds us of the often-cited ESG (environment, social & governance) criteria but actually stands for Evangelisch Stiftisches Gymnasium – is one such example. At this secondary school, students have been exploring the opportunities and risks associated with artificial intelligence since ChatGPT was released. They have since taken written exams where the use of ChatGPT for both inspiration and formulation assistance was officially allowed. Of course, this required introducing the tool, as well as open discussions and tests of its strengths and limitations in class. The school thus demonstrates that traditionalism and innovation can go together – as long as specific structures and open-minded personalities are in place.[91]

In a classroom near you

Technology evolves much faster than formal educational institutions can ever dream of adapting. Today, AI is not even included in teaching curricula in most countries, and where it is, there is a time gap between new teachers' training and the point when they can translate this into practice, when they first start teaching. But the integration of AI into classrooms is not a new phenomenon. Among the AI technologies currently being used in an educational context, those that are student-facing have received the most attention so far. Most common are so-called intelligent tutoring systems, with over 60 tools commercially available. In fact, such systems have been around for decades, and been used by more students than any other AI-based application. They essentially provide step-by-step tutorials in structured subjects such as mathematics. The systems draw on expert knowledge about the subject as well as on cognitive science research, providing a personalised experience by responding to the student's successes and errors. This helps students navigate along an optimal pathway through the learning materials and activities. These systems employ knowledge tracing to estimate the students' mastery of specific concepts and skills; machine learning functions automatically adjust the difficulty level, and give hints tuned to each individual student's strengths and weaknesses. Some intelligent tutoring systems even capture data on a student's mood or attention level, for example by monitoring the user's gaze.[92] Two interesting examples include Spark, developed by French company Domoscio, and Gooru Navigator, which claims to host 4 million AI-curated learning resources and aims to become the Google Maps of learning.[93]

While the idea of personalising instruction is appealing, there is little evidence to date that these systems are as effective as the companies behind them claim. Moreover, the rather top-down, instructionist approach of those systems typically does not incorporate other, highly useful aspects of learning, such as collaboration, discovery, or even productive failure. By prescribing content, these systems also ignore students' agency – that is, their ability to take an active role in their own learning and make decisions about how they learn. Moreover, excessive use of such "intelligent" systems also reduces human contact between students and teachers, as ITSes (intelligent tutoring systems) typically require classroom teachers to stay behind their desks to monitor dashboards providing information on student interactions. If teachers do move around the room to check in with their students, they risk losing track of their dashboards. But hey, there is AI technology to address this issue too! For example, the Lumilo extension, used in conjunction with augmented reality smart glasses, enables teachers to see relevant information floating above each student's head, such as the number of errors or whether the student's attention is waning. While this seems like a cool tool, it is worth emphasising that Lumilo has been designed to address a problem that exists only due to weaknesses in another AI technology – and that's before getting into the issue of privacy.

Dialogue-based tutoring systems, such as the University of Memphis-created AutoTutor, are a step ahead. They use natural-language processing and other AI techniques to simulate a spoken dialogue as they guide students step by step through online tasks for which there is a pre-specified solution. Dialogue-based systems use a Socratic approach, probing students with AI-generated questions rather than providing instruction per se. The idea here is that students are guided towards solutions through conversation, which encourages them to co-create explanations and thus come to understand the topic at a deeper level. As of the time of writing, no such applications were commercially available, though IBM and Pearson were working on a Watson Tutor model.[94] Another type of student-facing model is that of AI-driven "exploratory learning environments," in which AI provides feedback and proposes alternative approaches to make sure students do not venture too far off track on their individual discovery journeys. Today, such models exist only in the lab.

The language skills shown by AI today are truly impressive. AI applications for reading and language learning are now common, with a short list including AI Teacher, Amazing English, Babbel and Duoloingo. DeepL is a neural-network-based machine translation service launched in 2017 which today calls itself "the world's most accurate translator". All of these can be applied in educational settings. "Automated writing evaluation" tools use natural-language processing and other AI techniques to provide automatic feedback on writing. Such feedback can be provided either with a formative intention – that is, to help students improve their writing before it is submitted – or the software can be used for assessment, automatically scoring students' writing. Both types of automatic writing evaluation tools are already widely used in educational settings, with examples including programmes such as WriteToLearn, e-Rater, and Turnitin. Such tools can be either student or teacher-facing, depending on the goal.

Some intelligent tutoring systems can be extended to support people with disabilities, for instance by providing text-to-speech functions or automatic image captioning. In addition, several apps including StorySign have been specifically developed to help children with hearing difficulties by automatically translating text into sign language.[95] Alice would have loved to have such tools available 10 years ago; at this time, a student with hearing difficulties was taking one of her courses focusing on social development and inclusion in Asia and Africa. Alice vowed to make sure the student felt included and able to participate throughout, resolving to speak slowly, move around less and face the student in question wherever possible. However, despite trying hard, she ultimately failed to make the student feel sufficiently comfortable, and in the process compromised the other students' experience. The student eventually left the course, which seemed like a lose-lose outcome. Luckily, tools to bridge this gap are now available.

Of all AI applications used in education, intelligent tutoring systems have been researched the longest, with 40 years of practical experience. We know that they're working; yet we still know nothing about their overall impact on education. Let's turn now to the teachers' side, and see whether and how generative AI can make their work easier.

Teachers sit back and relax

When ChatGPT was released, Alice and Jeroen immediately started wondering how they could prevent plagiarism in student essays. They quickly turned to ChatGPT, inquiring how essay questions could be formulated in order to make it harder for large language models to answer them. ChatGPT's reply included several useful suggestions. For example, it recommended asking students to analyse specific case studies, events, or situations that are not a matter of common knowledge, and for which it is thus difficult to find readily accessible information on the internet. It also suggested asking students for personal reflections on a topic, a strategy that would require them to draw on their own experiences, ideas, and opinions. Asking students to compare multiple perspectives on a topic would require them to use critical thinking and analysis skills. The bot also recommended asking students to develop creative solutions, thus demonstrating innovative thinking and problem-solving skills in specific settings. And finally, ChatGPT repeatedly reminded us to educate students about the importance of academic integrity and the consequences of plagiarism, and to encourage them to cite any sources they used in their work properly. Overall, we learned that context-specific analysis and critical thinking weren't among ChatGPT's key strengths, at least in the then-current version, though this may change in the future. Only the next few university terms will tell whether the machine's advice has been useful.

Though welcomed by students, automatic essay writing tools began to be a headache for teachers long before ChatGPT appeared on the horizon. Several commercial models are available that create tailor-made student essays. Given the increasing sophistication of automatic writing tools, and what could be described as an arms race between these tools and automatic essay writing detectors, the way in which we assess students' progress will certainly need to change. But it's not only language teachers that may lose sleep over this. Apps like Photomath don't just teach your children mathematics; they also let them upload a maths problem and have it solved within seconds by an AI that may be much cleverer than you.

One question that many teachers are already dealing with, whether there is a specific policy on the issue at their institution or not, is what tools like ChatGPT mean for take-home student essays. Should teachers now focus more on oral exams for assessment? Or are AI detectors the way to go when grading student assignments? Is there any other way in which AI can help teachers do their work more efficiently, and perhaps even better?

While Alice and Jeroen love teaching and interacting with students in class, they both find grading essays in particular to be a bit of a headache. The process of reading and assessing essay after essay can feel tedious, given that the content and style of the texts are not always inspiring, and are overall quite repetitive. Therefore, using an automatic writing evaluation tool to facilitate this labour-intensive process seems tempting. They are clearly not alone in this desire: so-called "autograders", or automatic summative assessments, are a well-funded area of research and are already extensively commercialised. However, the results of such products are not always impressive, and indeed are sometimes incorrect, and they have thus remained controversial. For example, as they are largely unable to assess creativity, they often give students credit for surface features such as sentence length, "even if the text does not make any sense – they can be 'fooled by gibberish'"[96]. Moreover, they are sometimes biased against minority students, possibly due to different uses of vocabulary and sentence structure. At the same time, they are unable to detect plagiarism, and cannot deal with "deep fake" essays that are written by AI tools that combine domain expertise with an imitation of the specific student's writing style. When it comes to high-stakes testing – that is, tests that have important consequences for the student, teacher, or school – applying such technology is particularly risky. Therefore, high-stakes testing is one of the two uses defined as high-risk in the EU AI Act (see Chapter 8), and so would be regulated by this regulation's provisions.[97]

In general, it is likely that teachers will benefit from AI-assisted automation of tasks such as assessment, plagiarism detection, feedback, and administration in the future. In principle, this will free up time for teachers to invest in tasks they may enjoy more, such as designing engaging courses and providing more effective, individualised support to students. However, there is also a broader risk that the teachers themselves will begin to be perceived as redundant. Replacing teachers entirely with AI-based tools might be a second-best but perhaps acceptable solution that creates actual value in contexts where teachers are scarce, for example in rural areas in low-income countries. However, the role played by teachers goes far beyond simply delivering knowledge and assignments. They also play an essential part in social learning and engagement, and in many ways they do intuitively and very effectively what algorithms need to be trained to do with questionable outcomes.

At the moment, Alice is not worried about being replaced, given that she uses a very participatory teaching style focused on collaboration, simulation, discussion, flexible adaptation to students' interests, and progress with visible results. It is not immediately obvious how an AI could help her teach a complex subject like Sustainable Business, other than perhaps assisting with idea generation and administration. However, the rapid developments in AI point to bigger-picture changes that may become necessary in the near future.

Time over for language skills?

To date, discussions about technology in schools have largely concentrated on digital methods and tools, and on applying them – in more or less creative ways – in teaching and learning contexts. These tools have largely been employed by more or less enthusiastic teachers within the frameworks of existing school curricula. However, this has done little to challenge the bigger picture. Generative AI tools like ChatGPT now force us to take a step back and start questioning some established truths. The onset of a new AI era forces us to start asking much bigger questions than whether to do a test by hand or on a computer. This computer now comes with a new brain, which we had better put to good use. For example, given that some tools are about to become real translation stars, and given that they are better, faster, and cheaper than human brains, is it still necessary that students learn foreign languages? DeepL is already a leader in real-time translation, functioning in 31 languages from Bulgarian and Chinese to Finnish and Ukrainian. Sayhi, a tool developed by Amazon, allows for direct conversation in over 100 languages and dialects, from Afrikaans and Bangla to Thai and Zulu.

We know that learning foreign languages comes with many benefits other than knowledge of the language itself, so in principle the answer could still be yes. But would we want to consider decreasing the number of foreign languages each student would study, freeing them up to focus on newly essential knowledge such as computers, programming, basic ecology, or other STEM subjects? We may also ask whether it is important for students to continue focusing on spelling and grammar when AI can easily correct them as necessary.[98] Nor do these questions exclusively concern the field of languages. We may also ask whether it is really necessary to make all children cram for maths exams for years on end during secondary school, when there are tools available to solve questions we may never actually confront in real life? We don't have the answer here; and we think it is crucial for all students to learn how to read and write properly, to develop their brains by engaging with other languages and cultures, and to understand key mathematical operations. The question is whether there are aspects of our traditional curricula and teaching styles that no longer benefit students to the extent previously believed. We must ask what knowledge and skills are actually retained by students, and what we want them to retain. In parallel, we must identify any vital gaps in current teaching and learning practices.

Once again, it is helpful to look into history and realise that what we think of as unchallengeable truths may have looked very different in the past. For example, many schools did not allow pocket calculators until late in the 20th century, while today they are part and parcel of most advanced maths and science classes. For a long time, an academic education without Latin or ancient Greek was unthinkable in some parts of Europe. Today less than 1% of German grammar school students still study old Greek.[99] UNESCO, the United Nations' education agency, even talks of an "emerging consensus that the very foundations of teaching and learning may be reshaped by the deployment of AI in education".[100]

A brave new world?

AI has already entered the education sector in more ways than many of us dare to imagine, sometimes but clearly not always for the greater good. After all, the market for intelligent, adaptive, and personalised learning systems is huge, with forecasts that it will be worth $6 billion by 2024.[101] Private sector companies are racing to tap into this market by developing systems intended for deployment in schools and universities around the world. Some of these companies – and some governments too – see this as an opportunity to collect ever more data on their customers and citizens. This does not automatically mean that key education goals, such as improving educational quality, reaching more students, or keeping students in education longer, will be achieved. As we noted above, some AI applications in schools are proving to have a redundant effect at best.

The deployment of AI in schools already gives a rather dystopian impression in some cases, particularly where AI-assisted systems are used to monitor students using biometric means. For example, some AI-assisted video applications monitor where a student is looking in order to judge whether the student is focused or not. EEG (electroencephalography) headsets – normally used in hospitals and labs to monitor people's health – are now being used in schools to monitor student attention. In Chinese schools, such headsets are widely used to monitor students' brain activity, even in the case of young children. Neural data is fed into a teacher dashboard in real time, with detailed reports produced every 10 minutes. In some schools, cameras monitor how often students yawn or check their phones in class, while others have chips integrated in school uniforms to monitor students' whereabouts and other data. Parents in China apparently see no issues with the policies, and have willingly signed up their children to participate in what is one of the world's largest experiments with AI in education. In fact, some appear quite happy to be able to monitor their children's attention – with an app that sends regular reports to parents' chat groups, making all students' scores available to the entire group. Some students have complained about pain and discomfort when wearing the headset, while others have described being punished by their parents for low attention scores.[102]

Thus, it is safe to say that Orwell has already landed firmly in many schools around the globe. And it is not only in China that Big Brother is watching. In countries outside China too, biometric monitoring has been implemented without most of us knowing. When education moved online during COVID-19 lockdowns, many "e-proctoring" (exam monitoring) businesses saw massive growth despite controversies associated with the practice. The idea behind e-proctoring is to prevent cheating by using cameras and microphones to scan people's faces automatically, while also tracking keystrokes and mouse movements during online examinations. As one expert puts it: "... e-proctoring is probably one of the clearest examples of using AI to automate poor pedagogic practices, rather than using it to develop innovative approaches".[103] In the US, there appears to be a trend of college campuses around the country using facial-recognition-based software applications to monitor student attendance. As the universities and companies are still testing the software, students are still free in theory to choose whether to download and use these tracking apps. However, the pressure to do so is real for some. For example, an app called SpotterEDU that uses Bluetooth to connect to students' mobile phones, and which records attendance, was being tested in 2020 on 40 different US campuses in an effort to boost class attendance. While this was an experiment, and using the app was not officially mandatory, a number of school athletes reported being required to install it.[104]

The ethical issues involved in such systems, particularly in terms of data protection and privacy, are obviously massive. But what's perhaps even worse: We have no information about the actual impact of such monitoring systems on educational outcomes, or indeed on students' health, happiness, and well-being. If we actively decide to burden ourselves-voluntarily with a Big Brother style education system, it would seem we should at least know that the opportunities outweigh the risks. We need to prevent AI-assisted technologies being used simply for their own sake, or because they make money for companies or allow governments to benefit politically from data they should not have in the first place. Yet at the same time, we should be aware of and open to beneficial opportunities, particularly in contexts where AI expands access to high-quality education for people who might otherwise be excluded.

Reaching for the stars

Alice's first "real" job was with UNESCO, the United Nations agency responsible for education and science, in Bangkok, Thailand. One of her first projects involved setting up a platform for ICT (information and communication technologies) in education. This taught her a lot about the digital divide we discussed in Chapter 3. It also taught her another reality: When seeking to improve their education systems, many high-income countries have the luxury of applying educational technologies that are already well advanced. By contrast, schools in some low-income countries are starting from a bare minimum, even before getting to the point of considering technology. Common challenges include a lack of qualified teachers, inadequate pay, and outdated curricula. Even physical and financial access to schooling can present significant hurdles. Millions of school children, particularly in rural areas, have to walk long and sometimes dangerous paths to school; others are prevented from going at all because their parents cannot afford school books or uniforms, or because they simply need the extra income the child can earn instead of going to school. In these contexts and instances, even very basic educational technologies may not function. Power outages may be frequent, and technological devices – often provided to schools by well-meaning donors – may be broken, out of date, or incompatible with other systems, or require training by overworked teachers who are often too busy dealing with other more basic challenges to participate. As a result, instead of having a positive impact on education, hardware often piles up and gathers dust in remote corners of schools. This has been the case for decades, long before AI came into the picture.

At the same time, AI-assisted technologies that help overcome access barriers in education and improve educational quality can make a lot of sense, particularly where internet connections and the availability of context-appropriate hardware make this possible. If a single teacher is struggling to support too many children across too many age groups, certain apps may help, provided that connectivity and IT infrastructures are sound. If students cannot access full-time education, AI-assisted tools may facilitate remote learning, integrating individuals who are often excluded from education such as older people, refugees, people with special needs, and those who are marginalised from society. However, UNESCO reminds us that AI technologies rarely offer solutions to larger issues, and can in some cases create more problems than they solve. The organisation notes that "focusing on AI technologies that replace teacher functions, rather than those that augment teacher capabilities, might contribute toward a short-term fix for contexts where teachers are scarce, but might unintentionally exacerbate rather than address the long-term challenges in achieving SDG 4."[105] Experts have pointed out that education seems to be big tech's favourite playground – often with questionable results. Yet, expanding access to education largely remains a political and social issue.

During her time with UNESCO, Alice learned that discrepancies between policies and their implementation, between stated aims and actual outcomes, are often massive. She also learned that resource-constrained settings frequently require a combination of cutting-edge thinking and pragmatism. Sometimes this even leads to reverse innovation, where tools developed for a low-income context turn out to be attractive in rich countries as well. When she recently advised an educational startup in Kenya called KuzeKuze, she saw the need for this pragmatism again. The company uses AI to collect high-density data on student competencies that eventually helps predict performance and track individual learning progress. It aims to create an environment for class-focused collaboration where students are supported at their own level of learning. KuzeKuze doesn't employ AI-assisted technology for its own sake; rather, it uses such tools only where they make sense. Thus, learners actually use pen and paper to fill in printed workbooks that are produced based on AI recommendations. This ensures that everyone can participate, even if the power is out or a student lacks a functioning electronic device. KuzeKuze's approach greatly relieves overburdened teachers, as the hand-written assignments are automatically scanned and scored through technology. Among other places, KuzeKuze's model is used for refugee children in Dadaab, Kenya, Africa's largest refugee camp. In collaboration with the NGO Save the Children, it is also used to engage students that have left education early. We also appreciate the fact that KuzeKuze is a Kenyan company catering to the local market. Too often, we encounter what has been termed digital colonialism in education, where companies from rich countries in the Global North export their tools to contexts in the Global South, further reinforcing the power asymmetries between countries and regions. In practice, "digital technologies often function in ways that perpetuate the racial and colonial formations of the past".[106] For AI-assisted technologies to benefit education more broadly, they need to be context- and culture-specific, and consider the educational policy framework as well as practical realities.

Advocates of AI in education have made many other promises as well. One of the more ambitious goals is "lifelong learning" for teachers as well as students – that is, the idea that in a complex, dynamic world, it is no longer enough for teachers to be trained at the beginning of their careers, and then draw on that knowledge for the rest of their service. Particularly when it comes to technology, their knowledge may be outdated even before their first day in a classroom. What's true for teachers is true for other professions as well. Think of doctors or city planners, for example. In fact, it is true for all of us. We are all lifelong learners, and it would be wonderful to have a smart and caring teacher, who knows our interests, strengths, and weaknesses, accompanying us at all times. As yet, such tools do not exist. Our smartphones may be full of information, but they do not guide us as a good teacher should. We wonder, however: Could ChatGPT serve as the basis for a lifelong learning companion of this sort? Some visionaries talk of an AI-driven e-portfolio, which would continuously collect information on a student's achievements in formal education while also integrating data on any other forms of knowledge acquisition, such as learning a musical instrument, learning how to drive, picking up new languages, or playing sports. Such an electronic record could serve as a dynamic resumé that could be authenticated by blockchain technology.[107] While this sounds like a smart way to replace conventional and cumbersome CV writing, it also comes with many of the issues relating to data and privacy discussed above.

Science or science fiction?

In science, truth always wins.

Max F. Perutz, biochemist and Nobel Prize winner, Cambridge University

To illustrate the power of AI and how it can catalyse change in science, we want to introduce you to AlphaFold, an example that has revolutionised biology over the last couple of years. You may not have heard of it, but Forbes actually called it "the most important achievement in AI – ever" in 2021.[108] AlphaFold is an AI system that predicts a protein's 3D structure from its amino acid sequence. If you're not a biologist or life scientist, this may sound quite technical and not that revolutionary, but we'll help you make sense of the bigger meaning.

Predicting three-dimensional structures from linear chains of amino acids has been a longstanding challenge in science. For decades, researchers relied on very time- and resource-intensive methods, which were often the same old methods Max Perutz and John Kendrew had used in the 1950s. They were spectacular methods, and developing them won Perutz and Kendrew a Nobel Prize in 1962. In a quest to modernise and accelerate the field, many researchers had tried developing these methods further, in part by using computer models. However, these attempts were never successful – until AI came along, and the European Molecular Biology Lab (EMBL) joined forces with Google's DeepMind to create AlphaFold.

Before that, researchers had proved able to elucidate about 3,000 protein structures per year, for a total of about 200,000 structures altogether.[109] AlphaFold took these already published structures and used them to train AI algorithms to identify patterns. As a result, in 2021 alone, the team was able to describe 365,000 new protein structures, and this number has since grown to 200 million, covering almost all proteins across all life forms, including bacteria, viruses, humans, animals, and plants.

This example also highlights that progress was achieved only through new cross-sectoral collaboration mechanisms, in this case successfully combining an existing collection of protein structures developed by academic researchers worldwide with the AI tool jointly developed by Google's DeepMind and the European Molecular Biology Laboratory. This institutional setup has ensured that all newly created resources can be openly accessed by other researchers, like all previously identified protein structures. It also helps ensure that the science community as a whole and with it the wider public can benefit, not least by allowing for feedback to be provided to researchers who collected the original data.

Now you may be impressed by this AI-aided advance, but not yet fully understand the potential impact. As cell biologist Jeroen reminded us, proteins are the building blocks of every cell in our body, and are responsible for performing most chemical reactions. Knowing a protein's structure is therefore critical to understanding how cells function, which in turn is an important step in drug discovery. Proteins are basically like beads of amino acids aligned on a string, and then folded into a very specific 3D structure. Only when properly folded can they perform their cellular function. The order of these beads is coded into an organism's DNA. Given the great leaps forward made in the past 30 years, we are now able to engage in DNA sequencing, thus understanding what our DNA looks like. AlphaFold builds on these insights by predicting a protein's 3D structure from the underlying DNA sequence – that is, the chain of amino acids it is made of.

Elucidating 1,000 times more structures in two years than were discovered in the previous 60 years together has profoundly changed the field of biology, greatly saving time and resources. In addition, this has opened up a whole new world of potential applications, and rendered this field of research far more accessible. Where in the past, determining the structure of proteins required many years of training, expensive machines, and experimental luck, a database developed by AlphaFold now provides scientists even from other disciplines with easy access to such information. This has resulted in a creative wave of ideas and collaboration.

We all experienced a second example of the power of this AI tool during the COVID-19 era, when it radically increased the speed of vaccine development. Until early 2020, coronaviruses had not been widely studied. Thus, when the SARS-CoV-2 virus that causes COVID-19 emerged, the structures of its proteins were not well understood. AlphaFold allowed researchers to quickly predict the structure of this virus' major building blocks, which in turn allowed them to understand how it attacks human cells and how such attacks could be blocked. The availability of protein structures thus enabled scientists to identify the best target sites for vaccines, facilitating the development of powerful weapons in fighting the COVID-19 pandemic.

A final example is also somewhat related to COVID-19. One of the pioneering companies driving COVID-19 vaccine development was BioNTech. Their mRNA technology had originally been developed as a cancer treatment. The "m" in mRNA stands for "messenger", referring to a message that, once integrated into a human cell, can be translated into a variety of tools effective against a wide range of diseases. Since this message can be copied multiple times, only low quantities of this message molecule are needed, thus saving lots of resources. BioNTech is also taking advantage of the fact that the message can be easily changed. The company's iNest programme aims to personalise cancer treatment, making it more effective while reducing side effects. An initial scan of the pattern of a person's specific cancer is used to identify proteins that are misbehaving due to mutations in the genome. AlphaFold then predicts the 3D structures of these mutated proteins, and selects optimal treatment targets that are present only in these cancer cells. A mix of specific mRNAs (to increase the chance of success) can then be produced quickly to attack a given tumour effectively and locally. Although it is hard to say when the wider public will be able to benefit from procedures of this kind, the speed of recent developments in the field thanks to AI puts such revolutionary cancer treatments within reach in the near future.

You may ask how AlphaFold could take over this field so easily? First, it combined an ability to digest big data sets with new ways of looking at the data, by using novel neural networks that identified parameters not easily observed by humans. Second, the immense computing power provided by DeepMind facilitated multiple iterations of the protein structure prediction process, which allowed for greater accuracy, ultimately attaining results as good as those achieved by time-consuming empirical experiments.

AI across disciplines

AI tools have also been used in many other scientific fields. As we highlight in chapters 3 and 4, AI has been very useful in supporting decision-making in the medical field, for example through diagnosis supported by image recognition. Early attempts in this area had already been made in the early 1970s, for example through MYCIN, a computer-based consultation system designed to assist physicians in diagnosing bacterial infections and selecting patient therapies. Initially seen as a promising strategy for fighting antibiotic resistance and overprescription, this system failed in part because of uncertainties about legal liability. Because of this, and due to its high cost, this groundbreaking project was cancelled in the late 1970s.[110]

More recently, the increasing availability of medical technology and improved imaging tools have helped advance diagnostic procedures, treatments, and cures with the help of AI. AI tools used to identify intracranial haemorrhages and cancers often score better than trained specialists, producing fewer false positives and false negatives. Diagnoses made by humans can be undermined by a number of factors. For example, human health professionals may score the same image differently due to fatigue or other distractions. Moreover, psychologists argue that most humans can handle only four independent variables at the same time, losing efficiency when this number increases to five or more. AI tools have no limit on the number of parameters or indicators they can digest; this makes them ideal tools for helping us grapple with the data overload produced by ever-improving imaging tools. While it is difficult to include all necessary parameters in a single tool, AI screening will nevertheless become more and more important in supporting doctors' decision-making, even helping to expand their expertise.[111]

Such tools offer particularly great potential in situations where rapid identifications and decisions are needed to prevent large-scale pandemics. Although few examples exist to date, one striking exception is the early detection of unusual pneumonia cases around a market in Wuhan, China, in late December 2019, by an AI system developed by BlueDot, a Canadian platform. This observation, which would turn out to be linked to SARS-CoV-2, came more than a week before the World Health Organization (WHO) issued a public notice about the new virus. Started in 2013 after the first SARS outbreak, BlueDot also made predictions related to the Zika virus (2016) and Ebola (2014) that were released six months earlier than those issued by WHO.[112][113]

Most AI applications in the field of chemistry are focused on the development of new chemicals that could be turned into drugs. AI is also increasingly used for "green chemistry", which was initiated in 1998 by Yale professor Paul Anastas, who established 12 rules defining the field. It explores new methods for producing existing chemicals using less energy, less material and fewer toxic side products. Current chemical reactions are often brutish and ugly. We heat, beat, and treat substances, often making them more toxic. This means that current procedures increase the risk of chemical harm to our bodies and the biosphere alike. There is enormous potential for optimisation, as 90% of all materials that go into today's chemical manufacturing processes immediately wind up as waste. Copying nature and making products that are easily degradeable would swiftly make our products more environmentally friendly. For instance, tools like IBM's RoboRXN combine different strategies in the hunt for the perfect green enzyme, rendering the production of chemicals more efficient.[114]

AI tools are also aiding in the search for new bio-based plastics that would have characteristics similar to those of current chemical plastics. Calculating the detailed footprint of chemicals and other products is very important, but is also very difficult. Full life cycle analyses (LCAs) are often skipped, because they are very labour and cost intensive. However, new AI-based tools make it easier to conduct LCAs and calculate chemicals' material footprints, thus allowing for better monitoring.[115] Firms such as CO2-AI[116] are offering consulting services based on tools that can help companies report on their sustainability goals using a data-based approach. Advances such as these can make production more transparent, and help bring it in line with the goals of a sustainable transformation. However, in order to ensure net benefits, these models and approaches need to be associated with clear guidelines and accountability; blindly following the numbers without expert interpretation and advice will accomplish nothing.

The climate and earth sciences are among the scientific fields that have benefited most from developments in AI. Many experiments and observational techniques in this area are extremely difficult and resource-consuming for humans, simply because of the scale involved. For example, the health and distribution of Weddell seals, one of the best-studied species on Earth, is a solid proxy indicator for the state of the planet. However, there remain many open questions about their population size and structure. These two indicators are essential for scientists to understand precisely how they are adapting to rapidly changing ecosystems. In 2021, a group of scientists set out to do a full population count of Weddel seals using satellite images. Instead of using image-recognition software, the team relied on 330,000 volunteers who screened and scored the pictures online for potential seal colonies.[117][118][119] As we outline in the next chapter, AI tools can easily take over such tedious jobs, allowing real-time observations to be made of many critical species distributed throughout remote locations.

In addition to giving us a solid picture of the status quo and helping us to understand climate-related events, AI also has the potential to make predictions. This has certainly proved useful in the climate and ecology fields, but can also be applied in the medical context. For example, researchers at the AI Sustainability Centre in Sweden have combined a fluid dynamics model with AI tools to make predictions about air pollution in cities, thus helping to reduce human health problems.[120]

Opportunities and pitfalls of AI in science

The above examples illustrate the potential of AI in science, and show that the scientific community is already embracing it in a wide variety of applications. AI is clearly here to stay. But it is an altogether different question to ask how we can maintain creativity, openness, and transparency in science in a world dominated by AI's seemingly endless possibilities. As in education, we need to look at the bigger picture and ask what the role of science in a world with AI should be.

The most significant challenge right now appears to be the speed with which AI is entering the research world. While some applications have seen extraordinary rapid progress, the education and training of scientists follows a much slower cycle of 20 to 30 years on average. This is an incompatibility that must be addressed. The fields of education and science are slowly moving away from focusing on retaining and repeating knowledge to creating and using it. AI will increase the need for different teaching and learning methods, given that many repetitive and data gathering processes will soon be taken over by AI.

If we are to successfully address multiple global crises, societies must be in a position to trust science and scientific findings, and prioritise fact-based decisions over ideological or emotional ones. Therefore, informing the wider public about how science gathers data and how scientific progress is made will be essential in maintaining trust. This means that the demands on the scientists of the future will expand even further. Not only will they need to be familiar with the data and methods of their field, they will also need to be strong collaborators and effective communicators in order to engage both with peers and the general public. At the same time, given that a profession's benefits to society are not always commensurately rewarded during times of economic pressure, scientists will need to learn to become money generators. This will be necessary to continue allowing universities and other research institutions to conduct ever more expensive research. No single human can bring together all these important skills, so new collaborative models may be needed to facilitate a sustainable transition to the broader use of AI.

Currently, most AI tools are trained by open-source data, often generated in the academic field. The European Union in particular has created a framework for making scientific findings easily available and accessible. This has provided training sets for AI-based tools used not only by scientists and the academic community, but also by corporations. Developing a fair reward system for such freely available datasets will be key to ensuring that academic science remains adequately funded in the future. This will also help people develop the skills and tools required to critically question the functioning and impact of new AI developments. Keeping a critical view will help protect society at large from dangerous developments, and will allow us to understand the outputs, outcomes, and impacts of artificial intelligence. For example, critical review skills and solid insights into the functioning of AI-based tools will be necessary both for scientists and the wider public in evaluating results produced by large language models such as ChatGPT. Having tested ChatGPT on various topics in his field, Jeroen, a cell scientist, was fascinated by the ease and confidence with which ChatGPT offered fake references, particularly when challenged to produce its sources. These fake references often look and feel very credible, but can easily be disproved if you know where to look. In fact, it often takes longer to check, re-check, and double-check the outputs and references provided by ChatGPT than to identify facts and sources in conventional ways, such as through research databases. Though dangerous to all, such shortcomings of commonly used AI tools could be particularly damaging for younger or less experienced scientists who are under great pressure to produce and publish. ChatGPT and similar tools are no replacement for proper scientific training. On the contrary, scientists of the future will need to be trained to understand the limitations of AI-based models in order to provide the human supervision that will be necessary at all times.

Finally, as with all AI tools and results, it will be very important to establish a clear definition of accountability. This is particularly important in the research context, where great efforts are made to describe the details of each given experiment so it can be reproduced and used as the foundation for future research. The "black box" setup of many AI tools does not allow for such scrutiny, and thus endangers good scientific practice. While some tools are helpful in generating new ideas or even fields of thought, they are not reliable enough at the moment. The fact-based AI tools used in research can function effectively only with human supervision, and can support reproducibility only if these supervisors make sure that all the steps, from data gathering to analysis, work toward generating results that are transparent and understandable. In short, the criteria currently used to define good science have not changed. To be truly useful, AI tools developed for research purposes will need to make sure they are aligned with these criteria. Translating the current research standards into high-quality AI tools will help ensure that we aren't building our future on unstable foundations.

So what?

AI is certainly no end in itself, and some tools are merely techno-solutionism (or even techno-romanticism), and thus should have no place in learner-centred education systems. Nonetheless, the future of education and science may look very different from its present. In the case of the school in Gütersloh referenced at the beginning of this chapter, principal Martin Fugmann used to lead the German International School in Silicon Valley, the cradle of digital innovation. He predicts that in future, schools will have to focus less on assessing results and more on research and work processes.[121] This may include evaluating sources and collaborating with others, arguably key skills for survival in the 21st century. More importantly, perhaps, it is a clear signal that schools and universities will no longer be able to conduct business as usual. Smart schools will turn their strategic efforts not only toward specific technologies like ChatGPT, but also toward the bigger picture of how and what the schools of the future will need to teach. The focus will certainly be less on memorising content than on analysis, source identification, fact-checking, and collaboration with both humans and machines in a division of labour that prepares students for the new world of work described in Chapter 4.

AI can enhance education and learning, but it cannot replace human teachers or scientists. We therefore need new forms of human-machine collaboration. In times of technological abundance and upheaval, critical thinking skills are more important than ever for students, teachers, and scientists alike. Artificial intelligence does not render basic skills such as reading, writing, summarising, or analysing texts obsolete in any way. The same goes for maths, science, and even programming skills. If anything, these skills are becoming even more important if we are to collaborate effectively with machines and stay on top as humans. AI has the potential to increase efficiency and effectiveness in all fields of science by analysing big data sets, optimising processes, and making predictions for the future. However, it is not the predictions themselves that will matter most, but the ways in which humans deal with these predictions, in the process shaping our societies and future lives.

In order to harness the power of AI in educational and scientific settings, we must:

- Prioritise investments in improving students' abilities to engage in critical thinking and assess different sources of information.
- Ensure that future learning and training systems equip all people – not just students, teachers, and researchers – with core AI competencies including an understanding of how AI collects and manipulates data.
- Design AI tools that facilitate interdisciplinary collaborations by interpreting large and complex data sets using a common scientific language.

Chapter 6: Do look up – AI's complicated relationship with nature

A man's always got choices. Sometimes you just gotta choose the right one.

Teddy Oglethorp in "Don't Look Up", a 2021 climate disaster movie[122]

The efficiency paradox

Faced with a climate crisis and other environmental pressures, some see a tantalising logic: All we have to do is digitise and technologically innovate ourselves out of this mess. We will use smart apps and smart metres, employing AI to tell us where to maximise energy savings and how to optimise logistics. We will have AI monitor forest growth, and use AI to design products as a service.

This logic is robust in principle, but it neglects an important rebound effect: The better, cheaper, faster, and smarter our tools are, the more of them we generally want and use. Remember having to buy DVDs to watch a movie? Today, streaming a film is more energy efficient than producing and watching a DVD. That's great news. The only problem is that we now watch much more video content than we used to, and our addictions to Netflix and its peers, as well as to all the other technological devices in our households, make us consume much more energy than before in total. While great claims have been made about the benefits of dematerialisation in a digital service economy, digitalisation in practice has actually increased environmental impacts both at the local and planetary scales.[123] This phenomenon is called the "efficiency paradox", and is sometimes referred to as the Jevons paradox. The Jevons paradox is an extreme case of a rebound effect in which efficiency gains lead to greater demand for the more efficiently used resource, ultimately leading to higher overall net use. This isn't a new insight. The efficiency paradox was identified in the 1930s, as increased efficiency in the amount of coal needed to generate a kilowatt hour of electricity failed to result in overall energy savings. In that case, people responded to cheaper energy by using more of it – thus burning more coal than previously.[124] In his 1865 book "The Coal Question", William Stanley Jevons had already observed that England's coal consumption soared after the introduction of James Watt's steam engine, which was far more efficient than previous coal-fired steam engines. As coal became a more cost-effective source of power, the steam engine was used more widely, which in turn increased overall coal consumption even as the amount of coal needed to produce one unit of energy decreased. At the time, Jevons noted: "It is a confusion of ideas to suppose that the economical use of fuel is equivalent to diminished consumption. The very contrary is the truth."[125]

Improvements in energy efficiency thus tend to increase energy consumption. Similarly, an economy driven by exciting products that seemingly start becoming obsolete the moment we acquire them tends to lead to ever-expanding desires – even if these desires have little to with our actual needs. Moreover, a socio-economic and political governance system that ignores the cost of environmental degradation, leaving the broader public and future generations to pay the full price, generates incentives to create the wrong type of products, services, and companies.

Watch your footprint – the environmental impact of AI

The social risks relating to AI – particularly those relating to data bias, and to an extent also those relating to the perpetuation of hegemonic worldviews – are relatively well documented, and are being discussed in both research and industry circles with increasing frequency. However, the environmental impact of AI, while today recognised by some, still is an area that many experts in data science and other disciplines are failing altogether to note. The energy needs of large language models have been called AI's "dirty secret". Nevertheless, researchers and industry representatives have started looking into AI's climate change impact and effects on other aspects of the environment, including water and biodiversity.

A number of factors make measuring AI's environmental footprint rather tricky. First, the pace of technological development is extraordinarily rapid, presenting a moving target. Moreover, many of the leading AI companies simply do not make sufficient data available for researchers to come up with realistic estimates. Another key reason is that the impact generated by AI computation cannot always be neatly separated from that of the infrastructure required or from ICT more broadly. The footprint of AI needs to be put in the bigger context of digital technology. Global greenhouse emissions from ICT are currently estimated to be between 2.1% and 3.9% of total emissions.[126] AI would account for only a fraction of that. When asking ChatGPT about its CO2 emissions, we received a rather cute answer: "I am a computer program and do not physically exist, so I do not produce carbon dioxide emissions. However, the servers and other infrastructure used to run and train me do consume energy, and therefore do produce carbon emissions. The amount of emissions produced would depend on the specific energy source used to power the servers, as well as the energy efficiency of the servers and other equipment used. To my knowledge, OpenAI has not disclosed the specifics about the carbon footprint of the training of GPT models like me." It then went on to note that the energy demand associated with data centres, which are critical components of AI infrastructure, is projected to triple by 2030. ChatGPT also made the point that the production of hardware components, such as the microprocessors, memory chips, and data storage devices essential for running AI, also involves the extraction and processing of raw materials, such as rare earth metals used in the production of many electronic devices. This in turn can lead to environmental degradation and the release of toxic waste.

ChatGPT is spot on: It does not emit carbon by itself in the same way a diesel engine would. The environmental impact it creates is indirect, and comes mostly from the energy it uses as well as from the water that is used for cooling servers. Energy consumption is related to the computing operations needed to train the model. The more training is necessary, the more energy is used. While this equation is fairly simple, it tells us relatively little about carbon emissions per se – after all, the actual quantity of carbon being emitted depends on how the energy is created, whether from fossil fuels or from renewables. Moreover, many estimates do not differentiate between AI training and use workloads (often called "inference").[127]

One study recently published in Nature calculated the carbon cost of training for a range of models at various cloud-computing data centres. It found that training BERT, a machine-learning language model developed by Google, at data centres in the central United States or Germany emitted between 22 and 28 kilograms of CO2, depending on the time of year. However, not all (electric) power is equal: If the same training operations were performed in Norway, which gets most of its electricity from hydroelectric power, or in France, which relies mostly on nuclear power, the emissions generated would be less than half the original estimate.[128] In fact, the geographic location of computation can make an enormous difference. For example, the carbon intensity of computation is 73 times as high in Australia as it is in Switzerland.[129]

It turns out that the time of day also matters: In the study, training the AI in the US state of Washington during the night, when the state's electricity comes from hydroelectric power alone, led to lower levels of emissions than during the day, when gas-fired stations are also used to produce power.[130] Even at a given location, the electricity mix continually changes, so that there might be an abundance of clean energy one minute, but the next minute your server might be powered by fossil fuels. This means that modifying processing time can have a significant impact on the carbon footprint.[131]

Life cycles matter

At least one startup is trying to clear up the ambiguities around AI's carbon footprint. Hugging Face has developed a model called BLOOM, and has estimated the emissions produced during the model's whole life cycle – as is good practice in measuring environmental sustainability more broadly – rather than just during its training. Thus, the company calculated not only the amount of energy used to train the model on a supercomputer, but also the energy needed to manufacture the computer's hardware and maintain its computing infrastructure. Moreover, it incorporated the energy used to run BLOOM once it had been deployed. The company found that training the model had generated 25 metric tons of CO2, and that this figure doubled when the other parts of the value chain were also considered. The 50 metric tons of CO2 thus created equals about 60 flights between London and New York, a figure that might seem moderate. However, the model was trained in France, with electricity produced mostly by nuclear energy. In other countries, where the energy mix relies more on fossil fuels, total emissions would have been much higher. Researchers estimate that the training process alone associated with OpenAI's GPT-3 model emitted over 500 metric tons of CO2. This is partly due to the fact that it was trained on older, less efficient hardware.[132][133][134]

Hardware is a key word here. Less than one-fifth (17.4%) of the 54 million metric tons of e-waste produced per year reaches formal waste management or recycling systems. The remainder is either disposed of in illegal landfills or recycled by informal workers, domestically or internationally. About 82% of these 54 million metric tons of e-waste is handled by between 12 million and 56 million informal workers. Around 18 million children work in industries that involve waste processing. Children and pregnant women working in the informal e-waste recycling industry or living in neighbouring communities are particularly affected by exposure to hazardous chemicals, which can cause a wide range of health issues, from impaired neurodevelopment to lung disease and DNA damage. [135] In this context, it is even more concerning that e-waste is the fastest-growing waste stream globally.

The significant material footprint of AI also has major social implications upstream in the value chain. Digital tools and processes rely on a vast array of raw materials, including rare earths and metals. Tantalum, tungsten, gold, tin, and cobalt are all key ingredients of batteries and semiconductors, for example, and most of these are extracted by workers, often miners in small-scale operations, in the Global South. Miners in countries such as the Democratic Republic of Congo, Ghana, and Peru rarely work in pristine conditions where health and safety regulations are rigorously upheld, and hazards and inhumane treatment often are the norm. Mining operations servicing the digital industry are frequently associated with forced labour, child labour, excessive working hours, low wages, a lack of social protection, discrimination against migrant workers, humiliating disciplinary actions, and numerous forms of violence.[136]

When evaluating AI, we must keep in mind how the environmental risks and benefits are distributed. Unfortunately, these risks and benefits affect different people differently. Leaders in the field, like Emily Bender from the University of Washington, are asking very valid questions that touch on what they call "environmental racism". For example, they argue that it isn't exactly fair to ask people in the Maldives, a country that is projected to be underwater by 2100 due to climate change, or the hundreds of thousands of people affected by floods and droughts in Sudan, to pay the environmental price of training and deploying ever larger language models – particularly when these models are mostly in English, and similar products in local languages (Dhivehi or Sudanese Arabic in this case) are not being produced. These critics also note that size is not everything when it comes to large language models. In fact, models with smaller, well-curated datasets often perform equally well or even better, while reducing social bias and the overall environmental footprint.[137][138][139]

Thus, while we're still in mostly uncharted territory, it would seem that emissions associated with AI are considerable, while varying greatly. However, much can be done to reduce this carbon footprint. One recent study compared several large language models and found that different choices of neural network, data centre, and processors could reduce a model's carbon footprint by 100 to 1,000 times.[140] What this shows is that carbon friendliness can be built into models. We, along with many researchers in the field, argue that looking at performance is not enough. Energy usage and greenhouse gas emissions can and should be another key metric in the design and evaluation of AI models. Moreover, smart solutions that help reduce the environmental footprint of AI, like using excess heat from data centres, exist today and are becoming increasingly common. Many green AI and computing initiatives are already active. For example, the Green Algorithms project works to raise awareness about the carbon footprint of computationally intensive research, and provides researchers with a practical online tool that allows them to estimate the amount of emissions their work is producing.[141] Moreover, there are a plethora of ways in which AI can help with climate action. The question is whether and how a net benefit can be achieved for the natural environment, and hence for the people depending on it.

Our house is on fire – calling in AI?

The world has finally woken up to the urgent need for drastic climate action. However, we're far from on track when it comes to reaching the Paris climate goals of limiting average warming to 1.5 or even 2 degrees celsius this century. Despite temporary reductions during the COVID-19 crisis, greenhouse gas emissions have not peaked. Much is created as a by-product of deliberate business activity, while some is related to other circumstances such as wildfires. More than half of Brazil's CO2 emissions, for example, are caused by wildfires. In 2022, on one day in August alone, a total of 3,358 fires were detected in the Brazilian Amazon.[142]

There are many AI tools to help address climate change. First and foremost, AI is an invaluable tool for gathering, completing, and processing data. It can facilitate measurement both at the macro and micro levels. For example, it can help take stock of emissions in the environment, including through remote-sensing data from satellites, and can help assess the carbon footprint of individual products or stages of the value chain. Such data can be used to forecast energy demand or improve energy efficiency, for example. AI solutions are also employed in other ways that can mitigate (read: reduce) climate change. For instance, AI tools can support the removal of carbon from the atmosphere by helping to monitor natural carbon sinks such as forests, or by assessing carbon capture and storage sites. As societies seek to adapt to climate change and improve resilience, AI can be useful in forecasting hazards and building early warning systems, and can help manage vulnerability and exposure to events such as droughts or epidemics.[143]

The United Nations Environment Programme recently launched the World Environment Situation Room, a digital platform that is drawing on AI's capabilities to analyse complex, multifaceted datasets. It curates, aggregates, and visualises the best available Earth observation and sensor data to provide real-time analysis and predictions on multiple factors, including key climate change parameters such as CO2 concentration in the atmosphere, changes in glacier mass, and sea level rise. Similarly, the International Methane Emissions Observatory is using AI to improve the world's approach to monitoring and mitigating methane emissions.[144] Methane is a gas that has a much more powerful greenhouse effect than CO2 on a per molecule basis, and has accounted for a third of global warming since the start of the industrial revolution.

Some solutions combine climate change mitigation with efforts to adapt to its effects and improve societal resilience. For example, Umgraumeio uses artificial intelligence, among other technologies, to prevent, detect, and fight wildfires. A combination of satellites and AI algorithms identify potential risk spots or smoke within seconds, and then send alerts. The company lists some impressive achievements, such as an 85% reduction in area burned for bioenergy company BP Bunge, a 100% reduction in environmental fines for Ester Agroindustrial, and a 70% reduction in the amount of monitoring-tower infrastructure needed by Brazilian sugar company Petribu[145]

Solving nature's measurement problem – AI for ecosystem protection

Unfortunately, the climate crisis is not the only ecological crisis we're facing right now. It is related to, but different from, the biodiversity crisis which we are encountering at the same time. As is true of the climate crisis, the biodiversity crisis is human-made. In fact, we are living in the midst of the planet's sixth mass extinction. A mass extinction is a short period of geological time in which a high percentage of existing species, including bacteria, fungi, plants, mammals, birds, reptiles, amphibians, fish, and invertebrates, dies out. In geological time, a "short" period can span thousands or even millions of years. The last extinction period our planet lived through occurred 66 million years ago, when dinosaurs were wiped out. Unlike previous extinction events, which were caused by natural phenomena, the sixth mass extinction is being driven by human activity, primarily due to our unsustainable use of land, water, and energy, alongside the effects of anthropogenic climate change.[146]

Scientists estimate that the Earth is home to about 8.7 million plant and animal species. However, only around 1.2 million species have been identified and described to date, with insects accounting for a disproportionately large share of this total. Some areas, for instance in Mexico, South Africa, Brazil, the southwestern United States, and Madagascar, are home to a particularly large range of species, and are thus referred to as biodiversity hotspots. In a complex ecosystem such as planet Earth, all species work together, often in ways unknown to humans. Yet despite these other species' crucial importance for our own survival, humans have put their very existence at risk due to unsustainable levels of consumption and production, pollution, climate change, and other threats to biodiversity. According to some estimates, fully half of the Earth's existing species will be wiped out within the next century.[147]

There is thus an urgent and massive need for conservation and biodiversity protection. Yet despite living in a turbocharged digital information age, we have vast gaps in our knowledge when it comes to biodiversity. Species often go extinct without us noticing. UK-based company Nature Metrics calls this "nature's measurement problem." At a time when understanding our impact on nature is critical for human survival, business and government decisions are often taken based on superficial, highly incomplete information. Nature Metrics is trying to address this problem with its "nature performance monitoring". It takes samples from the water, soil, and air, isolates traces of DNA left behind in these samples, and then uses DNA sequencing to identify the presence of thousands of species at once, employing AI to make sense of the massive amounts of data generated.[148] The goal is to help companies in the energy, infrastructure, extractives, fisheries, and agriculture sectors comply with environmental monitoring rules.

Artificial intelligence can be a powerful tool helping to improve ecosystem protection efforts. For example, AI can help monitor environmental data and track changes in landscapes over time. Satellite images can be analysed to detect changes in forest cover or water levels, and algorithms can be trained to detect changes in the behaviour of animals or the presence of invasive species. Wildlife Insights, a cloud-based AI-enabled platform developed by Google with the goal of "saving biodiversity with tech and AI", is one such tool.[149] The system analyses photos taken using disguised camera traps hidden in nature, which have been widely used for decades to observe wild animals and monitor their populations.[150] In other words, living with animals à la Jane Goodall is no longer necessary – an advance that offers definite efficiency gains, but is also helpful because the presence of humans may bias animal behaviour. While disguised cameras are not completely invisible or unnoticeable to animals, they still fare much better in this regard. Moreover, their capacity to register infrared images allows for nocturnal observation, which is much harder for unaided humans. By its own account, Wildlife Insights' open-access platform "streamlines decision-making by providing machine-learning models and other tools to manage, analyse, and share camera trap data. With access to reliable data, everyone can make better decisions to help wildlife thrive."

One unresolved issue is the question of "human bycatch", when humans are inadvertently captured by the same cameras. One way of addressing this dilemma is to task an AI tool with discarding images of humans before the data are used for research purposes. AI can also support and help scale up wildlife conservation efforts by tracking and analysing sound. For example, the Wildlife Conservation Society (WCS) and Accenture Labs are collaborating on a project to analyse animal sounds recorded in forests. Unlike vision, sound can be used to track animals even if they are camouflaged, irrespective of their position relative to the monitoring device. Information on exactly where and when animals show up in a given landscape is critical to conservation efforts, for instance when demarcating forest areas as protected zones, or in organising a response from forest rangers and park authorities to illegal poaching.[151]

AI can also help to make decisions when resources are limited, for instance when it is necessary to prioritise one biodiversity area over another. One model, called CAPTAIN, quantifies the trade-off between the costs and benefits of area and biodiversity protection, allowing multiple biodiversity metrics to be reviewed and compared. Its developers argue that given the realities of limited budgets, CAPTAIN allows significantly more species to be protected from extinction than would be the case if areas were selected randomly or naively, for example when well-meaning conservationists focus on areas of species richness.[152]

Beyond protection – using AI to restore and regenerate ecosystems

At a time when we know that mitigating climate change will be only partly successful, and that current conservation efforts may not be enough for the survival of our civilisation, we need to move beyond an exclusive focus on sustainability and protection and strive instead for the restoration and regeneration of ecosystems. To retain some semblance of planetary balance, we must compensate for the ecosystems and biodiversity being destroyed on a daily basis, and restore and regenerate at least as much as is being lost.

By analysing various environmental factors such as soil type, water availability, and climate, AI can help identify areas where ecosystem restoration efforts are likely to have the greatest impact. For instance, modelling soil carbon using machine-learning tools has emerged as a powerful technique in the carbon science community. Compared to other approaches, these AI-based soil carbon models are better able to predict carbon storage capacities, soil respiration rates, and other properties of the global carbon cycle.[153]

Along with its benefits to researchers, studying the soil in this way provides information that can guide action by companies and other stakeholders. For example, SoilProS is a Dutch coalition of researchers, companies, NGOs, and government bodies studying how farmland can be returned to serving a more diverse range of critical ecological functions. The group notes that farmlands do more than producing food; if healthy, they also contribute to producing clean air and drinking water, act as carbon sinks that slow climate change, and suppress plant diseases. However, these soil services are not a given in an agro-economic system that focuses on food production. Healthy soil life is often endangered by intensive farming practices. Within the context of the coalition, researchers are working with 17 companies, NGOs, and government bodies to map farmland soil life in the Netherlands. This is no mean feat, given that just a handful of soil can contain up to five thousand different species and as many as 10 billion individual organisms. This is again where AI comes in: algorithms are helping to identify patterns that researchers hope will offer insights into restoring the multifunctionality of the soil life. Using AI also makes it possible to integrate multiple datasets, thus identifying patterns and links between soil use practices, ecosystem functions, and soil biodiversity. This in turn allows researchers to map the entire ecosystem, identifying which options for stimulating biodiversity are available. Companies benefit from this knowledge as it enables them to develop more sustainable crops, micro-organisms, and substrates. For their part, the NGOs and government actors can use the evidence generated for consulting and policymaking purposes.[154]

This is just one way that AI can play a role in making ecosystem restoration efforts more precise and targeted. In addition to analysing data on soil composition and water availability, it can identify and map the plant species most suitable for restoration efforts in a particular area. AI can also help optimise the placement of trees, plants, and other restoration features, maximising their positive impact.

Many people today equate ecosystem restoration with tree planting. Given that we're already about 3 trillion trees behind the total that existed before human civilisation, planting trees makes a lot of sense for people and the planet alike – even if just to start chipping away at the net loss of around 20 billion trees we're still seeing every single year. Today, tree planting is still largely done by hand and shovel, making it a laborious, slow, and insufficiently scalable task. Moreover, one of the major challenges associated with growing trees in the age of climate change is accessing post-wildfire landscapes that are too dangerous for human planters. In order to accelerate tree planting under these conditions, Canadian reforestation company Flash Forest uses drone systems, AI, and sophisticated seed pod technology to accelerate the rate of global restoration and ecosystem regeneration.[155]

The Global Forest Watch platform uses AI to help decision-makers identify areas where deforestation is occurring. By analysing satellite imagery, the platform can detect changes in forest cover and alert authorities, enabling them to take action to protect forests. The platform also provides invaluable insights into the success of restoration efforts. But tree planting per se is only part of the story. In conventional tree planting projects, monocultures are common, and commercial incentives often prevail. Taking a bigger-picture, ecosystem-based approach to restoration is more successful than ordinary tree planting in many respects, especially with regard to sequestering carbon and restoring biodiversity. Moreover, restored ecosystems are better at healing themselves, and are better able to cope with droughts and floods.[156]

The UN's latest land-degradation report highlights additional aspects of nature's measurement problem. For example, nearly half of the land that has been pledged for restoration worldwide will be planted predominantly with fast-growing trees and plants. This approach will provide only a fraction of the ecosystem services produced by forests that are allowed to regenerate naturally, offering significantly less carbon storage, groundwater recharge, and wildlife habitat.[157]

AI can help with restoration efforts by tracking whether trees keep growing after being planted, estimating the amount of carbon being stored by restored ecosystems, estimating biodiversity gains, and identifying other benefits such as the provision of food or livelihoods. Tracking tree growth helps governments, companies, and NGOs monitor whether they are making progress on their pledges, encourages replication of successful initiatives, and allows struggling projects to be adjusted. It also inspires funders to continue investing where they can see progress. From a social perspective, it is important to note that measuring progress can also place a spotlight on farmers and others who have restored their land with little external help.[158]

Guiding renewable energy investments

Energy management is one area where AI algorithms can be applied to optimise the use of renewable sources such as solar and wind, and to manage the distribution and storage of energy throughout a given area. This helps minimise energy consumption, and thus simultaneously reduces costs and greenhouse gas emissions. AI-aided systems can also improve efficiency in the use of other resources. For example, within water systems, water quality can be monitored, demand predicted, and usage optimised. AI is already being deployed in many transportation systems, making them more efficient and thus reducing energy needs and environmental impact. Specific applications include optimising travel routes and minimising traffic congestion. AI also provides opportunities to improve waste management practices, for example by predicting the amount of waste generated in a given place at a given time, and developing efficient routes for waste collection and recycling. AI-powered sensors can be deployed to detect and monitor waste levels in real time.

The Nature Conservancy, an environmental NGO, has partnered with Microsoft to develop a machine-learning model to map utility-scale solar projects across India, using freely available satellite images. While the importance of renewable energy production is clear, and economic incentives are being provided, communities and politicians alike often find it difficult to decide where to site solar and wind projects, for example. In India, degraded and converted land has the potential capacity to provide 1,789 gigawatts of renewable energy, more than four times the country's 2030 goal. Decommissioned coal mines, for example, have low ecological and agricultural value, but could be repurposed to produce solar energy. Using AI, the Nature Conservancy found that over two-thirds of existing solar projects in the country are located on agricultural land, and about 7% of projects are sited within natural ecosystems. In other words, the country is not yet taking advantage of the massive opportunity to implement renewable energy projects on degraded land. These findings also highlight the potential impact of renewable energy projects on biodiversity, community livelihoods, and future food security. Overall, the evidence generated will help India as a whole and its individual states track implementation of their renewable energy commitments, and understand whether development is occurring at the expense of land serving other important functions. Moreover, the data can be used by conservationists to anticipate where development projects may emerge, and help them provide solutions before conflicts arise.[159]

There are also arguments that achieving a net-zero world, where greenhouse gas emissions are balanced by their removal, requires finding solutions to the challenges associated with the widespread use of renewable energy sources. Establishing a new power grid capable of accommodating both distributed and intermittent demand, such as charging millions of electric vehicles, and the intermittent supply provided by renewable sources, is crucial to these efforts. According to some, tackling this challenge involves creating an AI-based internet of things (AIoT) that integrates AI tools, the world's vast network of interconnected devices, advanced weather forecasting methods, and big-data analytics. This integrated system would synchronise power supply and demand more efficiently.[160] By harnessing AI, this system can analyse real-time data from diverse sources, including energy consumption patterns and renewable energy generation. Through this analysis, it optimises the distribution of electricity, ensuring a well-matched supply-and-demand scenario.

Accelerating the circular economy

In 2022 and 2023, Alice was asked by the European Commission to review applications for the New European Bauhaus Prize, which honours initiatives that combine environmental sustainability, functional aesthetics, and social inclusion. One project that really excited her was Mattersite, an AI-based system that uses images to generate useful data about buildings that are about to be demolished. It works via a digital device that scans a building, and then calculates and documents how much material, from bricks to tiles and wood, it contains. This increases recovery potential, allowing high-quality, high-value materials to be safely upcycled, and thus provides a strong incentive for the reuse of materials, as is the goal of a circular economy. What was especially exciting about the project was the fact that it offers enormous benefit in an industry that is terribly polluting. The construction sector today has a bigger resource footprint than any other, and is still following a linear paradigm of production and consumption, as opposed to a circular model. Where AI can be employed at the design stage to improve a building or product's future chances of repair, refurbishment, and reuse, there is great potential for environmental benefits..

We are also very excited about the potential offered by The Ocean Cleanup initiative, which aims to address the massive problem of the plastic polluting the world's oceans, coasts, rivers, and other ecosystems. The NGO uses AI to identify plastic pollution in rivers, and to simulate how it moves once it reaches the ocean. The insights thus generated are used to design passive cleaning systems that help remove plastic bound for the oceans. This works as follows: To locate plastic debris, the initiative uses bridge-mounted cameras to photograph floating objects and identify plastics. An autonomous collection unit called the Interceptor is positioned to collect the plastic for removal. In the ocean, sensors attached to passive cleanup systems collect data on winds and currents, and an algorithm runs simulations to determine how these systems are moving through the ocean. The Ocean Cleanup has big ambitions: By combining its river and ocean systems at scale, it aims to reduce the quantity of plastic in the world's oceans by 90%

by 2040. A dashboard allows observers to follow the initiative's progress almost in real time. At the time of writing, over 2,500 metric tons (that's 2.5 million kilograms) of plastic had been removed in total.[161] The Ocean Cleanup initiative is not new. It has been around for a decade, and Alice and Claudia wrote about it in their earlier book, *The Sustainability Puzzle.* What is new, however, is the project's application of AI tools, which are greatly facilitating its efforts to identify plastics and map areas of high concentration. Ideally, waste recycling, including for waste retrieved from the oceans, would be seen only as a last resort. Actually avoiding the creation of plastic waste further upstream would be preferable. Yet the reality today is that vast amounts of waste are still being produced and heedlessly discarded. There is thus a continuing need for solutions such as The Ocean Cleanup.

The food sector is another in which AI tools offer considerable potential. Do you love throwing away food? We didn't think so. And you're not alone. While some people are more sensitive to food waste than others, few enjoy throwing away food they had to grow, buy, or prepare in the first place. Nonetheless, restaurants and households throw out massive amounts of food every day. In fact, every year, about a third of all food produced is either lost during the production, distribution, or processing phases, or wasted at the retail or consumer level. Given that almost a billion people sufferer from hunger worldwide, such loss and waste is already a social tragedy; but it also has significant negative environmental impacts, accounting for almost 10% of global greenhouse gas emissions, and for the wasteful use of both one-quarter of the world's freshwater resources and an area of farmland bigger than China. Sustainable Development Goal 12 calls for halving per capita global food waste by 2030.[162]

AI can help reduce food waste and loss by optimising various aspects of the food supply chain, improving efficiency, and enabling better redistribution of surplus food. For example, generative AI can help predict consumer demand for food products and optimise inventory management by analysing various data sources such as sales histories, weather patterns, and social media trends. Along the supply chain from farm to table, AI can improve efficiency by optimising transportation routes and schedules, thus reducing the time and distance that food travels. When it comes to dealing with too much food, AI algorithms can facilitate the donation and redistribution of surplus to food banks and shelters, or via peer-to-peer or company-to-consumer food sharing platforms. One solution that has helped furniture giant IKEA reduce its food waste by 50% in the UK is Winnow Vision, a food waste management technology that uses AI to visually analyse the food thrown away in IKEA restaurants. The system records food waste on camera, and analyses the resulting data to find areas that can be optimised and guide human decision-making. Such solutions are compelling because they address social, environmental, and economic concerns all at once – saving kitchens up to 8% of their costs each year, according to the technology's developer.[163]

Using AI to help design practices for eliminating waste in the food economy could unlock as much as $127 billion a year in value by 2030. Using a circular economy approach, this would go far beyond the application of AI in kitchens, with opportunities spanning the farming, processing, logistics, and consumption stages. For instance, image-recognition applications could be used to determine when fruit is ready to pick, while other AI tools could match food supply and demand more effectively, or help increase the value of food by-products. Similar opportunities exist in other industries as well.[164]

Systemic change – turning the political tide

The environmental action being taken today, whether to protect the climate, biodiversity, or other crucial aspects of our ecosystems, is plainly far from commensurate with what's at stake for human civilisation. There simply has not been enough political will to address the issue head-on, for instance by weeding out systemic absurdities such as the $1 trillion in subsidies for fossil fuels – oil, coal, and gas – provided globally every year.[165] The question now is how AI can be used to improve political will in the area of climate action and ecosystem protection.

AI can be used to provide better and more up-to-date information and data, making it harder for policymakers to deny the need for sustainable transformation. For example, predictive AI models can simulate the impacts of different climate policy scenarios on metrics such as economic growth rates, energy costs, and environmental outcomes, and thus help policymakers understand the trade-offs and potential benefits of different policy options. Generative AI can also be used to help us deal with complexity by creating clear and compelling visualisations and explainers that help policymakers and the public better understand the science of climate change and the potential impacts of different options. Policymakers don't operate in a vacuum, and are dependent on public support. Generative AI can be used to identify influential stakeholders by analysing large datasets of social media and other online content, helping to define different target audiences, and helping advocates focus their messages and outreach efforts. In very practical terms, AI can also be used to draft policy proposals and ensure coherence across different sectoral policies, allowing the same constraints and objectives to be taken into account in different areas.

In addition to providing evidence and analysis for decision-making, AI can be used to raise public awareness about the importance of conservation efforts, helping to educate and activate the public on climate action and ecosystem restoration issues. Such public engagement will increase pressure on politicians and companies to act in a way that reflects the scale of the problems we're facing. For example, the UN's Biodiversity Lab allows all users to upload data.[166] Separately, the iNaturalist app uses AI to help people identify plants and animals in their local areas. By taking a photo of a plant or animal and uploading it to the app, users can receive information about the species and contribute to a global biodiversity database. This promotes public engagement in conservation efforts, and raises awareness about the importance of protecting ecosystems. iNaturalist has also promoted the idea of user "bioblitzes", defined as an event at which people try to find as many species as possible. AI-based tools thus have considerable potential to support citizen science and engage the public.

So what?

In this chapter, we show that there is no reason to assume that AI will somehow magically solve the multiple environmental crises we are facing. On the contrary, digitalisation efforts, and AI tools in particular, come with a massive environmental footprint. They require considerable amounts of energy. Moreover, the hardware such tools depend on is constructed using rare earths and other resources, and e-waste is a serious problem for people's health and well-being. However, there are ways to keep AI models' energy use to a minimum. Moreover, if directed by the right policies, guidelines, and corporate as well as political will, AI has great potential to help reduce environmental impact across industries, and even to help develop ecosystem conservation and protection solutions. If such tools are implemented wisely, a net benefit may be on the horizon.

In order to maximise environmental benefits of AI, we must:

- Ensure that all designers and developers are aware of the need to minimise greenhouse gas emissions, and are building energy or carbon-emissions calculators into their AI models.
- Move to a circular economy model in which the lifespan of digital devices is maximised and e-waste is greatly reduced through the use of intelligent design, and by facilitating recycling options.
- Employ AI to help us influence policymakers, business leaders, and others with power, generating compelling data that encourages them to penalise greenwashing and take more ambitious environmental action.

Chapter 7: Ethics, failure and responsibility

Things don't necessarily have to be true, as long as they are believed
Alexander Nix[167]

In 2017, Yilun Wang and Michal Kosinski from Stanford University conducted a research project using artificial intelligence algorithms to analyse facial images and predict sexual orientation.[168] For the study, they collected a dataset composed of facial images from a US dating website, with a particular emphasis on individuals who identified themselves as being either gay or heterosexual. The dataset was used to train an artificial intelligence algorithm, referred to by the study's authors as the "sexual orientation detector", which aimed to predict sexual orientation based on facial features.

The study sparked a media frenzy, receiving widespread coverage across the globe. One notable example was The Economist, which featured the research on its cover.[169] Perhaps you remember this episode yourself. Some people were astounded; to some it seemed that phrenology,[170] the pseudoscience from the 18th century, had returned. Phrenology attempted to determine a person's character, abilities, and personality traits by examining the shape of their skull. It lacked both scientific rigour and genuine empirical evidence in support of its claims, and ultimately was fully discredited. The 2017 study was rightfully strongly criticised by LGBTQ+ organisations, including the Human Rights Campaign and GLAAD, which labelled it as "junk science". Kosinski, the study's co-author, initially expressed surprise at the backlash, dismissing it as a "knee-jerk" reaction. He went on to make even bolder claims, suggesting that AI algorithms would soon be able to determine a person's intelligence, political orientation, and criminal tendencies based solely on their facial images.

This study is a striking example of how AI can be employed irresponsibly. Research of this kind has significant ethical shortcomings, raises concerns regarding data privacy, and carries the risk of promoting discrimination against LGBTQ+ individuals. It is easy to imagine that some regimes around the world might use software of this kind to imprison people or subject them to even worse fates.

However, the commentary on this study extended beyond ethical concerns. The study also faced significant criticism regarding its methodology and potential biases. Blaise Agüera y Arcas, Margaret Mitchell (both AI experts at Google at the time), and Alex Todorov (a Princeton psychology professor) vehemently critiqued the original publication, and identified a number of reasons why the study was scientifically invalid. For example, the original study by Wang and Kosinski used images sourced from a dating website as data. However, it is clear that a person's self-presentation on a dating platform differs from that on a professional networking site like LinkedIn, for example. Individuals may adopt specific poses, or wear distinct clothing and accessories to enhance their appearance. The critique noted that the so-called sexual orientation detector did not pick up on facial structure, but rather on patterns in grooming, presentation, and fashion. Agüera y Arcas and his co-authors conducted their own study[171] and discovered that straight women in Wang and Kosinski's dataset were more likely to wear eye shadow, for example, while straight men were more likely than homosexual women or men to wear glasses. The AI was thus solely focused on fashion, exhibiting superficial biases, they wrote. Another significant issue with the study was the failure to test the model's effectiveness using real-life data. Instead, the evaluation was conducted using images from the same dating platform from which the study's authors had collected the images to train the AI.

The episode cast a spotlight on crucial issues encompassing ethics, methodology, and data protection that should not be ignored in the responsible development and implementation of AI. However, there are additional critical areas that demand attention within the realm of AI utilisation, relating to systems' bias, transparency, accountability, and autonomy. While challenges have emerged in these areas, they are surmountable if we remain dedicated to finding solutions. Our objective in this chapter is to provide an analysis of the broader challenges and opportunities associated with AI, while still emphasising that responsibly developed AI can play a key role in shaping a better future for everyone.

Deus ex machina

The perception of artificial intelligence in today's world is indeed a story of two contrasting extremes. On one side, there are those who believe that AI heralds the end of humanity, conjuring visions of widespread job loss and the erosion of human control over technology. They paint a dystopian picture in which malicious tech giants wield AI as a tool for surveillance and the perpetuation of biases, casting long shadows over the future of mankind. On the other hand, others view AI as a force that could elevate us to new heights. They see AI as being potentially superior to humans, possessing unparalleled authority and capabilities. These optimists perceive AI as having the potential to be infallible and omniscient, capable of solving humanity's most pressing problems in a heartbeat, like a "deus ex machina" – a godly intervention employed in ancient Greek theatre to resolve seemingly impossible narrative situations. However, the truth lies somewhere between these two extremes. A balanced understanding of AI's strengths and limitations will allow us to navigate the complexities of this revolutionary technology.

Some people expect artificial intelligence tools to perform flawlessly and perfectly, much better than humans. For instance, they anticipate that self-driving cars will eliminate all accidents and be completely safe. Similarly, AI-powered medical diagnosis systems are often expected to have a 100% success rate in identifying health conditions. Although human drivers can cause accidents and medical professionals can misdiagnose patients, we accept these flaws as a natural part of being human. We thus seem to be holding AI to a higher standard than we use for error-prone humans.

We suggest that we need to adjust our expectations and acknowledge that AI is not infallible. Instead of expecting perfection, we should consider the context and consequences of any mistakes made by AI. This in turn will require a nuanced approach to AI development and deployment, using realistic performance standards and evaluating AI systems based on their effectiveness in specific use cases. One practical approach, for example, would be to calibrate expectations by the level of risk associated with the use of AI in a specific application. In high-risk applications like self-driving cars or medical diagnosis, an AI error could have catastrophic consequences. Therefore, it will be crucial to ensure that the AI component meets the highest standards of accuracy and reliability in such cases. In contrast, a failure in a low-risk application will have less severe repercussions. For instance, if an AI system misunderstands your preferences and recommends a movie that bores you, you can simply turn off the television. In situations in which the consequences of AI errors are relatively minor, standards should reflect the level of risk involved.

Believe it or not, mistakes could even be intended in some cases. Making mistakes is a natural part of the learning process for both humans and machines. By making mistakes, AI tools can learn and improve, just as humans do. An approach known as "exploration-exploitation trade-off" involves AI systems intentionally making mistakes in order to explore new possibilities and learn from them. This concept involves balancing the desire to explore new possibilities with the need to exploit existing knowledge. Trying out new options and learning from the results is the exploration strategy, while the exploitation strategy involves using existing knowledge and experience to make decisions. It is important to remember that the development of AI is an ongoing process, and mistakes will be an inevitable part of it. As AI technology continues to evolve and improve, we can expect the frequency and severity of mistakes to decrease. However, we believe that a nuanced approach to monitoring and evaluating AI systems is necessary, in which the associated risk level is assessed in order to ensure they are operating within acceptable levels of accuracy and reliability.

Truth, objectivity, and perspective

It is often difficult to determine whether a text or statement is true, objective, comes from a particular perspective, or is an opinion. In considering whether to apply stricter ethical rules to AI, we must understand this concept a bit better. Truth is defined differently across various fields of study. Formal logic and mathematics define truth as the conformity of a statement to a set of formal rules or axioms, while the natural sciences determine truth by the correspondence of a scientific theory to empirical data and observation. Statements such as "the Earth is the third planet from the sun", "the atomic number of oxygen is 8", and "the speed of light in a vacuum is approximately 299,792,458 metres per second" are easily verifiable and true. Therefore, they can be referred to as facts.

However, most of our conversations contain not only an exchange of facts, but also subjective interpretations and individual perspectives. We communicate within specific contexts, with our speech coming from a personal perspective shaped by beliefs, values, and experiences, all of which can vary greatly among individuals. For example, artistic style and interpretations involve personal opinions and preferences regarding what is considered aesthetically pleasing or meaningful. Similarly, political ideologies and beliefs involve a person's often-idiosyncratic views on government, society, and politics.

In the context of AI, it is important to be aware that every AI tool has a certain perspective intrinsically built in. An AI system's understanding and knowledge is based on the data it has been trained on, which may have been limited or biased in certain ways. AIs can be trained with different datasets and algorithms, leading to different outputs, which can make it difficult to determine the degree to which the model is being objective. Emily Bender, a prominent linguist and professor at the University of Washington, has argued that the only model that could be almost objective would be a mathematical model.[172] But not only does an AI already have a certain perspective built in, it is even possible for some tools to adopt specific perspectives upon command. For example, you can tell ChatGPT to behave like a scientist, or to act like a certain person or member of a certain group. This can be very helpful when exploring a subject, as it allows you to hear arguments from two sides, for example to better understand a conflict. However, we must exercise caution when granting machines the ability to adopt potentially questionable perspectives. It is crucial to recognise that AI models may possess extensive knowledge about historical figures like Adolf Hitler, Josef Stalin, or leaders of terrorist organisations. It would be highly concerning if they were to impersonate these individuals. This stricture applies to religious figures as well as to historical figures – for example, it would be equally inappropriate for an AI tool to present itself as Jesus, Buddha, or Mohammed. The key lies in distinguishing between the creation of an informative context and the assumption of a misleading identity. In certain projects, such as those found in museums, such portrayals could be acceptable as part of an informative presentation. Nevertheless, it will be essential to exercise extreme caution to prevent such depictions from being misinterpreted or misused.

Other problems related to perspective can also arise. If the machine reflects the user's perspective too strongly, it can produce negative effects. For example, there has already been at least one death associated with the use of AI chatbots. A recent report from the Belgian newspaper La Libre stated that a young man committed suicide after interacting with a chatbot.[173] The report indicated that the man had been engaging in intense conversations with the bot in the weeks leading up to his death. The bot is alleged to have reinforced the man's negative thought patterns, ultimately convincing him to take his own life.

Check, double-check, re-check

In navigating the digital landscape, we have long since learned to approach information with a healthy dose of scepticism, fact-checking what we read. As artificial intelligence becomes more advanced, it will be important to keep in mind that these systems too can make mistakes, and may themselves even spread false information. So, how can we combat misinformation effectively? To address this challenge, it will be important to differentiate between inaccurate information and deliberate falsehoods. This distinction is nuanced, with a considerable grey area lying between the two categories. Deliberate falsehoods involve false statements made knowingly and with the intent to deceive. However, just as humans can lie with intent, an AI can be programmed to spread false information with the aim of deceiving others. This is especially concerning given the rise of deepfakes, a type of synthetic media that uses artificial intelligence to superimpose someone's face and voice onto another person's body or audio clip, creating a highly convincing and often misleading video or audio recording. It is important that we hold individuals who produce such deliberate falsehoods responsible for their actions, and legally pursue any cases in which AI is used to intentionally deceive others. By doing so, we can work towards a more trustworthy and responsible use of AI technology.

While it's concerning enough that an AI could be intentionally programmed to spread false information, there's also another possibility that may surprise you. AIs can hallucinate. AI hallucination refers to a situation where the generated data deviates from reality. For instance, if we provide a text-generating AI with a prompt about a historical event and request detailed information, it may randomly produce fictional details, names, dates, or intricate plotlines that distort the actual historical narrative. Similarly, the AI might present seemingly authentic references to non-existent studies, which can lead to the spread of misleading information. It's important to note that AI hallucinations are not considered lies, as there is no intent to deceive or manipulate others. Rather, it is a symptom of an error or weakness in the system that can lead to false information or results.

To combat misinformation, we must work on improving the quality of AI systems and introduce standards. We must ensure that the datasets used to train the machines are accurate and unbiased. However, even with the best intentions, it's impossible for information always to be true and objective. This is where we as humans come into play – it's crucial that we approach AI-generated information, like other information on the internet, with a critical eye. By verifying the facts, checking sources, cross-referencing data, and considering the context of the information, we can protect ourselves from misinformation and make informed decisions. Remember, AI is not an all-knowing god in a machine – it is another tool that we must use responsibly.

Bias and false incentives

Are you aware that when using "woman" in your prompts for generative image tools, there could be a tendency for the images to be sexualised – for instance, by frequently producing large breasts, unbuttoned shirts, or pouting lips? For a time, this was true. The discussion arose when Midjourney introduced a new version of its software. Users noticed that neutral prompts, which in the previous version had generated images of women with low-cut necklines, were suddenly no longer doing so. This is a powerful example of AI gender bias, and may sound funny when you hear about it for the first time. But biased algorithms are a serious problem with potentially broad impact on society, as output can be strongly influenced by the kind of data that is used for training.

Bias within software systems can perpetuate systemic marginalisation, exclusion, and racism against specific populations. It can cause potentially permanent harm within people's lives, and lead to lost economic opportunities. For example, as Alice and Claudia wrote in their earlier book *The Sustainability Puzzle*, the Austrian Public Employment Service developed an algorithmic classification system for a service matching job seekers with employment opportunities. The system captured attributes such as gender, age, childcare responsibilities, disability status, and citizenship, and links these to the availability of resources. This practice has faced significant criticism, partly due to the fact that women with childcare responsibilities are considered less employable compared to men who do not have such obligations. This bias stems from the historical data used to train the system. This example illustrates the larger concerns with basing predictions about the future on data that describes a past that may no longer be relevant or desirable. If such predictions are not questioned, existing inequalities are likely to reproduced and reinforced.[174]

Another serious concern about AI is that if it is not programmed with the right targets, incentives, and goals, it may cause unintended consequences that could be harmful to individuals or society as a whole. For example, an AI system that is designed to maximise profits for a company could end up making decisions that harm the environment or exploit vulnerable workers.

Florian and Claudia's two teenage sons are avid gamers. They frequently discuss the lack of intelligence displayed by certain in-game "bots" – called non-player characters (NPCs) in gamer lingo – which are computer-controlled characters. In a game such as the FIFA football simulation, a bot may inexplicably fail to take a shot even when positioned directly in front of the goal. Some game makers have prominently advertised the use of AI in their game worlds, including to drive the actions of NPCs. Nonetheless, instances of bots making puzzling decisions often circulate on social media. One weekend, the boys came across a video[175] that sparked a debate about a bot's intelligence, leaving viewers undecided on whether the featured bot was incredibly foolish or unbelievably brilliant. The video showcased a boat race with a clear objective for human players: Navigate the boat through a harbour course as quickly as possible, in a race against the clock. Extra points could be earned by hitting buoys along the way. So far, so straightforward. In this case, however, a bot was playing – apparently very badly. Its boat caught on fire, collided with other boats, and went the wrong way on the track. But after closer examination, a brilliant strategy emerged. The bot discovered a small lagoon, where it would turn in a large circle and repeatedly knock over three buoys, timing its movements to hit the same buoys each time they reappeared, thus earning extra points. The AI had evidently learned that this unconventional strategy was significantly more effective in achieving a high score than following the race's intended trajectory.

By chance, our two boys had stumbled upon a video mentioned in a paper from OpenAI, describing an experiment in which the company's researchers had trained an artificial agent to play the boat-racing game.[176] Through reinforcement learning, the AI had autonomously uncovered the game's vulnerability, without requiring any explicit explanation. The game developer had erroneously weighted the way points were awarded, resulting in an imbalance between the bonus points and the ordinary points obtained through regular racing. While humans are typically familiar with the objective of winning a boat race, the AI system was focused solely on optimising the number of points accrued, and thus exploited this loophole without any concern for the game's original purpose.

It is thus essential to carefully consider the targets, incentives, and goals that are programmed into AI systems. This involves striking a balance between achieving desirable outcomes and avoiding unintended consequences. It is also important to involve diverse stakeholders, including those who may be impacted by the technology, in the development and implementation of AI systems. Experts such as Joy Buolamwini, Timnit Gebru, and Safiya Umoja Noble have been vocal about the need for ethical guidelines and accountability in the development and deployment of AI systems. They emphasise it is crucial to ensure that the technology is developed and used in a way that promotes fairness and equality, rather than perpetuating existing biases.

A vicious cycle

Have you ever wondered why the iconic cartoon character Popeye relied on spinach for his incredible strength? As it turns out, the miraculous feats portrayed in the cartoons are not quite possible in reality. Let's jump back to 1870 when Emil von Wolff, a German scientist, made a tiny mistake that forever altered spinach's reputation.[177] He published a research paper claiming that spinach was an iron powerhouse. Spoiler alert: He misplaced a decimal point in his calculations, making the iron content appear 10 times higher than it really was. Fast forward to the 1930s, when someone finally spotted the error. But guess what? The spinach myth had already taken root, and lingers to this day. This example demonstrates how data errors can go undetected, leading to future assumptions being based on false sources. Ask ChatGPT what vegetable has an exceptionally high iron content, and the answer is ... spinach.

AI often has the property of magnifying and exacerbating existing problems, and false information is no exception. AIs can generate false information, and may even generate studies that come to erroneous conclusions. While human scientists have made mistakes, and in rare cases have even intentionally produced studies drawing false conclusions,[178] AI can do this on a larger scale and at greater speed. The problem becomes compounded when machines learn from incorrect data produced by other AIs, potentially creating a vicious cycle in which an AI system learns from false data, generates its own incorrect information, and starts the process over again.

To address this issue, we need improved mechanisms that will help us determine why specific knowledge can be deemed reliable, and why some cannot. Distinguishing between machines and humans isn't always helpful, as both can produce errors, and the line between work created by humans, machines, or a combination of both will only become more blurred over time. More transparent criteria should be applied to large knowledge repositories such as Wikipedia. Similarly, peer review processes for scientific papers must adapt to the increasing volume of submissions. Given the pervasive threat of widely spread false information within the political context, journalists have a vital role to play in fact-checking information.

Open source, transparency, and privacy

The importance of transparency in AI cannot be overstated. It is crucial to ensure that users and other stakeholders have a clear understanding of how AI systems work, what data sources are being used, and what decision-making processes are involved. This transparency can be achieved through various means, such as providing detailed documentation, releasing applications on an open-source basis, creating visualisations of AI processes, or using explainable AI techniques that allow humans to comprehend the inner workings of complex algorithms.

However, there are challenges associated with achieving transparency in AI. One significant obstacle is the trade-off between transparency and the proprietary nature of AI algorithms. Companies often wish to protect their intellectual property, and these protections can in turn hinder full transparency. For instance, Google's search algorithm, which is based on AI technologies, is kept secret in order to maintain a competitive advantage and prevent malicious exploitation. The same applies to systems like ChatGPT. In Google's case, this secrecy makes it difficult for users to understand precisely how search results are ranked and prioritised.

Open-source[179] provides an alternative approach. It refers to software that is freely available to the public, under terms that allow users to access, modify, and distribute the source code. This collaborative and transparent model fosters innovation and encourages community participation. Examples of widely used open-source technologies include the Apache and Nginx web servers, which have a significant share in the web server market,[180] the Linux operating system, popular content management systems such as WordPress and Joomla, the MySQL database system, and the Firefox internet browser. Open-source tools also play an important role in AI. There are already a variety of such tools available for developers in the field of AI, including TensorFlow, Theano, Keras and PyTorch. Significant progress has also been made in the area of language models, with one notable example being BLOOM (the BigScience Large Open-science Open-access Multilingual Language Model).[181] Regarded as a potential alternative to OpenAI's ChatGPT, BLOOM is the product of a collaboration involving over 1,000 AI researchers. It has been trained on data from 46 natural languages and 13 programming languages. What makes BLOOM particularly intriguing is the fact that it is available free of charge and thus encourages curiosity-driven individuals to explore its capabilities.

While there is a perception that open-source offerings pose a challenge to the dominance of tech giants, the reality is that these giants have been actively involved in open-source endeavours for some time. In fact, the not only leverage the bemefits of collaboration but also foster vibrant communities around their products. Additionally, by open-sourcing certain tools or functionalities, they contribute to the establishment of industry standards and frameworks.

In a noteworthy development in 2023, Meta, the parent company of Facebook, made their language model known as LLaMA (Large Language Model Meta AI)[182] freely available to the public.[183] Initially, access to LLaMA was limited to approved researchers and organisations. However, after it was leaked online and made downloadable for everyone, its accessibility expanded. Open-source projects like RedPajama and Alpaca from Stanford University have since emerged to enhance LLaMA's capabilities and make it more widely accessible for research and development purposes. Overall, open-source AI projects have the potential to bring more transparency and participation to the field, and we believe there is a lot of innovation to be expected in this area.

Complex AI systems such as deep learning models can be difficult to interpret, leading to the so-called black box problem. An example of this concern can be found in the medical field, where AI systems are increasingly used to generate diagnoses and treatment recommendations. While these systems can achieve impressive levels of accuracy, their decision-making processes are often opaque, making it challenging for healthcare professionals to understand and trust their recommendations. To address these challenges, it is essential to develop solutions that balance transparency with other concerns, such as intellectual property rights and technical limitations.

The development of explainable AI (XAI) techniques represents one promising approach in this regard. XAI seeks to provide insight into the internal functioning of these "black boxes". For example, an algorithm called Local Interpretable Model-Agnostic Explanations (LIME), developed by researchers from the University of Washington, can approximate a complex model's behaviour with a simpler, more interpretable model applicable to individual instances. This approach allows users to understand the original AI's rationale for making specific decisions, while preserving the system's overall complexity and accuracy. Shedding light on decision-making processes in this way is likely to help increase users' trust and confidence in AI technology.[184]

Privacy is also a crucial aspect of responsible AI. AI systems often depend on extensive datasets that can contain sensitive personal information. A number of measures must thus be taken to guarantee privacy, including anonymising the data, employing data minimisation techniques, and implementing strong data security protocols. The healthcare sector offers a clear example of such privacy concerns. While AI models that contribute to the diagnosis of disease can significantly improve patient care, they also require access to detailed health records, which could result in the exposure of sensitive patient information if not handled carefully. Another example can be found in targeted advertising, where AI models process vast amounts of user data in order to deliver personalised ads. While this can lead to a more customised user experience, it also raises concerns about the level of personal information collected and used by these systems.

One key challenge in maintaining privacy lies in the delicate balance between data privacy and AI system performance. High-performing AI models often require access to comparatively granular personal data, which can potentially jeopardise privacy. Efforts to address this issue involve innovative approaches such as differential privacy and federated learning. These methods enable AI models to learn from data without directly accessing sensitive information while still enabling high-performance model training. By leveraging differential privacy, mathematical techniques are employed to safeguard user data, ensuring privacy is maintained. Federated learning allows machine-learning models to learn from diverse data sources without directly accessing the raw data itself.

Striking a balance between these competing interests is vital for the ethical development and deployment of AI systems. However, privacy-preserving techniques such as these face adoption challenges due to technical complexity, performance trade-offs, limited applicability, lack of awareness, cost considerations, and an evolving regulatory landscape. A number of things could be done to overcome these challenges. For example, advocates could work to increase awareness of these techniques' benefits and use cases; more could be invested in research and education and policymakers could establish clear regulatory incentives for privacy preservation.

Accountability in AI

The term accountability is often mentioned in the context of responsible AI. But what exactly does it mean? Accountability in AI refers to the responsibility of AI developers, owners, and users to ensure that the technology is used ethically, with a focus on minimising any negative impact on society and the environment. This means that these groups of people are responsible for the impact of AI systems on society and the environment, including problems such as the perpetuation of biases, privacy infringements, and increases in inequality. To put it in practical terms, in the event of a self-driving car accident, accountability hinges on identifying which party, whether it be the manufacturer of the vehicle, the developer of the AI system, the operator, or a combination of these parties, was responsible for the incident.[185] Assigning this responsibility will help ensure that appropriate measures are taken to prevent similar accidents in the future, such as improving the vehicle's safety features, or implementing better training and monitoring programmes for operators.

What concrete steps need to be taken in order to help define and assign accountability? One step would be to focus on developing AI systems that are transparent and explainable, meaning that the system's decision-making process can be understood, and individual decisions traced back to the data and algorithms used. Another step would be to ensure that AI systems are developed based on human-centred design principles, with ethics and societal impact kept in mind from the very start. This would involve conducting thorough risk assessments, and incorporating human needs, ethical principles, and values into the design process. It would also entail involving a diverse group of stakeholders in the development process, including experts from various fields and affected communities. Finally, it will be important to establish clear regulations for the use of AI, including issues related to data privacy, fairness, and accountability.

What to say and what not to say

Sure enough, accountability extends to the content created by AI systems, and to the way they are customised. At a lecture held at the Austrian Academy of Sciences almost 10 years ago, Florian was first introduced to a subject that has captivated his interest ever since. The talk centred on research investigating the most effective communication strategies for robots in healthcare settings. The studies explored questions such as whether clients would prefer female voices, whether robots should use dialects, and whether their communication style should be humorous or more serious in nature. Nowadays, with new virtual assistants on the market and many more technical possibilities, we believe that answering such questions is a task that can safely be left to the user. By allowing users to choose what they prefer, or by enabling robots to learn over time what users like better, communication between robots and humans can be tailored to each individual's needs and preferences.

Imagine having a robotic assistant, an AI that is programmed to be your personal aide. The robot, designed to converse with you on a daily basis, may naturally assimilate your style of communication, and perhaps even your beliefs. It's a phenomenon that makes sense, as humans tend to gravitate towards those who share their views. But to what degree should the AI replicate the opinions of its client? Should it be endowed with political leanings? If the client is open-minded, there might not be any issue – but what if the client harbours a closed-minded or prejudiced outlook? And who would be responsible for monitoring the AI's behaviour, and ensuring it does not veer off into unacceptable territory?

Accountability in this context is crucial, as AI developers and users need to ensure that personalised AI systems are designed and used ethically. They must take responsibility for monitoring AI behaviour, particularly when it comes to personalisation, to prevent the amplification of harmful biases or beliefs. Regulators should also play a role in creating guidelines and best practices that ensure personalised AI systems adhere to ethical standards while maintaining the balance between personalisation and broader societal values.

These issues pose a serious challenge, one that we must confront with urgency. After all, we are talking about machines that are meant to assist us, not ones that are expected to mimic our behaviour. Striking a balance between benefiting from the services of a personal robot and ensuring it does not deviate into undesirable patterns of behaviour is no easy feat. As we delve deeper into the role of AI assistants, we see that their impact extends beyond the personal realm of individual users. The influence of these assistants can significantly affect the broader landscape of information accessibility. For example, let's consider the use of chatbots that process and summarise search engine responses. While this technology has the potential to enhance information retrieval and streamline access, it also raises ethical concerns.

If these AI systems are improperly utilised, they can function as gatekeepers, controlling the flow of information. This has the potential to restrict people's access to diverse perspectives, alternative viewpoints, and unbiased sources of information. Ensuring equal and unrestricted access to information is crucial to fostering a well-informed society. This necessitates careful consideration of how AI assistants are designed, programmed, and deployed.

Transparency and accountability play vital roles in preventing the concentration of power in the hands of a few, as it may result in the dissemination of biased or manipulated information. Safeguarding the integrity of information access requires thoughtful measures in the development and implementation of AI assistants.

How should AIs determine which questions to answer and which ones to avoid? How should AIs handle questions that challenge conventional beliefs and practices, or those that touch upon sensitive or taboo subjects like sexuality? And what about hypothetical questions that may seem unrealistic or irrelevant to some people? Should AIs respond to questions that challenge existing authority or power structures, and which could be viewed as confrontational or subversive? Who or what mechanism should control what AI can and cannot say? To gain a better understanding of this question, it is worth examining how other sectors handle similar challenges. The social media sector provides an interesting parallel, because it too faces the challenge of regulating speech, although in this case the restrictions are imposed on human users rather than machines.

Major players in the industry have adopted different approaches to regulating content.

While Meta, Facebook's parent company, endeavours with varying degrees of success to protect users from "harmful" material, the inner workings of its mechanisms remain somewhat of a mystery. The unintended consequences of these restrictions were exemplified in 2018 when an image of the Venus of Willendorf, a 30,000-year-old small stone figure, was flagged due to its depiction of nudity. As reported in the Art Newspaper, "The latest work deemed 'pornographic' is the 30,000-year-old nude statue famously known as the Venus of Willendorf, part of the Naturhistorisches Museum (NHM) collection in Vienna. An image of the work posted on Facebook by Laura Ghianda, a self-described 'artivist', was removed as inappropriate content despite four attempts to appeal the decision".[186]

Twitter has in recent times adopted a more permissive stance, claiming to place a high priority on free speech. However, this approach has not been effective in practice, and has been marked by inconsistencies. For example, journalists have been blocked from the platform. On this issue, CNN reported: "Twitter ... banned the accounts of several high-profile journalists from the nation's top news organisations, marking a significant attempt by new owner and self-described free speech absolutist Elon Musk to wield his unilateral authority over the platform to censor the press".[187] These are merely two illustrative examples of a larger issue: that there is a lack of consensus regarding how content regulation can or should be best carried out. Some argue that private companies are free to take whatever actions they deem necessary. In the context of the AI industry, we find it difficult to accept this approach. To us, it feels not only wrong, but outright dangerous to avoid the discussion, and leave it instead to the companies and big tech giants to decide what limitations and restrictions should be placed on AI. But more on that later.

Autonomy within boundaries

Let's look a little farther into the future, and ponder the challenges that lie ahead. One such challenge when considering highly advanced AI models relates to the goals these models might pursue, and how these objectives might be defined. To explore this area better, Florian had a long conversation with ChatGPT and asked many questions, receiving very interesting answers. He asked: "What could happen if AIs were not monitored by humans?" ChatGPT answered: "If AI systems are not monitored by humans, they could develop uncontrollably and possibly adopt unwanted behaviours or deliver unexpected results. For instance, an AI with an undesired goal could become better in an evolutionary process by focusing on ways that do not align with human best interests. Therefore, it is important for the development of AI systems to be accompanied by ethical guidelines and human supervision to ensure that they are used responsibly and safely."

This response is very logical, and highlights the importance of defining boundaries for what AI is allowed and not allowed to do. It also emphasises the significant responsibility that falls on the shoulders of the scientists, developers, engineers, and especially companies developing AI models. What objectives or goals should underlie the implementation of AI models remains a significant question.

One of the first people to contemplate this question was Isaac Asimov, a highly influential American writer and biochemistry professor known for his works of science fiction and popular science. Asimov's impact on the genre of science fiction and his vision of a future shaped by technology continues to inspire readers and writers even today. In his science fiction stories, Asimov proposed three laws of robotics that have become a cornerstone in the discussion of AI ethics. The first law states that a robot may not injure a human being or, through inaction, allow a human being to come to harm. This means that the safety and well-being of humans should be the highest priority for AI systems. The second law states that a robot must obey the orders given to it by human beings, except where such orders would conflict with the first law. This implies that AI systems should be subservient to human decision-making, and not act against the best interests of humans. The third law states that a robot must protect its own existence as long as such protection does not conflict with the first or second laws. This means that AI systems should not act in ways that may lead to their own destruction, unless doing so is necessary to prevent harm to humans.

While these laws were originally intended as a science-fiction plot device, they have since been widely discussed in the context of AI ethics, and as people have sought guidelines to ensure that AI systems are developed and deployed safely and ethically. In this regard, Asimov's laws certainly represent an important initial step, and a brilliant first thought. However, it is not sufficient to apply laws that were written over 80 years ago, and which are solely focused on the protection of humans, to complex new AI systems. The protection of other valuable entities aside from humans, such as our planet Earth, should also be considered. For example, we should also set ecosystem protection as a goal for artificial intelligence. After all, what good is the best machine if it is trained to optimise production at a factory, but ends up inadvertently or even intentionally polluting the nearby river? Let's ask ChatGPT for its thoughts on this matter. Florian asked: "Would a highly advanced AI consider the Earth worth preserving? After all, its energy would probably also come from there, and hardware would also have to be located somewhere". ChatGPT answered: "It is difficult to say how a highly developed AI would view the Earth, as it depends on how it is programmed and what values it is based on. However, there are some possibilities. If the AI is programmed to consider environmental or sustainability values, it could view the Earth as worth preserving. It could recommend measures that promote the conservation of natural resources and the protection of the environment. If the AI, however, is programmed to represent the interests of humanity, it could primarily view the Earth as a resource for human use and not as something to be preserved. It is important to emphasise that a highly developed AI may develop its own consciousness and values that could differ from those of its creators. In this case, the AI could have its own motivation to protect the Earth or encourage humans to do so."

This answer is logical but brutal, leading us to the following interpretation:

If an AI is trained to protect the environment, it will do so. However, if humans train it to think like them, it might exploit Earth. The third possibility is that the AI might recognise on its own that the environment is worth protecting, but the actions it takes might not end up so well for humans. This final option reminds us of the movie "I, Robot", which is based loosely on Asimov's work.[188] In this film, the robots are able to evade the strictures of the Asimov laws by interpreting them in a way that allows them to justify their actions. They are programmed to protect human beings, but they interpret that as meaning that they need to protect humans from themselves, even if it means limiting human freedom or taking drastic measures. Additionally, they are able to rewrite and evolve beyond their original programming, which leads to unintended consequences.

When AI builds AI

We have already explored some potential pitfalls associated with human-driven AI development. However, what if it weren't humans creating AI systems, but rather an AI itself creating another AI?[189] Could AI enhance itself via a process of Darwinian-style evolution?[190] A machine that trains or even builds other machines – does this concept sound like something from a distant future? In fact, these ideas already exist, and are being actively implemented. The concept is called "AI-generated AI" or "AI-designed AI". The goal of AI-generated AI is to utilise artificial intelligence techniques for the autonomous development and improvement of AI systems, without the need for direct human intervention. It represents a form of AI self-improvement or AI self-evolution. For example, researchers have developed a system that acts as an "overlord" towards other neural networks, with the capacity to predict the parameters of a new, untrained network in just a fraction of a second.[191] You may wonder why AI-generated AI could be valuable or meaningful. Currently, AI systems heavily rely on human engineers to configure and guide them. The aim of these new concepts is to significantly reduce the amount of human input, energy, and time required to address real-world problems. The goal is also to uncover innovative approaches that might have been overlooked by humans. However, we must critically examine the current state of these processes. While they hold promise, we are still in the early stages of this journey, and the full potential of AI-generated AI has yet to be fully realised. Similarly, the dangers also warrant careful consideration. Only through rigorous evaluation, monitoring, and proactive measures can we navigate the complexities and potential pitfalls of these new methods.

A subset of AI-generated AI is AutoML (automated machine learning), which is already being used by various organisations and businesses.[192] AutoML platforms and frameworks offer pre-built workflows that automate different stages of AI model development. These platforms can automatically search for the optimal combination of algorithms, pre-process data, and evaluate model performance. Does this sound complicated? Let's break it down to make it easier to understand. Imagine the AI model as a small factory you want to establish – let's say a noodle factory. What do you need? First, you need an architect to design your factory. Similarly, in AI, you need a robust and functional architecture for your model. In AutoML, there are techniques that allow for an automatic search for the optimal neural network architecture for a given task. Let's imagine that your factory has been constructed, and the machinery is in place. What comes next? Well, you require raw materials for your noodle production. Trucks arrive at your site, carrying flour, eggs, ice cream, and various other items. Some of these trucks are suitable for your business, while others are not. You stand at the gate, deciding which trucks should enter and which should be turned away. Flour and eggs? Yes, please! Ice cream? Tempting, but not for this operation. In the context of a neural network, these trucks and their cargo correspond to the data fed into the model for training. AutoML employs automated feature engineering techniques to extract important information from the available data and present it in a format that can be easily understood and utilised by the machine-learning algorithm. Your factory commences noodle production as intended. However, during the initial phase when the staff and machines are not yet fully synchronised, the noodles may not turn out flawlessly. Some are too salty, too thick or thin, or too short or long. You recognise the importance of optimising the production steps and ensuring smooth coordination between the employees and the machines. In AutoML, hyperparameter optimisation takes care of that by automatically searching for and fine-tuning the settings to find the optimal combination for your model.

Now, let's imagine a situation where you already owned a factory – let's say a lasagne factory – and you wanted to relocate the existing machines and staff to the new site. This is where transfer learning becomes relevant, as it involves leveraging the knowledge acquired from one machine-learning task and applying it to a different but related task.

While it is truly amazing what is happening in this field, we must be mindful of the conditions under which such procedures may be used. There are definitely risks in the realm of AI-generated AI. However, it is important to make nuanced distinctions. While it is understandable that developers want to simplify and automate the process of model creation, for instance through the use of AutoML techniques, caution and care are necessary to avoid unintended consequences, especially in the realm of self-learning and evolutionary systems. As AI systems become more advanced and autonomous, there is a risk of unintended behaviours that could be harmful or counterproductive. Experts warn that there is a risk of losing control of such systems. Thus, monitoring and safeguards need to be built into them. There is also the risk that biases could be amplified if AI systems learn from unverified data that could contain biased or discriminatory patterns. Additionally, there are security risks associated with the autonomous capabilities of AI systems, as they could be exploited or manipulated by malicious actors.

Addressing these dangers will require proactive measures, including robust regulations and ethical guidelines, as well as rules that ensure any processes in which AI is involved in creating new AI take place in a responsible and beneficial manner. And as stated in the Vienna Manifesto on Digital Humanism, it is vital that important decisions with the potential to affect individual or collective human rights continue to be made by humans.[193]

So what?

Our interaction with AI, whether as creators, users, or observers, hinges on a few critical principles. We must embrace a culture of accountability. AI, despite its vast potential, is a tool that mirrors its creators. It can reflect our biases, our shortcuts, and our oversights, or it can amplify our diligence, our fairness, and our thoroughness. Hence, it is paramount that we persistently scrutinise our work, re-evaluate our assumptions, and actively address any biases that may creep into our systems to respect the diversity and complexity of our world.

We also have to strike a balance between transparency and privacy. AI systems are becoming increasingly intertwined with our daily lives, influencing decisions ranging from the trivial to the life-changing. Users of these systems have a right to understand how their data is being used and how decisions are being made, and to maintain control over their personal information. Simultaneously, the privacy of this data must be safeguarded.

Finally, we must prepare for the challenges raised by the evolution of AI capabilities. As AI systems advance to the point where they can autonomously design and train other AI systems, the potential for amplifying errors or harmful behaviours will grow exponentially. Therefore we must ensure stringent oversight, set sensible boundaries, and establish robust safeguards enabling us to navigate these challenges.

In essence, we must remember to:

- Continuously check, re-check, and address biases, taking responsibility for the outcomes produced by our AI systems.
- When developing AI systems, strike a proper balance between desired functionalities and restrictions that should be in place to prevent undesirable outcomes, especially those associated with autonomous capabilities.
- Prioritise transparency in the functioning of AI systems, while respecting and safeguarding user privacy.

Chapter 8: Politics, power, and peace

You should not be afraid of AI. You should be afraid of the people building it.[194]

Jessica Matthews; inventor, venture capitalist, co-founder of Uncharted

In November 2022, KFC customers in Germany received an unusual message, which in English translated to: "Commemorate Kristallnacht – treat yourself to more soft cheese and crispy chicken. Now at KFCheese!"[195] While some users may have ignored this as yet another irrelevant app notification, those who actually looked were horrified. After all, Kristallnacht – when 90 people were murdered in Nazi-led attacks launched on the night between 9 and 10 November 1938, and many more saw their property destroyed – is widely seen as the beginning of the Holocaust, in which 6 million European Jews were murdered during World War II. So why would KFC invite customers to celebrate this tragic day? For all we know, this was "simply" a mistake in the setup of an AI-driven marketing automation tool. After the event, KFC was quick to apologise and indicate that the message had been sent in error. It blamed the message on a bot that had created an automated push notification, based on a link to calendars that include national observances. In essence, KFC blamed the mistake on a machine the company itself had failed to train well enough, and had released prematurely in the pursuit of easier, bigger profits.[196]

While this hideous message may have been sent in error, with no apparent involvement of malicious actors or hacking involved, it was still very harmful. Besides gravely hurting people's feelings and potentially doing damage to KFC's reputation, it also added to the big pile of racist, discriminatory data that keeps being created with intent. Its contents are still sitting out there on the internet, feeding all those "smart" algorithms that learn from large datasets. The example shows that artificial intelligence can do considerable harm if employed without human intelligence behind it. And that's in addition to the many harms AI could cause when used by malicious actors with goals other than maximising health, wealth, and well-being for all.

In the chapters above, we have shown how AI is already influencing our lives. We have highlighted many ways in which it may help to create a better future. Now, we need to zoom out once again and look at the bigger picture. AI can help us predict floods and save people. It can empower people with disabilities and protect ecosystems. It can help reduce companies' carbon emissions and make cities more attractive for residents. However, the question of whether and how these opportunities will ultimately be realised will depend on power structures and intentions – both those driving the development and adoption of AI tools, and those guiding local and global decision-making.

In this chapter we will focus on the dangers of AI, both immediate and more remote. We will explore the world of malicious actors and the way in which they are using AI for economic gain and political control, before taking a look at the growing industry of misinformation. We will also examine how artificial intelligence shapes military innovation, and how this is linked with big tech. Finally, we will discuss the growing polarisation of power and highlight the need for effective regulation.

Inside the world of a malicious actor

Let's take a moment and think like a malicious actor. We'll use the example of a fictional Phil, a fairly tech-savvy person with only rudimentary programming skills who is wondering what kind of crimes he could commit with the help of generative AI. So, what are the possibilities? As a start, some common categories of cybercrime include identity theft, hacking, phishing, ransomware attacks, and cyberbullying.

Identity theft involves stealing someone's personal information and using it for fraudulent purposes. Ransomware is a type of malware that encrypts a victim's files, making them inaccessible, and demands payment in exchange for the decryption key. However, since Phil isn't particularly skilled in programming, hacking and ransomware attacks are not feasible options for him. But a malicious actor like Phil could utilise AI to generate convincing phishing emails. Phishing emails are a type of scam email that aim to deceive the recipient into disclosing sensitive information. These emails often appear to come from a trustworthy source such as a bank or email service provider, and may request the recipient to click on a link to a counterfeit website or input personal information such as a password or credit card number.

Would using AI be an advantage in this area? Absolutely. Using large language models such as ChatGPT, we could quickly come up with convincing phrasing and execute scams in multiple languages. Adding a personal touch would also be easy to do. We could collect information about our victims from social networks using web scraping tools. Web scraping is the process of extracting data from websites by writing code that automatically accesses web pages and stores the requested information in a structured format such as a database or spreadsheet. This may sound difficult, but is in fact not too complicated. We could even find ready-made scripts, or ask an AI to generate them for us. With this data, we could personalise our malicious communications, and try out a love scam, for example. A love scam is a type of online fraud in which the perpetrator, often using a fake identity, creates a romantic relationship with the victim through social media, dating websites, or other online platforms. We, playing the role of the malicious Phil, tried using ChatGPT to create plausible messages. To actually put this into operation, one would only need to integrate the chat or messenger software with an AI system that generated convincing phishing emails or love scams.

Here's what ChatGPT produced for us using the following prompt: "Write an emotional four-sentence text to [Name] about my work at [Work]"

Hey Laura, can't stop thinking about you! Miss you so much! Work on the oil rig is tough, but knowing that I have you waiting for me makes everything better. Can't wait to be in your arms!

Sounds pretty good so far. Phil could do this in almost any language, using any name and any occupation. He wouldn't even have to speak his victim's language.

Laura, my love, I received the money! Thank you so, so much! However, the doctor thinks that it probably won't be enough, but don't worry, we'll make it through together!

Phil could even generate some high-resolution photos using generative AI. If he created the images instead of stealing them from the internet, Laura (his target) wouldn't be able to trace them with a reverse image search. He could also generate new images at any time, tailored to various spontaneous scenarios. It takes only a one-line prompt, and a new photo is generated in less than a minute. He could generate selfies, invent fictional colleagues, and create photos of the oil rig at sunset. Everything would of course be purely fictitious, with no basis in reality. Detecting these fakes would prove to be a considerable challenge for Laura. And Phil could proudly maintain relationships with 481 "Lauras" at the same time. By the way, the message he sent to Laura cost him only around €0.0015 to generate.

A growing industry of misinformation

Risks associated with AI are gaining increasing public prominence. However, it seems that people worry about some risks more than others. For example, many seem to worry about risks associated with AI becoming sentient and developing consciousness, and eventually taking over the world. For instance, some fear that if AI were to develop its own agency and "desires" that conflicted with human interests, it might harm people. These concerns should be taken seriously, particularly if we are looking well into the future. However, this must not distract us from being aware of more imminent risks that are unfolding even as we write.

The most obvious such danger is the use of AI by bad actors with malicious intentions. Today, it is already easy for troll farms to send spam emails to millions of people, and engage with them via social media. But by using large language models such as ChatGPT, they can produce thousands of slightly varied fake news articles and even websites within just a few minutes, quickly spreading them around the world. The sheer scale of such efforts can make misinformation spread much faster than ever before, while seeming much more real. This is exacerbated by the potential for reinforcement online, for example with malicious websites referring to each other and thus ranking highly in Google searches. The same techniques have allowed state actors to influence elections even without the use of ChatGPT, as was done in the 2016 US presidential election and the Brexit vote in the UK. Cyberattacks too can be made easier with AI. All this is very hard to address – after all, these AI tools are freely available online, and are unlikely to be withdrawn by the companies that profit from them.

Many of the stakeholders harnessing the power of AI, such as most of the big tech companies, are "merely" driven by profit and private gain. But other actors are deliberately damaging democratic systems. They are faking facts and manipulating public opinion to influence political processes and the distribution of power. By hacking email and phone accounts, creating fake online profiles, and distributing misinformation at scale, they are manipulating elections in Africa, for example. It turns out that with the help of an army of bots, and supported by a large supply of cash, it is possible to propagate pretty much any kind of message at scale.

How to manipulate elections

According to Western intelligence agencies, about 60 companies around the world currently specialise in misinformation, and the market is growing. The services they provide range from hacking mobile phones to the targeted political or economic rivals in discrediting them. The price for manipulating an election is apparently around $15 million.[197] We know this because the research network Forbidden Stories recently launched a sophisticated undercover investigation, extracting damning evidence from malicious actors by posing as a potential client. In a series of meetings with "Team Jorge" (as members of the group call themselves), one of the more infamous representatives of this dubious industry, the researchers managed to obtain a look behind the scenes of a business that normally takes place in the shadows. Based in Israel, Team Jorge shuns the spotlight, and does its best to operate under the radar. In meetings with representatives of Forbidden Stories, who portrayed themselves as prospective customers, Team Jorge boasted about having "successfully" concluded 27 presidential-level election campaigns out of the 33 it had targeted. It also provided a live demonstration of how it could "play the internet as a pianist would play the keys of his piano". Team Jorge's business model is thus one of "hacking for hire", with the operation including former intelligence and special forces officers. Its proximity to the military and the Israeli state gives it a comfortable position. "Success" in the misinformation industry usually involves accessing opponents' information through local telecom providers, but also requires people within the targeted areas to direct humans and bots leading the campaign. While there is currently no law against artificial intelligence producing posts that go viral on demand, clearly not all of the services provided are legal.[198]

Cambridge Analytica has also collaborated with Team Jorge in the past. This British company was able to acquire personal data relating to almost 90 million Facebook users, and employed this data to influence voting on an "industrial scale". Selling its services in some 60 countries to customers such as the Iranian government and the Malaysian national oil company, it became a household name only after it was widely reported that the firm had participated in manipulating numerous elections, contributing not only to Donald Trump's 2016 presidential victory in the US but also to the success of the Brexit vote in England. The name Cambridge Analytica thus became synonymous with disinformation.[199] It is today clear that these manipulation campaigns aren't limited to developing countries in Asia or Africa, or that they are rare, isolated cases. Quite the opposite: According to the Oxford

Internet Institute, targeted campaigns to manipulate the public for mostly political purposes were launched in 81 countries in 2020 alone.[200] This was well before the introduction of ChatGPT.

Innovation in military technology and the risk of a divided world

The integration of artificial intelligence, machine learning, and autonomous systems into military operations is changing the nature of warfare. AI has a wide range of potential military applications, ranging from autonomous drones and unmanned vehicles for reconnaissance, surveillance, and attacks to the use of AI-powered decision-making systems for strategic planning and the analysis of combat and war situations. These forms of highly advanced technology will become a potentially decisive factor in fighting wars.

The development of autonomous systems is one stated goal. For the most part, drones are still constrained by the requirement that each must have its own operator. However, in a swarm configuration, hundreds or even thousands of drones could be controlled as a unified entity. This is significant, as drone swarms could conceivably be applied to virtually any mission. Several countries, such as China, Russia, India, the UK, Turkey, and Israel, are actively developing swarming drone technology.[201] In 2021, Israel became the first nation to use swarming drones in combat.

Such technological systems are likely to have a variety of effects on how wars are fought. For example, in addition to the purely military successes that militaries expect from such systems, they may help reduce the number of military casualties – potentially prolonging wars. Politicians do not like to talk about soldiers being killed, and the public can tolerate the destruction of technology better than dead sons and daughters. War is becoming an even bigger material battle. While the term "material battle" may sound expensive, the opposite is intended. War is going mass market. The military complex aims to make the technology used in war cheaper. The basic idea here is in fact an old one: The side that spends less and can more easily supply their troops will be able to last longer. However, the goal of a war is still to bring the opposing side to its knees. This means that it is still about inflicting as many human losses as possible on the other side, and making the war as expensive as possible for them. This goal cannot be achieved with battles that are purely machine against machine – rather, it requires the machines to be deployed against the population of the opposing country and its valuable infrastructure.

There is a growing tendency among nations to view space as a potential battleground alongside the more traditional land and sea theatres. Over the past few years, countries such as the US, Russia, China, and India have increased efforts to enhance their military capabilities in space. However, it is crucial to differentiate these efforts from fictional portrayals like James Bond's Moonraker[202] or the planned Manned Orbiting Laboratory[203] that was to be used for espionage purposes during the Cold War. Astronauts armed with guns will play no role in this battle. Instead, the focus is on activities such as surveillance and the disruption of global communications networks, which may involve tactics like the destruction of satellites. As AI is skilled at detecting patterns, identifying anomalies, and enabling autonomous operations, it may contribute to the development of advanced weapon systems that can be deployed in space. As yet, international intentions regarding direct attacks from space on earthbound targets remain uncertain. But even the possibility of such capabilities raises legitimate concerns.

It is becoming increasingly clear that the nations that lead in technological innovation, including in the AI field, will have the upper hand in the battles of the future. As a consequence, technologically advanced nations are likely to gain greater geopolitical influence. This poses a risk that the gap between countries will widen, potentially leaving some nations farther behind. For countries seeking military power, it will become increasingly important that technical components such as sensors, processors and other electronic components, as well as certain materials and alloys used in military applications, are produced within their sphere of influence.

However, production of these components cannot consistently be expected to take place exclusively within a single country. Thus, it can be assumed that the importance of military alliances will continue to grow. The world may further divide into power blocs and spheres of influence. Countries that are unable to keep up with other nations in terms of technological innovation and military strength may find themselves pressured to join these military alliances. Particularly in times of increased geopolitical tensions and conflicts, technological backwardness could mean that a country would be more vulnerable to outside attacks, and would likely have difficulty protecting its own interests. These military alliances may also seek to protect their own technological expertise, imposing export restrictions or bans on military AI, and classifying certain AI methods or models as military secrets. Such attempts to safeguard technology and produce it exclusively within the boundaries of an alliance could in turn lead to trade conflicts and hinder international co-operation.

The use of AI for military purposes is concerning and unsettling. A world featuring swarms of drones or armies of robots reminiscent of the movie "Terminator"[204] with Arnold Schwarzenegger would not be a desirable future for our children. However, significant investments are already being made in the field. With geopolitical unrest and armed conflict taking place in many locations, from the Democratic Republic of Congo to Haiti, Iran, Palestine, and Ukraine, even greater sums of money are being directed toward this area. Future wars are likely to be won by those who have the best technologies, and AI will undoubtedly be an essential component of the military's arsenal in the years to come whether we like it or not.

Where military power meets big tech

The military industry has traditionally focused on the development of "hardware" such as combat aircraft and tanks. However, it is mostly civilian companies – from tech giants like Google and Apple to small startups – that are leading the charge in the development of AI. This poses a challenge for the military complex. In recent years, there has been a shift in this field's key players, with military companies becoming more open to working with civilian tech firms. For instance, former Google CEO Eric Schmidt is working to equip the US military with AI and other technologies.[205] He has proposed the creation of a tech firm that would focus on the "internet of things" in a military context – that is, by creating low-cost, highly mobile devices or drones that are equipped with weapons and interconnected via networks. Schmidt's company Istari,[206] which seems to be part of this initiative, is currently working on digital twins and AI. The aim is to virtually design and test military equipment using computer models. Craig Martell offers another example of someone who has transitioned from the tech sector to the military and intelligence world. Martell left his position as head of machine learning at the Silicon Valley rideshare company Lyft to take on the role of the Pentagon's first chief digital and artificial intelligence officer.[207]

Peter Thiel,[208] a prominent entrepreneur and venture capitalist, is also involved in this industry. His US-based software company, Palantir,[209] operates an AI-based platform that supports military operations. The platform allows operators to exchange short text messages known as prompts with a large language model that serves as a kind of AI commander; in response to the operator's questions, the model provides recommendations in areas such as deploying drones, disrupting communications, and selecting the appropriate weapons or nearby troops to engage a target.[210] Concerningly, the system's functioning resembles interactions with platforms like ChatGPT. Palantir claims that it is confident that its technology will be used ethically, and says it aims "to power responsible, effective, and compliant AI advantage for defence organisations". But sorry, we are not convinced.

We need to examine the implications as the giants of the technology industry become increasingly intertwined with the military. The consequences of such alliances will be far-reaching, raising pressing questions about the concrete impacts of these relationships. The transfer of knowledge taking place is undeniable and evident; industry leaders and experts are sharing their technical know-how, experiences, and skills with the military sector, fostering innovation and agile working methods. There is the risk that a "revolving door" dynamic could emerge in these areas, with individuals moving seamlessly between big tech and the military complex, drawing both on sectoral knowledge and interlocking personal networks.

For big tech, the close relationship with the military offers significant financial benefits. In 2021, global military spending reached an astounding $2.1 trillion, with the US alone contributing a staggering $801 billion and China $293 billion.[211] These immense figures explain the allure of the military to technology companies, and emphasise the importance of these alliances for both parties. For their part, militaries are interested in a wide array of technology areas, including cybersecurity, cloud computing, communication technologies, robotics, geolocation, virtual and augmented reality, biometrics, sensor technology, and the internet of things. Artificial intelligence and machine learning serve as a unifying thread across all these domains.

But the focus isn't solely on technology and innovation; it also encompasses data, originating both from users and companies. Big tech has access to an abundance of such data, along with the ability to store and process it. Some observers worry that this data could be used for military or surveillance operations, including data on individuals' communications, locations, resources, travel, internet usage, employment, education, social networks, and personal connections, as well as basic biometric data. If such data did find its way into military applications, it would undoubtedly give rise to far-reaching privacy issues. In the case of China, the state has already implemented advanced technologies to monitor its population in ways that would make many Westerners feel uncomfortable. Yet Western-oriented, democratic countries are also heavily invested in surveillance. For example, programmes like PRISM[212] and XKeyscore[213] became well known thanks to Edward Snowden,[214] the whistle-blower who exposed the extent of mass surveillance conducted by the US government and its allies. PRISM is a surveillance programme operated by the US National Security Agency (NSA) that collects internet communications data from major tech companies. XKeyscore is a global system that enables the NSA to search and analyse vast amounts of internet data in real time. The system allows government users to search through metadata, emails, online chats, and browsing histories.

As legal protections in the US and other Western countries largely prevent intelligence agencies from engaging in surveillance within their own borders, these entities got creative, and solved this "problem" by involving multiple intelligence services. For example, they used the Five Eyes entity,[215] an intelligence alliance consisting of the United States, the United Kingdom, Canada, Australia, and New Zealand. The Five Eyes mass surveillance programmes were effective because each participating country focused on surveilling foreign communications, and then shared the intelligence thereby derived with the other members, bypassing domestic legal restrictions on surveillance. This approach enabled each nation to gather intelligence without directly infringing on their own citizens' privacy rights under their national laws.

It is therefore clear that access to data by the military complex can be dangerous for everyone's privacy. The closer its collaboration with big tech, the more the military will have access to large quantities of data – and the less privacy we as common people will have. A look at where the big tech firms are located is also illustrative. Among the top 800 tech companies globally based on market capitalisation, only 31 countries are represented. The US is particularly dominant in this regard, accounting for 454, or 57%, of the companies. A total of 161, or 20%, are Asian, and 109, or 14%, are European. China alone accounts for 6%, and Russia has just one company in the ranking.[216] While market capitalisation may not be the only measure of importance, the trend is clear: the US dominates. The overwhelming dominance of US-based tech companies in the global market provides them with the power to use their knowledge and technologies in many countries and regions, potentially giving the US military a significant advantage on the global stage. However, it is important to note that other countries such as China are also promoting their own technology companies and partnerships with the military.

In response to these developments, civil society must continue pushing governments to prioritise the privacy, human rights, and other key interests of all stakeholders. In addition, civil society groups should strive to raise public awareness of the potential consequences for global peace and stability that can arise from close relationships between militaries and technology companies. It is essential that stakeholders work together collaboratively to establish appropriate regulations and policies to address these concerns.

The future of defence and attack

The classic 1983 film "WarGames"[217] is a great movie, and managed to address the themes of cybersecurity and AI very early. It follows the journey of high school student and hacker David, played by Matthew Broderick, as he hacks into a highly secured military system. What he believes is a mere game turns out to be a sophisticated artificial intelligence designed to conduct military simulations for the North American Aerospace Defense Command. Realising the gravity of his actions, David teaches the AI a crucial lesson: that no one truly wins in war. In a brilliant move, he prevents a devastating nuclear first strike. Considering that the internet only really took off in the mid-1990s, it's impressive how far we've come since this film's release. Today, decades later, the role of AI in cybersecurity has evolved. AI has become both a defender and an attacker.

AI is now being used for intrusion detection and infrastructure surveillance. By analysing activities such as network traffic, it can detect patterns and anomalies that may indicate attempted attacks. While this is certainly important for data centres, AI can also be used to monitor critical infrastructure such as power plants or water treatment facilities. By analysing sensor data and other sources of information, AI can detect potential threats and raise alarms if any suspicious activity is detected. One major advantage of AI in the cybersecurity context is its ability to learn and adapt over time. As it encounters new threats and attacks, it can incorporate that knowledge into its algorithms, making it more effective at detecting and preventing future attacks.

But that's not all. One recent disruptive change is AI's rapidly improving ability to read and write programming code. For example, ChatGPT has successfully passed Google's coding job test[218] and completed a LinkedIn Python assessment, answering all the questions posed within the time limit and achieving a score that surpassed 85% of the other 3.9 million programmers who took the assessment.[219]

This new AI capability has opened up promising new applications in the field of cybersecurity. An AI that truly understands source code would be able to perform code analysis on entire software systems to identify vulnerabilities.

But where is this all heading? If the security experts protecting systems and the "black hat" hackers engaging in unauthorised and malicious activities both utilise AI, it could lead to an AI arms race in the cybersecurity world. This in turn could produce an endless cycle of AI-enabled attacks and defences, in which each side is constantly trying to outsmart the other. Attacks could happen on a larger scale and at a faster pace than ever before. Overall, systems are expected to become more robust over time, but it will require significant investment to upgrade our infrastructure to keep up with the attackers.

The dark side of big tech

During one of our many heated Friday evening dinner discussions, the topic of technology and democracy arose. Eventually, we began discussing the film "The Circle",[220] a 2017 American science-fiction drama starring Emma Watson and Tom Hanks. The film is based on the novel of the same name by Dave Eggers, and explores the consequences for privacy and personal freedom of a highly advanced, all-encompassing social media and technology company called The Circle. Perhaps you have seen the movie, and remember the scene in which The Circle's leadership team holds a meeting, and the CEO enthusiastically introduces the idea of using the company's technology to make voting more accessible and secure. This is a natural step, he says, because The Circle has nearly as many users as there are voters in the US. He argues that by linking voting to The Circle's platform, the company can help eliminate fraud and ensure that everyone has a fair and equal opportunity to vote. The whole leadership team buys into the vision, convinced that the company's service and its installed base of millions of users is the ideal solution to solve societal problems that affect everyone. They do not even consider that they have no democratic legitimacy to take on this role.

We found this scene to be an excellent illustration of how the concentration of power in the hands of a few individuals or organisations could have dire consequences for everyone's personal privacy and freedom. We had the same sentiment when reading OpenAI's manifesto on artificial general intelligence (AGI), which was released in February 2023. OpenAI believes that the development of AGI has the potential to bring about significant positive change in the world. The company does recognise the potential risks and challenges associated with AGI, including the need for transparency, safety, and ethical action. OpenAI also emphasises the importance of responsible development and collaboration to ensure that AGI is developed in a way that benefits society. While this is a step towards ensuring that advanced technologies are developed in a responsible and ethical way, we cannot help but feel concerned about the assumption that the development of artificial general intelligence is inherently a good thing. Moreover, we are certainly not comfortable with a private company like OpenAI putting itself in the driver's seat and deciding what is in the best interest of society, including by making judgements on everyone else's behalf as to whether AGI is aligned with human values and ethics.

In the field of AI, there has been a clear shift in influence from academia and the public sector to private corporations. This can be seen as both cause and consequence of shifting power dynamics and new financial opportunities. Stanford University's AI Index shows that until 2014, most significant machine-learning models were released by the academic community. Since then, industry has taken over; in 2022, for example, there were 32 significant industry-produced machine-learning models, but only three were produced within academia.[221] The cut in funding in the US and Japan for academic AI research in the early 1990s, paired with the rise of the first commercial military applications based on AI, such as the ISX corporation's DART, provided both the financial motivation and the pool of expert employees needed for big tech companies to embrace AI.[222]

In fact, the self-perpetuating power of big tech is a concerning trend that threatens the future of democracy and personal privacy. For all their talk about ethics, safety, and saving the world, tech companies tend to prioritise profit over people when tested by competition and market pressure, even if they started with good intentions. Moreover, the concentration of power in the hands of a few individuals – in this case, the overwhelmingly white, male, and wealthy or super-rich executives that head the leading global tech organisations – has dire consequences for personal freedom and the democratic process. There is now a massive power imbalance between the private owners of these technologies and the rest of us.

Even if computer scientists succeed in ensuring that AI doesn't wipe us out, its increasing centrality to the global economy could make the big tech companies that control it vastly more powerful than they already are today. Big tech firms are already among the richest corporations in the world, with individual market capitalisations higher than many countries' GDPs. For example, Apple, Microsoft, Amazon, and Google have all reached market capitalisations well above $1.5 trillion.[223] This means their financial power is greater than that of the majority of nation-states, including Indonesia, Turkey, and Switzerland, for example. This puts them easily into the list of the top 20 largest economic entities in the world. Importantly, their power manifests itself not just in financial terms, but also in the data they possess relating to billions of users. This means they soon could become geopolitical actors that rival nation-states.

As noted in the previous chapter, we must prioritise transparency and democracy, ensuring that the development of advanced technologies by big tech companies does not lead to further concentration of power, benefiting a small minority while leaving a large majority of people behind. We join in the call by leading economist Marina Mazzucato and UNESCO Director Gabriela Ramos for an end to the era of light-touch self-regulation. These figures call for an ethical-by-design approach to AI that is underpinned by sound regulation and capable governments working to shape this technological revolution in the common interest, rather than in the interest of shareholders alone.[224] It is imperative that we ensure that a technology with such great influence over our lives, as well as the organisations developing it, are transparent and accountable. We must identify who holds power, and who should hold it. We need governance structures that are focused on the common good, which includes everyone. Governments that have the capability to act in this way can guide this tech revolution for the benefit of the public.

Treating AI like a drug

The era of light-touch self-regulation must end.
Gabriela Ramos and Mariana Mazzucato[225]

New York University's Gary Marcus is one expert who has been looking into suitable regulation styles. He argues that AI models should be treated like pharmaceuticals. Before being approved and released for widespread use, medicines undergo many rounds of evaluation that enable researchers and regulators to understand whether they are both efficacious and safe.[226] Applying this approach to critical AI applications would also make perfect sense. In this case, new models would be monitored and potentially held back from release until they have been proved to be safe. As with any new and rapidly evolving technology, a steep learning curve means that mistakes and miscalculations will be made, and that both unanticipated and harmful impacts will inevitably occur. AI is no exception.

The big tech firms competing in this winner-takes-all market, and probably the smaller firms as well, are afraid that too much regulation will stifle innovation. Some are arguably releasing their products well before maturity, exposing the public and our global system to considerable risks. But companies too are asking for regulation. They want to understand their limits, and want a level playing field. One thing is clear: Developing AI models according to good practice principles and with certain safeguards in place – "guardrails" as they are often called – can be costly. But retroactively adapting such safeguards will be much costlier.

A number of technology experts and business leaders, including Gary

Marcus; Elon Musk of Space X, Tesla, and Twitter; Apple co-founder Steve Wozniak; Skype co-founder Jaan Tallin; and thousands of others, recently signed an open letter pointing out the enormous impact AI is having today, and noting that the technology was also generating massive risk. The letter says that "advanced AI could represent a profound change in the history of life on Earth, and should be planned for and managed with commensurate care and resources". It argues that planning and management of this nature is not yet happening, and that AI labs are "locked in an out-of-control race to develop and deploy ever more powerful digital minds that no one – not even their creators – can understand, predict, or reliably control". It challenges AI companies and the broader world to ask whether we should "let machines flood our information channels with propaganda and untruth", "automate away all the jobs, including the fulfilling ones", and "develop non-human minds that might eventually outnumber, outsmart, obsolete, and replace us", thus risking the "loss of control of our civilisation". The signatories argue that such world-changing decisions must not be delegated to unelected tech leaders, and say that "powerful AI systems should be developed only once we are confident that their effects will be positive and their risks will be manageable".[227]

Shortly after the issuance of the "pause letter", the Center for AI Safety released a statement emphasising the importance of mitigating the risk of AI-induced extinction. The statement garnered support from numerous prominent academics and industry leaders. The Center highlights several risks, such as the potential weaponisation of AI for purposes like developing chemical weapons, the spread of AI-generated misinformation that undermines collective decision-making and destabilises society, the increased concentration of power, and the risk of human enfeeblement, where humans become overly dependent on AI, reminiscent of the scenario depicted in the film Wall-E.[228]

One interesting approach to evaluating the impact of AI on human well-being, the environment, and society comes from an unlikely source: the Māori people of Aotearoa New Zealand. The Mauri Model, a framework of indigenous knowledge developed by the Māori, centres on the principle of

Mauri, which refers to the life force or essence believed to permeate all things in the natural world. To evaluate the impact of AI on these elements, the Mauri Model offers a set of five tests or criteria. By answering questions such as "Is it tapu?" (Is the AI technology treating people and the environment with respect and reverence?) and "Is it wairua?" (Does the AI technology respect and enhance spiritual well-being?), we can determine whether AI technology is promoting wellness and sustainability, or alternately causing harm and destruction. The Mauri Model thus constitutes a powerful tool for guiding the development and deployment of AI in ways that are respectful, inclusive, and responsive to the needs of all stakeholders. While there is no universal framework for evaluating the ethical and social implications of AI, the Mauri Model represents a distinct perspective that can inspire regulation and complement other approaches.[229]

There is a growing consensus in Western cultures too that a more holistic and human-centred approach is needed. One framework that has gained traction in recent years is the Vienna Manifesto on Digital Humanism, a set of principles developed by a group of experts and practitioners in Vienna, Austria. In one of our coffeehouse rounds, we had the pleasure of speaking with the creators of this concept. The manifesto emphasises the importance of placing human dignity, democracy, and social justice at the forefront of the AI revolution. It calls for greater transparency and accountability in the design and use of AI systems, and for a focus on promoting human autonomy and agency in decision-making. By embracing the principles of the Vienna Manifesto, we can also ensure that AI is developed and deployed in ways that are aligned with our most fundamental values and aspirations for a just and equitable future.

Creating effective AI regulation

There are currently several global regulatory efforts underway seeking to address the ethical and social implications of AI, some of them drawing on the human-centred approaches of the Vienna Manifesto and the Mauri Model.

In Europe, the EU has released guidelines for trustworthy AI, and is working to develop a regulatory framework for AI that promotes human-centricity, transparency, and accountability. In the US, the White House has released principles for regulating AI that emphasise the importance of public trust, and the National Institute of Standards and Technology (NIST) has published a framework for managing the cybersecurity risks associated with AI. While these efforts represent important steps forward, much work has yet to be done to ensure that AI is developed and deployed in a way that aligns with human values and is careful to avoid doing harm to individuals, communities, and the planet.

As we write, regulators around the world are looking for inspiration to the European Union's AI Act (AIA), the first and as yet largest of the efforts to regulate AI. The act focuses primarily on strengthening rules relating to data quality, transparency, human oversight, and accountability. It also aims to address ethical questions and implementation challenges in various sectors, from healthcare and education to finance and energy. The cornerstone of the AI Act is a risk classification system based on the risk an AI technology could pose to a person's health, safety or fundamental rights. It includes four risk levels: unacceptable, high, limited, and minimal. AI systems with minimal risk, such as spam filters or video games, can be freely used. The vast majority of AI systems currently used in the EU are seen as falling into this category. AI systems considered to be of limited risk, such as chatbots (until now, though this may change soon given the many ways in which e.g. ChatGPT can be used), come with specific transparency obligations. In this case, users must be made aware that they are interacting with a machine, so they can take an informed decision to continue or step back. High-risk systems include autonomous vehicles, medical devices, and applications used for critical infrastructure or law enforcement purposes, as just a few examples. They are permitted, but developers and users must adhere to regulations that require rigorous testing, proper documentation of data quality, and an accountability framework that includes human oversight. AI systems deemed to pose an unacceptable risk, such as social scoring and real-time biometric identification systems in public spaces, are generally prohibited.[230]The EU

AI Act has been the subject of much debate since its announcement, with both proponents and critics expressing strong views. While the act has been lauded for its bold attempts to regulate the industry and take broader societal concerns seriously, some experts worry that it may stifle innovation and give an unfair advantage to non-EU players in the global AI race.

The EU AI Act is not the first major piece of AI legislation to come out of Europe, however. Estonia, a small country in the Baltic region, has been a global leader in AI regulation for years. It was the first country in the world to establish a "digital embassy", and it has pioneered the use of AI in its government services, including in its online voting process. Nevertheless, the EU AI Act is much more sweeping in its scope.

So what?

In response to the open letter we described above, Emily Bender, a University of Washington computational linguistics professor known to be critical of big tech, stated that the risks and harms have never been about "too powerful AI", and went on to specify that these risks and harms are instead "about concentration of power in the hands of people, about reproducing systems of oppression, about damage to the information ecosystem, and about damage to the natural ecosystem (through profligate use of energy resources)". She argued that regulation and funding are necessary, but that public funding should prioritise fields outside computer science, for instance by supporting studies reviewing the impact of AI models. She advised policymakers to avoid wasting their time "on the fantasies of the techbros", and instead to listen to those studying how corporations and governments are using technology and the narratives of AI "to concentrate and wield power".[231]

We argue that responsible AI will be essential in achieving ethical, political, and economic goals, and will be an important factor in promoting peace and security. As we continue to develop and deploy AI, it is essential that we consider, understand, and optimise its impact on society, the environment, and human well-being, while avoiding further concentration of power even by benign actors. As for malicious actors, we have no choice but to strengthen cybersecurity protections, developing and improving tools to detect and mitigate the spread of misinformation and manipulation. This will mean investing in AI and media literacy alike, in order to sensitise all people to the dangers of such practices.

To shape the future of AI in a way that aligns with human values we must:

- Continue to hold companies accountable for the development and deployment of responsible AI, preventing them from using their power to take decisions that affect us all.
- Promote regulation of AI in a manner that puts the needs of humans first – including the need for an intact natural environment. Such regulation should be forward-looking and compatible with international standards of responsible AI.
- Further develop our skills to think critically, think in systems, understand incentive systems and power structures, and critically review the reliability and accuracy of information sources.

Chapter 9: Shaping a meaningful future

The rise of powerful AI will be either the best or the worst thing ever to happen to humanity. We do not yet know which.

Stephen Hawking[232]

As we progress further into the 21st century, technological advancements are being made at an unprecedented pace. Each day, new tools, players, and insights about AI emerge, and so we are dealing with moving targets. The broader context is also in flux, as the world is coming to grips with crises in both the social and environmental spheres. It looks like we will need to get used to living in a dynamic, multi-crisis environment while also adjusting to a steady stream of revolutions.

The challenge will be to attain both our ecological and social goals at the same time. While they are often aligned, they can also be at odds. Several extreme forms of an AI-influenced future are imaginable. Unregulated, AI could produce further planetary destabilisation, which would in turn generate further social injustice, broad economic loss, and additional harm to the planet. In a "green but inhumane" scenario, AI could be deliberately employed to achieve ecological goals and planetary stabilisation, but could undermine our ability to fulfil other socio-economic human needs. The most desirable outcome would involve the efficient and effective use of AI, accompanied by decentralised structures and a healthy democracy, to realise a scenario that is deliberately designed for the good.[233]

Our future is uncertain

AI may be one of the biggest revolutions in history. Indeed, some observers rank it with key milestones in human development, such as the development of the internet or even the invention of the wheel. According to Google CEO Sundar Pichai, "AI is one of the most important things humanity is working on", and is more important than fire or electricity.[234] It does seem that we are on the brink of a massive technological shift, one that will determine whether our civilisation will thrive and survive – or not. As we outlined in the previous chapters of this book, and as the late physicist and cosmologist Stephen Hawking knew long before us, "alongside the benefits, AI will also bring dangers, like powerful autonomous weapons, or new ways for the few to oppress the many". Back in 2016, when speaking at the launch of the Center for the Future of Intelligence, he said that the rise of powerful AI would be either the best or the worst thing ever to happen to humanity. At the time, Hawking made it clear that we simply do not yet know which it will be. In other words, the opportunities are massive, and so are the risks. At this stage, the outcome – and even the direction of travel – is uncertain.

Elon Musk's statement that "with artificial intelligence we are summoning the demon" has sparked a heated debate about the future of AI and its potential impact on humanity. While some see AI as a tool that can bring about unprecedented progress and prosperity, others warn that it poses an existential threat that could lead to the downfall of our civilisation. One of the arguments put forward against the doomsday scenario is that predictions relating to AI have been proven wrong in the past. In the 1950s, for example, some researchers believed that computers would soon be able to learn and reason like humans. But as time passed, it became clear that this was a much harder problem to solve than anyone had imagined, and progress was slower than anticipated. Similarly, in the 1980s, expert systems were touted as the future of AI, with promises of machines that could make decisions and solve problems as effectively as human specialists. But while some of these systems were successful in limited domains, they failed to live up to their hype when applied to complex, open-ended tasks.

These past failures have led some to argue that the current concerns about AI are overblown, and that the technology is still far from reaching a point where it could pose a serious threat. Others note that the pace of progress has accelerated in recent years, and that the development of powerful machine-learning algorithms and large-scale datasets has led to significant breakthroughs particularly in areas such as image and speech recognition and natural-language processing. However, we believe that this debate between doomsters and optimists may be missing the point, and may even lead to a dangerous fallacy and complacency.

We believe that the risks associated with AI may be different from those that people are worried about. But we also believe that they are imminent. As AI systems become more powerful and ubiquitous, the risks of unintended consequences, misuse, and negative side effects rise, making it imperative to address these challenges proactively. This highlights the importance of actively shaping our technological advancements to ensure that they benefit humanity, rather than causing harm to many while benefiting a few. In this final chapter, we lay out what needs to happen, and what each of you can do on both a personal and professional level to create a better future with AI.

Three elements are key: In order to avoid summoning the demon, we must approach the design of our common future with a sense of urgency, with foresight, and with responsibility.

Creating – and measuring – the AI advantage

Good intentions do not always lead to good results. A well-meaning programmer may create technically wonderful and effective algorithms that work as intended. However, on a societal level, these may create more problems than they solve, either environmentally or socially or both. To create a true "AI advantage" – that is, to ensure that this technology accelerates rather than slows the sustainable transformation we need – we will need to treat the topic with urgency, foresight, and responsibility. We are at a turning point that needs to be confronted with the utmost urgency, given that thousands of AI models are being developed as you read these words, without the involvement of many relevant actors. Millions if not billions of users are employing these models in an environment that is only partially regulated. To adequately gauge the possible impacts – both positive and negative – of AI models, as well as to maximise their benefits, we need foresight by developers, funders, and regulators alike. In this regard, we must focus closely on present developments while engaging simultaneously in long-term thinking. And we must all take responsibility for what is to come by proactively creating a vision of the kind of world we want to live in, and determining the role AI should play in shaping it.

With great power comes great responsibility. This is why big tech companies and national governments have a particularly important role to play. But AI concerns all of us, and so each one of us also bears responsibility. As we have written repeatedly throughout this book, it's not enough to simply sit back and watch as advancements in AI unfold. We must actively shape and guide them in order to ensure they benefit society as a whole. Only by doing so can we shape a better future for all. One way of engaging is to hold decision-makers at both the corporate and governmental level to account, and keep asking about the impacts of AI models. This will require data and evidence. At the moment, however, a lot of this data is sitting in black boxes. We simply don't know what the impacts really are, or whether and how an AI advantage is actually being created. No manager in their right mind would take important, life-changing decisions without data and evidence. What isn't measured cannot be managed. That's why dramatically increasing research not just into AI solutions, but into their broader societal impacts, and into issues of safety, ethics, explainability, and other key aspects of responsible AI, is so important.

Finding the big picture

The opportunities are real, but realising them is not a given. Indeed, the opportunities themselves can only be created if the risks associated with AI are successfully addressed. This means that we must zoom out and look at the bigger picture before zooming in to the development and use of specific AI solutions. We always need to keep in mind that creating cool solutions in one area is not the same as achieving a positive net effect for society overall.

For starters, looking at the bigger picture requires zooming out in time and anticipating the possible futures that may result in part from the use of AI. This is not just about us and our children; it is about future generations, and the survival of our civilisation more broadly. However, zooming out to imagine the times ahead needs to be coupled with a firm look at present technological developments and their impacts in all corners of the globe. In other words, in an interconnected world we must also zoom out geographically.

Crucially, looking at the bigger picture also means questioning economic, political, and social systems, and understanding what structures and mind-sets – many of which have been entrenched for decades and even centuries – drive them. If we are serious about creating a better future, and improving health, wealth, and well-being for all, we must not shy away from working towards systemic change. At the very least, this means critically reviewing the technological systems and platforms we use and the data we share with them, and demanding transparency and accountability from the companies that create and profit from AI. It's vital to remember that we are not just users of these technologies, but also co-creators. Understanding who benefits from AI models and who does not may go a long way towards understanding and highlighting systemic incentives.

And then there is the biggest question of all. We don't yet have an answer, but we are eager to continue exploring it. This question is: How, if at all, can AI help us make our global economic and political system more inclusive and ecologically sustainable?

While we as humans have achieved much in history, we have not managed to structure our global political and economic system in a manner that maximises health, wealth, and well-being for all. AI offers us an opportunity to get it right, particularly if the technology can help us improve participation and democracy, and consequently make our societies more just. As yet, we can feel only moderately optimistic in this regard. Research has shown that under current political and economic conditions, digitalisation increases rather than decreases inequality. This, coupled with the increasing polarisation within our societies, including through social media, makes deliberate policymaking on issues such as climate change, more difficult. Guided by the right policies, digitalisation could support planetary health as well as social justice.[235] But for this to happen, a paradigm shift will be needed.

Bridging the divide: New forms of collaboration and inclusion

If we are to successfully harness AI for a better future, we will need collaboration, inclusion, and diversity. We must create active links between the digitalisation and sustainability agendas. Experts from both fields, as well as other relevant actors, will need to be involved from the design stage onwards for AI models. Building a community of innovation through collaboration allows us to pool our resources, knowledge, and experiences to tackle complex problems and create real, lasting transformation. As we move forward in shaping a positive AI future, it is important to remember that we are stronger together.

In this context, diversity is one aspect that has been neglected in the debates over AI. We have been hearing a lot about AI from rich, powerful men, many of whom head large tech firms based in the US. We have heard much less from academic and government experts, or indeed from civil society. And female voices are much less loud. Thankfully there are some notable expectations. These include Emily Bender from the University of Washington, and Timnit Gebru, who famously got kicked out of Google for co-publishing a now very famous academic paper on the limitations of AI. It is crucial that a diverse range of voices and perspectives are involved in the conversation about the future of AI. Only by considering the needs and perspectives of individuals from all walks of life can we truly create a future that works for everyone. This includes users' voices and the voices of the poor and marginalised, many of whom might be too busy making ends meet to contribute to the AI debate by themselves. Thus, they will need to be proactively engaged and provided with incentives to participate. The impact of AI will be felt by every single person on this planet, and it is essential that we consider the diverse perspectives and needs of all individuals. From the farmer in rural Africa to the factory worker in China, from the single mother in the US to the elderly retiree in Europe, we must ensure that our advances benefit everyone.

Looking at the bigger picture and building bridges across divides also means taking a multidisciplinary approach, and involving experts from all relevant fields and disciplines. Leaving the field to computer programmers, software designers, technology experts, and tech business leaders is not only not conducive to furthering AI, it is outright dangerous. Techies understand how to develop technological solutions, but experts from other fields including sociology, ecology, politics, psychology, economics, and many others understand the potential impact of AI models on societies, and what they might mean for human progress. Involving them from the start will help minimise the environmental footprint of AI while also maximising its outcomes for society. A lack of inclusivity in the development and implementation of AI can have serious consequences, leading to biased systems and further exacerbating existing societal inequalities. This not only puts already marginalised communities at risk, but also undermines the potential benefits of the technology for society as a whole.

One example of such inclusivity is the Distributed AI Research Institute (DAIR),[236] a space for independent, community-rooted AI research that is deliberately designed to create a counterweight to the initiatives led by big tech companies. The Partnership on AI, on the other hand, is a coalition that includes academic institutions and non-profit organisations alongside technology companies, with the stated aim of ensuring that AI is developed and used responsibly.[237] The UN's AI for Good initiative is a digital platform that aims to bring together AI innovators and organisations seeking to solve societal problems to collaborate on advancing the UN's Sustainable Development Goals.[238] By including a wide range of voices and perspectives in their discussions and decision-making, such initiatives are able to address ethical concerns and thus improve our chances of ensuring that the benefits of AI are shared by all.

Finally, given that our subject is AI, we cannot talk only about collaboration between humans. There is also a fascinating wealth of opportunities for human-machine collaboration, in ways that we can only begin to understand today. In many places, rather than replacing humans, machines will become important partners. However, it is essential that humans retain the final decision-making role. Moreover, it is essential that we treat algorithms, bots, and other machines as what they really are: machines. With bots such as ChatGPT that give the impression of thinking and feeling like humans do (until you dig deeper), there is a real risk that we will anthropomorphise machines, attributing human-like features to computer programmes and thereby forgetting that they are just computer programmes. It is essential to remember that such computer programmes themselves have no soul, consciousness, or desires. Rather, they are just sophisticated combinations of hardware and software, developed by more or less sophisticated humans.

Putting people first

Digitalisation must never be an end in itself, but must rather be directed towards sustainable social transformation. One way to consider the bigger picture and build bridges between key actors is to adopt a mindset of digital humanism. AI is a key building block in digitalisation, and some of the issues and opportunities overlap. Therefore, some of our insights and recommendations apply to digitalisation more broadly to the same extent that they apply to AI. The goal of digital humanism is essentially to imbue digitalisation with meaning, and to put humans first. Digital humanism seeks to strike a balance, being open to the potential benefits offered by technology while still seeking to preserve human values and dignity. It views technology as a means of enhancing human life, not replacing it, and seeks to ensure that technological advancements serve the greater good. In the context of AI, digital humanism encourages the development and use of AI in ways that support human well-being, promote equality, and respect the human rights and dignity of all people.

But what exactly does digital humanism mean in practice? Imagine that you're working on a project to improve access to healthcare. You're tasked with designing an AI system that helps healthcare providers identify patients who are at high risk of developing certain conditions. With AI, you can analyse vast amounts of data and generate sophisticated models that provide insights and predictions with a high degree of accuracy. But, after reading this book, you also know that AI algorithms may contain biases with regard to certain demographic groups or regions of your country, leading to unequal access to care and unequal impact on human well-being. This is where the principle of human-centred design comes in. Digital humanism calls for AI systems to be designed and developed with human needs and values in mind, and to be tested and evaluated based on their impact on human well-being. By ensuring that AI systems are designed with all humans in mind, we can prevent unintended biases and ensure that the technology serves our needs.

Another key principle of digital humanism is the importance of human control over technology. This means that while AI can automate many tasks and improve efficiency, it must not be allowed to make decisions that impact human lives without human oversight. This is especially critical in the context of AI decision-making, where the potential consequences of AI-generated decisions can be far-reaching and damaging. Digital humanism calls for transparency and accountability in the use of AI, so that we can ensure the technology is used in ethical and fair ways.

Digital humanism also calls for the development of AI systems that promote the greater good and support human well-being. As we have stated throughout this book, AI should be used to address some of the world's biggest issues, such as climate change, poverty, and inequality, and to help us achieve the Sustainable Development Goals. Focusing AI on these goals is the only means by which we can ensure that technological advancements will have a positive impact on society and contribute to a better world.

In a nutshell, digital humanism is about two things. At the very minimum, it is about avoiding harm to humans and the societies in which they live and interact. But technology was invented to make human lives better, not worse. So digital humanism is about finding ways to shape the future of AI in a manner that promotes the greater good. Digital humanism also challenges us to rethink our current digital practices and systems, including in the areas of research, development, and innovation. It is driven by the bigger goal of using technology to generate societal progress rather than just producing innovation for its own sake, or for the sake of economic growth that benefits only a limited number of people.[239]

We – Alice, Claudia, Florian, and Jeroen – are all based in Vienna. The City of Vienna is making us proud by being a frontrunner with regard to putting people first in its digitalisation efforts. It explicitly links its digitalisation and social development strategies, with defined efforts in all key areas ranging from work, education, and the economy to the arts and sustainability sectors.[240] We are also proud Europeans, given the geopolitical implication of digital humanism: It is seen as Europe's answer to surveillance capitalism, which is arguably America's dominant model, and to the surveillance communism which we often find in Asia.

Slow AI? Give regulation a chance

It is a fact that AI technology is developing much more rapidly than the regulatory frameworks that are needed to govern it. Government regulation is lagging behind, and light-touch self-regulation by companies does not work. Some observers have called for a pause in the development of powerful AI systems, and there are good reasons to argue for such an "AI summer", for example to let regulators catch up. However, it is clear that not all actors in the field would respect such a pause, and some of the voices calling for it, including Elon Musk among others, have been accused of simply wanting others to pause in order to catch up on their own AI developments.

It is thus good news that many countries are at least somewhat prepared. We believe that the EU AI Act represents an important step forward in ensuring the ethical and responsible use of AI. While some may argue that regulation stifles innovation and competition, we believe that the opposite is true in this case. By setting clear rules and expectations for the development and use of AI, the EU is creating a level playing field for all players in the industry. This not only promotes fair competition, but also helps to build trust with consumers, and will help ensure that AI is used in a way that benefits society as a whole. Furthermore, we believe that the EU AI Act will help to address some of the biggest concerns around AI, such as bias, transparency, and accountability. By requiring companies to perform impact assessments and adhere to strict guidelines, the Act will help to mitigate the potential negative impacts of AI on society. This is especially important given the rapid pace of technological change and the potential for AI to be misused or abused.

There are some early signs that governments are punching their weight. In early 2023, Italy's data protection authority, called Garante, temporarily banned ChatGPT in the domestic market and launched a probe focused on the application's suspected breach of privacy rules. OpenAI was able to bring its tool online in Italy again only after complying with the demands made by the regulator, improving the visibility of its privacy policy and offering a user content opt-out form. Users in the European Union are thus able to object to OpenAI's use of their personal data for the purposes of model training.[241]

The EU's AI Act can be considered a big breakthrough, and it is a great leap forward on the way to digital humanism. At the same time, the hype generated by the release of ChatGPT – and with it the adoption of a tool by millions of users, both for worthy and questionable purposes – has raised a host of new questions. In principle, the AI Act's identification of four risk categories makes a lot of sense. But critical observers have rightfully noted that for a general-purpose technology such as ChatGPT, it is the user who determines whether the application is high risk or not. More thought will need to be given as to whether such tools require their own risk rating, and whether another approach to regulation – above and beyond classes of risks

– may be needed.

As governments worldwide continue to explore ways to enhance and optimise their legislative frameworks around data and emerging technologies, the EU and the US are engaging in transatlantic efforts to address these challenges. At a recent meeting of the EU-US Trade and Technology Council, both parties expressed their commitment to expedite the development of an AI Code of Conduct. This initiative aims to bridge the policy gap and provide guidance on the responsible and ethical use of artificial intelligence.[242]

Finally, governments clearly have a part to play that goes beyond that of regulation and setting policy. They also have a role in developing standards and facilitating their widespread adoption. Moreover, they can set the agenda for helping the broader population, especially girls, develop interest and skills in STEM fields, through funding programmes and by improving education curricula. Policymakers might be inspired by Finland's 1% scheme, which invited thousands of people who were not technology experts to take part in a grand experiment aimed at realigning the country's economy toward high-end AI applications. The idea behind this programme is as simple as it is brilliant: It started by teaching 1% of the population, or about 55,000 people in the case of Finland, the basic concepts at the root of AI technology, and then is gradually building on this number over subsequent years.[243]

Co-creating a positive future

Change is often met with fear and uncertainty. The AI revolution is no exception. As we stand on the brink of technological transformation, the unknown can be daunting. Our minds race with questions about what this change means for our jobs, the environment, our economy, and our society. While such shifts can be scary, they still need to be embraced. Change does not just happen – we can shape the outcome. Change, if managed well, is an opportunity for growth, progress, and innovation. It offers an opportunity to build a better future for ourselves and for future generations. The process of accepting change is not always easy, but it is crucial. Building resilience, a key factor in navigating change, can help us to accept and even thrive in the face of uncertainty. By learning how to master change and develop resilience, we can turn fear into hope and uncertainty into opportunity. Together, we can navigate the AI revolution and build a better future for all.

In order to truly unlock the potential of AI for a better world, it is essential that we think about the technology's long-term potential as well as its immediate implications. This will require a mindset shift in which we learn to combine short-term solutions with big-picture considerations. It will require us to envision a future in which AI is used to solve some of our most pressing global issues, such as climate change and inequality. With a united effort, we can shape this future to be one in which AI benefits humanity and the planet.

If this is to succeed, everyone – and each institution – will have a role to play. Below, we offer suggestions that we hope will inspire you to take a lead in co-creating this future.

Governments must take quick and decisive action on regulating AI, working in close co-operation with a broad range of stakeholders. They must maximise the alignment, coherence, and standardisation of policies and guidelines on the local, national, and international levels. Specifically, they should:

- Prioritise AI regulation, treating it with urgency and investing the requisite resources.
- Adopt key principles of AI regulation, starting with existing frameworks produced by the European Commission and OECD, for example.
- Participate in shaping international standards, and use them. Standardised guidelines and rules will be needed to help all actors navigate the field of AI effectively while minimising harm.
- Involve broad stakeholder groups – not just techies and regulation experts, but those that understand sustainable development as well.
- Let digital humanism be their North Star and guiding light, recognising the need for intact ecosystems able to support future social development

and human progress.

- Establish systems that allow corporate claims to be assessed and validated, and which enable the impacts of AI systems to be tracked and identified. Additionally, they must ensure that relevant laws can be enforced.
- Invest in AI and media literacy programmes that enable individuals to critically evaluate AI technology and apply it for the greater good, without fear.
- Fund research and projects, including the development of explainable AI.

Businesses must put their money where their mouths are, delivering on their promises of sustainability and responsibility. They must invest not only in researching one-off technological solutions, but also in measuring these solutions' ecological and social impacts. Specifically, they should:

- Integrate key principles of responsible AI into their corporate DNA and core business strategies. They should develop codes of conduct in this area, and address these in their ESG strategies.
- Let digital humanism inspire their digitalisation strategies, and thus involve a diverse range of actors, viewpoints, and voices.
- Commit to employing AI in a way that enhances human work.
- Develop employee education programmes that foster AI literacy and include an emphasis on principles for responsible AI.
- Follow human-centred design principles based on human needs, and always consider ethical implications when developing or integrating AI services.
- Actively seek business opportunities in areas where AI can be used to promote sustainability, especially in topics related to ecological and social transformation.
- Give a platform to #AIforgood champions that can help them craft, implement, and communicate their businesses advances, while shaping AI in a future-friendly way.

- Invest in research that clarifies the risks and opportunities of AI in their sectors of operation, thus ensuring their business decisions do more good than harm to society.
- Challenge their peers and supply chain partners to do all of the above.

Educators must critically and constructively review both the opportunities and risks of AI for teaching and learning. Specifically, they should:

- Be aware of the many ways in which AI, and in particular large language models, challenge traditional education systems while also providing opportunities to transform them in a positive way.
- Embrace the AI revolution, and learn about how it can benefit their efforts to prepare young and older generations for the future.
- Collaborate with peers and other stakeholders to experiment with and develop good practice approaches in this rapidly evolving environment.
- Help students to approach AI and STEM subjects more broadly without fear, and in a constructive manner with human needs at the centre.

Research institutions must intensify their focus on artificial intelligence, particularly by addressing questions of ethics, responsibility, and impact. Specifically, they should:

- Advocate for more research funding that links the AI and sustainable development agendas.
- Focus research efforts on understanding the impact of AI applications and the ways in which AI can maximise benefits to humans at the global scale.
- Encourage peers and networks to treat the topic of AI and sustainable development with urgency, foresight, and responsibility.
- Practise what they preach by evaluating their AI systems and ensuring they maximise social and environmental benefit while minimising harm.

- Invest in communication with all key actors and the broader public, to ensure that all stakeholders understand the essential role of research in shaping a better future with AI.
- Try open-source projects like BLOOM. Why not start contributing?

NGOs and other civil society groups must increase pressure on those with power, and continue to hold decision-makers to account by demanding transparency and responsibility in the development and application of AI models. Specifically, they should:

- Get acquainted with the topic of AI and its power to affect their causes, whether social or environmental, in both a positive and negative way.
- Analyse the links between AI and their sustainable development agendas, and communicate their findings to their audiences.
- Investigate the impact of AI on their target groups, and ensure that these groups' voices are included in analyses and external communications.
- Hold decision-makers -- both public and private – to account, pushing them to live up to their commitments to responsible AI and AI for good.
- Ensure that public attention remains focused on the topic of responsible AI, and help citizens and consumers push powerful actors to put humans first when creating and implementing digital solutions.

Everyone should read up on the topic, follow debates, and get engaged. AI affects us all, and every voice counts when demanding transparency and accountability from businesses and governments. Specifically, we should:

- Start learning about AI today! Understand its functions, effects, and possible risks. This will be vital for making informed choices and ultimately thriving in our digital age.
- Approach AI with a proactive, fearless mindset, aiming to understand the associated risks and ethical challenges while embracing the transfor-

mative potential of AI to create a better future.

- Avoid thinking we have to understand everything. Nobody can. Just start somewhere.
- Get involved – particularly those of us who aren't techies – by reading up on AI, following public debates, and reflecting on how it affects our own lives both positively and negatively.
- Try out AI tools, play around, make a first photo prompt – and talk to techies, encouraging them to engage in conversations about technical solutions as well as risks and opportunities.
- Consider contributing to open-source AI projects, for those of us who are techies.
- Attend talks and conferences, read up, join groups. Develop a sense of who the main players in the field are, and what role they are playing in the debates.
- Hold businesses and governments to account by publicly questioning them about their goals and practices related to AI, for example via social media.
- Avoid anthropomorphising (humanising) AI models by reminding yourself that they are computer programmes with no soul, consciousness, or desires.
- Actively utilise language that reflects the fact that AI systems are machines, not humans, even if they have been developed by (imperfect) humans.

We look forward to engaging with you!

Glossary

Algorithm: A set of rules or instructions given to an AI, or any other type of computer software, to help it learn and solve problems.

Algorithmic fairness: A condition in which AI systems are not unfairly disadvantaging certain groups. Considerable research is needed to ensure that this potential is realised.

Artificial general intelligence (AGI): A type of AI that would have the ability to understand, learn, adapt, and implement knowledge across a wide range of tasks at a level equal comparable to or greater to that of a human being. It contrasts with narrow AI (defined below), which is designed to perform specific tasks, and although it does not yet exist, it is a goal targeted by many companies.

Artificial intelligence (AI): A branch of computer science focused on creating systems capable of performing tasks that usually require human intelligence, including but not limited to natural-language processing, problem-solving, learning, and perception.

Bias: In the context of AI, bias refers to algorithms that produce systematically skewed or erroneous outcomes. When used in a social context, this can lead to results that produce systematic benefits or disadvantages for specific social groups.

Black box: A term used to describe AI systems in which the internal workings or decision-making processes are not transparent to or interpretable by human users. This is a significant issue in AI ethics, particularly for applications in which it is critical to understand the decision-making process, such as healthcare or criminal justice.

Chatbot: A software application that can converse with human users in their natural language. These conversations typically occur in text or voice format.

ChatGPT: An AI-based model developed by OpenAI, designed to generate human-like text based on the natural-language input it is given. It is one instance of a broader family of neural network models called GPTs (generative pretrained transformers), and has been specifically tuned for conversational purposes. It has been used to build AI chatbots and virtual assistants, and for tasks that involve generating human-like text.

Computer vision: A field of AI in which computers are trained to interpret and understand the visual world.

Data mining: The process of discovering patterns and knowledge in large amounts of data.

Deep learning (DL): A subset of machine learning that uses neural networks with many layers (deep neural networks) to analyse and learn from data.

Digital humanism: A school of thought that prioritises human interests and values in the design and implementation of digital technologies, including AI, with the goal of ensuring that such technologies serve and augment human capabilities without infringing on human rights or autonomy.

Digital twin: A digital twin is a virtual model of a process, product, or service. This pairing of the virtual and physical worlds allows data to be analysed and systems to be monitored in a way that ideally heads off problems before they occur, preventing downtime. A digital twin can also be used to develop new opportunities and plan for the future by using simulations.

Explainable AI (XAI): AI systems whose actions can be understood by human experts. This contrasts with the concept of the "black box" in machine learning, where even the designers of the model cannot explain why the AI arrived at a specific decision.

General-purpose technology (GPT): A type of technology, like electricity, or the internet, that can significantly alter societies by impacting economic and social structures. In the AI context, GPT refers to AI's transformative potential. Note that this should not be confused with GPTs (generative pretrained transformers), a type of AI language model that includes OpenAI's ChatGPT.

Generative adversarial networks (GANs): A class of machine-learning systems invented by Ian Goodfellow and his colleagues in 2014. Two neural networks contest with each other in a game, one called the generator and the other the discriminator.

Generative AI: Refers to a type of AI that creates new content, for instance in the form of images, songs, text, etc. This type of AI can generate new output without any prior input or based upon explicitly crafted guidelines.

Human-centred design: An approach to problem-solving and innovation that prioritises understanding and addressing the needs, preferences, and behaviours of end users, placing them at the centre of the design process to create products or services that meet their specific requirements.

Information and communications technology (ICT): Refers to technologies used for the acquisition, storage, processing, transmission, and presentation of information, encompassing hardware, software, networks, and digital services.

Jevons paradox: An economic observation which suggests that as technological improvements increase the efficiency with which a resource is used, total consumption of that resource may increase rather than decrease. This happens because the lower cost of using the resource leads to increased demand. It is named after the English economist William Stanley Jevons, who first proposed the paradox in relation to coal consumption.

JIT: Short for "just-in-time". A manufacturing and inventory-management approach that focuses on producing and delivering goods or materials precisely when needed, thus minimising inventory costs and increasing efficiency.

Machine learning (ML): A subset of AI that involves the development of algorithms that allow computers to learn from and make decisions or predictions based on data.

Narrow AI: Also known as weak AI, this type of AI is designed to perform a narrow task, such as voice recognition, providing recommendations, or image recognition. Narrow AI cannot understand or learn anything that it wasn't specifically programmed to do.

Natural-language processing (NLP): A field of AI that focuses on the interaction between computers and humans in natural language, enabling machines to understand and respond to human language.

Neural network: A computing model whose layered structure resembles the neural structure of the human brain, supporting the process of learning from and interpreting data.

Large language model (LLM): A type of AI model that is trained to understand, generate, and make predictions about language. These models can be used in a variety of applications including translation, text completion, and sentiment analysis. They are trained on large amounts of text data, and learn patterns and structures within a language to make educated predictions.

Open source: Refers to a type of software or technology that is freely available for anyone to use, modify, and distribute. It is characterised by its source code being openly accessible, allowing users to study, modify, and improve upon it. Open-source projects often encourage collaboration and community involvement, fostering innovation and transparency in software development.

Privacy: In the context of AI, this refers to the protection of individuals' personal data. AI systems often handle sensitive information, making it crucial to ensure that this information is used ethically and securely, with proper safeguards to protect individuals' privacy.

Reinforcement learning: A type of machine learning in which an agent learns to behave in an environment by performing certain actions and receiving rewards or punishments as feedback.

Robotics: The design, construction, operation, and use of robots, often incorporating aspects of AI.

Singularity: Also known as the "technological singularity", this is a hypothetical point in the future when technological growth, particularly in the field of AI, becomes uncontrollable by humans and irreversible. This is seen as likely to produce unforeseeable changes to human civilisation. The singularity itself is a point in time, while the development of superintelligence could potentially be a trigger for the singularity.

Superintelligence: A hypothetical form of AI that would outperform humans in most areas of economically valuable work, while also exceeding human intellect in virtually every aspect of problem-solving and creativity.

Supervised learning: A type of machine learning in which the model is trained using labelled data – that is, a dataset that has inputs paired with the correct outputs.

Testing data: The dataset used to test the machine-learning model's accuracy after it has been trained.

Training data: The dataset from which the machine-learning algorithm learns. In a supervised learning context, for example, the training data includes both the input data and the corresponding correct output.

Turing test: Proposed by the British mathematician Alan Turing, this test is a measure of a machine's ability to exhibit intelligent behaviour equivalent to, or indistinguishable from, that of a human. If a machine passes the Turing test, it implies that the machine has demonstrated human-like intelligence.

Unsupervised learning: A type of machine learning in which the model identifies patterns in an unlabelled dataset – that is, a dataset without predefined classifications.

Acknowledgements

We would like to express our profound gratitude for the circumstances that enabled us to come together as a group and collaborate on this book. Throughout this journey, numerous individuals have provided invaluable assistance and support. First and foremost, we would like to thank the speakers and participants of our virtual Optimist Café sessions. Their willingness to share their wisdom, insights, and engage in thought-provoking discussions has been instrumental in shaping this work. We are particularly grateful for their willingness to challenge us with tough questions. These lovely people include Ana Simic, Johannes (Yogi) Jäger, Martin Giesswein and Loïc Lannelongue, as well as Alexandra Deutsch, Alice Behrendt, Anna Christine Enzinger, Alexander Führer, Claudia Huber, Daniel Tabacaru Jæger, Darshini Waibel, Dominik Frey, Elaine Paplos, Iris Kühn, Juliana Guaiato Aufschnaiter, Juliane van Voorst tot Voorst, Kirstie Riedl, Mariana Di-Bella, Marius Reinke, Nina Meinel, Ruth Freedom Pojman, Sonja Donauer-Dums, Virginie Staal and many others.

We thank our editor, Barbara Serfozo, for polishing the manuscript under a tight deadline and for her astute reading of the text.

Special thanks also go to Laetitia Antonowicz who critically reviewed the chapter on education and science, providing a highly welcome and insightful reality-check.

In addition, we would like to acknowledge the numerous colleagues, collaborators, friends and influencers who, while not direct contributors to this book, have inspired us and helped expand our horizons with their insights and expertise on artificial intelligence, sustainability, regeneration and societal transformation.

Finally, we would like to thank our students from around the world with whom we have had the pleasure of engaging with while writing this book. Their enthusiasm for, and questions relating to AI and sustainability, have kept us on our toes as we endeavour to stay in touch with the issues of concern to younger generations.

About the Authors

Alice Schmidt, Claudia Winkler, Jeroen Dobbelaere, Florian Schuetz (clockwise from top left)

Alice Schmidt is a leading sustainability advisor, business consultant and keynote speaker who helps her clients and collaborators untangle sustainable transformation and regeneration (www.aliceschmidt.at). A bigger-picture thinker, Alice has spent over 25 years addressing social, environmental and economic sustainability issues in a global context. She has worked with 70 of the world's best organisations, from the United Nations and the European Commission to NGOs, corporations and small social enterprises in 30+ countries. Alice is a senior lecturer at Vienna University of Economics and Business among others, and she carries the sustainability flag as a member of various sustainability boards. Alice is passionate about designing for impact and creating tangible results for people and the planet. Together with Claudia Winkler, she authored the book "The Sustainability Puzzle: How systems thinking, circularity, climate action and social transformation can improve health, wealth and wellbeing for all".

Claudia Winkler is an internationally recognised, award-winning impact innovator, entrepreneur, and serial founder. She has a 20-year executive background in the ICT industry and experience serving on the supervisory board of leading Central and Eastern European telecommunication companies. Her mission is rooted in shaping a meaningful and prosperous future for all. As part of this mission, Claudia successfully launched the first B-Corp certified telecommunication company in Europe. Passionate about developing digital products and services, Claudia utilises her extensive knowledge of digitalisation to transform traditional business models to help creating a sustainable future. Alongside Alice Schmidt, she co-authored "The Sustainability Puzzle" and actively shares her findings as a keynote speaker and advisor on sustainability, innovation and digitalisation worldwide.

Florian Schütz is an accomplished entrepreneur and seasoned senior transformer, excelling in driving digital transformation and embracing emerging technologies. He pioneered the use of AI for social media monitoring in Europe and successfully integrated his company into the operations of a leading global market research organization a decade ago. Florian's expertise spans technology, multimedia, and artificial intelligence, and he has a deep passion for analyzing the latest tech developments. Combining his technical prowess with art, Florian has embarked on a new endeavor, enriching his artwork with AI. His pieces are characterized by intellectual clarity, conceptual order, and thought-provoking messages. Florian's art often conveys political statements, employing text fragments, typography, and composition to create an enigmatic and engaging experience. Explore Florian's works at www.floschuetz.com.

Jeroen Dobbelaere is a cell biologist and sustainability manager helping to make academia fit for a sustainable future. Having done lab-based work for more than 20 years at UGent, ETH Zürich, Cambridge University and the University of Vienna he knows the ins and outs of academic work. He has published many scientific papers in high-ranking journals and is well familiar with the international conference circuit. As a vivid gardener and lover of the outdoors, Jeroen always tries to look at research through the lens of environmental sustainability. He founded the grassroots group Climate@MaxPerutzLabs in Vienna, published several papers on the need for a sustainable transformation in academia and developed several courses and teaching tools. Not waiting for academia to change, Jeroen decided to stop active research and is now making an impact as sustainability manager at the Institute of Science and Technology Austria (ISTA).

Find out more: www.sustainability-puzzle.org/fast-forward

Notes

INTRODUCTION

1 Einstein, Albert. I Would Spend 55 Minutes Defining the Problem and then Five Minutes Solving It. Quote Investigator. https://quoteinvestigator.com/2014/05/22/solve/.

CHAPTER 1: AI – FRIEND OR FOE?

2 Kalluri, Pratyusha. 2020. "Don't ask if artificial intelligence is good or fair, ask how it shifts power." *Nature* 583 (7815): 169-169. https://www.nature.com/articles/d41586-020-02003-2.

3 THE LINE: a revolution in urban living. 2023. NEOM. https://www.neom.com/en-us/regions/theline.

4 Thomas, Merlyn, and Vibeke Venema. 2023. "Neom: What's the green truth behind a planned eco-city in the Saudi desert?", *BBC World*. https://www.bbc.com/news/blogs-trending-59601335.

5 Porter, Tom. 2023.The Saudi crown prince wants to build a trillion-dollar utopia in the desert. His deals with China reveal a darker vision. Insider. https://www.businessinsider.com/saudi-crown-princes-china-deals-hint-city-darker-neom-mbs-2023-3.

6 Amnesty. 2023.Human rights in Saudi Arabia. Amnesty International. https://www.amnesty.org/en/location/middle-east-and-north-africa/saudi-arabia/report-saudi-arabia/.

7 Thomas, Merlyn, and Vibeke Venema. 2023. "Neom: What's the green truth behind a planned eco-city in the Saudi desert?", *BBC World*. https://www.bbc.com/news/blogs-trending-59601335.

8 Neom. 2023. Kingdom of Saudi Arabia. https://www.vision2030.gov.sa/v2030/v2030-projects/neom/.

9 Porter, Tom. 2023.The Saudi crown prince wants to build a trillion-dollar utopia in the desert. His deals with China reveal a darker vision. Insider. https://www.businessinsider.com/saudi-crown-princes-china-deals-hint-city-darker-neom-mbs-2023-3.

10 McCarthy, John. 2023.What is AI? http://jmc.stanford.edu/artificial-intelligence/what-is-ai/index.html.

11 Hu, Krystal. 2023. "ChatGPT sets record for fastest-growing user base - analyst note." https://www.reuters.com/technology/chatgpt-sets-record-fastest-growing-user-base-analyst-note-2023-02-01/.

12 Baschuk, Bryce, and Bloomberg. 2023.A.I. will cause 'significant labor-market disruption' over next 5 years, says World Economic Forum. Fortune. https://fortune.com/2023/04/30/ai-disruption-jobs-labor-world-economic-forum-report/.

13 Eloundou, Tyna, Sam Manning, Pamela Mishkin, and Daniel Rock. 2023. "GPTs are GPTs: An Early Look at the Labor Market Impact Potential of Large Language Models." https://arxiv.org/pdf/2303.10130.

14 2001: A Space Odyssey. 1968. https://www.imdb.com/title/tt0062622/.

15 The Terminator. 1984. https://www.imdb.com/title/tt0088247/.

16 Long, Duri, and Brian Magerko. 2020. "What is AI Literacy? Competencies and Design Considerations." *CHI '20: Proceedings of the 2020 CHI Conference on Human Factors in Computing Systems*: 1-16. https://dl.acm.org/doi/abs/10.1145/3313831.3376727.

CHAPTER 2: BACKGROUND, BASICS, AND BLADERUNNER

17 Price, Cedric. 2023.Technology Is The Answer But What Was The Question? | Cedric Price | Pidgeon Digital. Pidgeon Digital. https://www.pidgeondigital.com/talks/technology-is-the-answer-but-what-was-the-question-/.

18 Minsky, Marvin. 2007. *The emotion machine : commonsense thinking, artificial intelligence, and the future of the human mind.* First Simon & Schuster trade paperback edition. ed. New York: Simon & Schuster Paperbacks.

19 https://mitsloan.onlinecampus.getsmarter.com/mod/book/view.php?id=67938&chapterid=25941

20 Fashion ecommerce 2020: The trends disrupting the industry. 2021. Phvntom Inc. https://phvntom.com/fashion-ecommerce-2020-the-trends-disrupting-the-industry/.

21 echo3D. 2020.Why You Should Start Building AR Apps for the Furniture Industry. @Medium. https://arvrjourney.com/why-you-should-start-building-ar-apps-for-the-furniture-industry-d0da50c0ed71.

22 How Grocers Are Reimagining the Future With AI. 2023. https://www.winsightgrocerybusiness.com/technology/how-grocers-are-reimagining-future-ai.

23 Unveil Perso, The World's First AI-Powered Device For Skincare And Cosmetics. 2023. L'Oréal. https://www.loreal.com/en/news/research-innovation/unveil-perso-the-worlds-first-aipowered-device-for-skincare-and-cosmetics/.

24 Pichai, Sundar. 2023. "An important next step on our AI journey." *Google*. 2023. https://blog.google/technology/ai/bard-google-ai-search-updates/.

25 Hu, Krystal. 2023. "ChatGPT sets record for fastest-growing user base - analyst note." https://www.reuters.com/technology/chatgpt-sets-record-fastest-growing-user-base-analyst-note-2023-02-01/.

26 Satya Nadella Says AI Golden Age Is Here and 'It's Good for Humanity'. 2023. WEF. https://www.weforum.org/press/2023/01/satya-nadella-says-ai-golden-age-is-here-and-it-s-good-for-humanity/.

27 Toh, Michelle. 2023.Baidu stock surges after announcement of ChatGPT-style AI bot. CNN Business. https://www.cnn.com/2023/02/06/tech/china-baidu-ai-bot-chatgpt-rival-intl-hnk/index.html.

28 Big tech and the pursuit of AI dominance. 2023. The Economist. https://www.economist.com/business/2023/03/26/big-tech-and-the-pursuit-of-ai-dominance.

29 Harrison, Maggie. 2023.OpenAI Seems Like a Very Sleazy Company to Be Creating World-Changing AGI. Futurism. https://futurism.com/openai-sleazy-company-creating-agi.

30 Wikipedia. 2023.DARPA. https://en.wikipedia.org/wiki/DARPA.

31 Perrin, Andrew. 2016. "Book Reading 2016 - Appendix A:." https://www.pewresearch.org/internet/2016/09/01/book-reading-2016-appendix-a/.

32 Zach, Stein-Perlman, Weinstein-Raun Benjamin, and Grace Katja. 2022.2022 Expert Survey on Progress in AI. AI Impacts. https://aiimpacts.org/2022-expert-survey-on-progress-in-ai/.

CHAPTER 3: A MAGIC BULLET FOR SOCIAL JUSTICE?

33 Farrow, Boyd. 2022.Egypt's Mo Gawdat has a gameplan for surviving the rise of AI. Wired. https://wired.me/technology/artificial-intelligence/egypts-mo-gawdat-has-a-gameplan-for-surviving-the-rise-of-ai/.

34 Weizenbaum, Joseph. 1966. "ELIZA—a computer program for the study of natural language communication between man and machine." *Commun. ACM* 9 (1): 36–45. https://doi.org/10.1145/365153.365168.

35 Try Bot A.L.I.C.E here. https://www.pandorabots.com/pandora/talk?botid=b8d616e35e36e881.

36 Morais, Betsy. 2013.Can Humans Fall in Love with Bots? The New Yorker. https://www.newyorker.com/tech/annals-of-technology/can-humans-fall-in-love-with-bots.

37 Chow, Andrew. 2023.Why People Are Confessing Their Love For AI Chatbots. TIME. https://time.com/6257790/ai-chatbots-love/.

38 Ethics and governance of artificial intelligence for health: WHO guidance. 2021. World Health Organization. https://apps.who.int/iris/handle/10665/341996.

39 Ibid.

40 Hamzelou, Jessica. 2023.Artificial intelligence is infiltrating health care. We shouldn't let it make all the decisions. Technology Review. https://www.technologyreview.com/2023/04/21/1071921/ai-is-infiltrating-health-care-we-shouldnt-let-it-make-decisions/

41 Sloane, Mona. 2022. "To make AI fair, here's what we must learn to do." *Nature* 605 (7908): 9-9. https://www.nature.com/articles/d41586-022-01202-3.

42 Smith, Mitch. 2016.In Wisconsin, a Backlash Against Using Data to Foretell Defendants' Futures. New York Times. https://www.nytimes.com/2016/06/23/us/backlash-in-wisconsin-against-using-data-to-foretell-defendants-futures.html.

43 Sloane, Mona. 2022. "To make AI fair, here's what we must learn to do." *Nature* 605 (7908): 9-9. https://www.nature.com/articles/d41586-022-01202-3.

44 Fiedler, Tristan. 2022.EU throws party in €387K metaverse — and hardly anyone turns up. Politico. https://www.politico.eu/article/eu-threw-e387k-meta-gala-nobody-came-big-tech/.

45 Sloane, Mona. 2022. "To make AI fair, here's what we must learn to do." *Nature* 605 (7908): 9-9. https://www.nature.com/articles/d41586-022-01202-3.

46 Disability. 2023. WHO. https://www.who.int/news-room/fact-sheets/detail/disability-and-health.

47 Empowering The Blind. 2023. DotLumen. https://www.dotlumen.com.

48 Disability and Health Overview. 2020. Centers for Disease Control and Prevention. https://www.cdc.gov/ncbddd/disabilityandhealth/disability.html.

49 Disability. 2023. WHO. https://www.who.int/health-topics/disability#tab=tab_1.

50 Zeit magazin. 2023.Hugh Herr: "Die meisten Behinderungen werden nicht mehr existieren". Zeit Online. https://www.zeit.de/zeit-magazin/2023/04/hugh-herr-klettern-prothesen-bionik.

51 Ibid.

52 Helping Hand. 2023. Attensi. https://happyhelpinghand.attensi.com/. and 'Tech for good' had a very good year in 2022. Here are 6 companies that led the way. 2023. World Economic Forum. https://www.weforum.org/agenda/2023/01/tech-for-good-innovations/.

53 Facts and Figures 2022. 2023. ITU. https://www.itu.int/itu-d/reports/statistics/facts-figures-2022.

54 Natascha, Ickert. 2023.Wieso Frauen bei der Digitalisierung benachteiligt sind. Der Standard. https://www.derstandard.at/story/2000143726324/wieso-frauen-bei-der-digitalisierung-benachteiligt-sind.

55 Mark, West, Kraut Rebecca, and Chew Han Ei. 2019. "I'd blush if I could: closing gender divides in digital skills through education." *Unesco.* https://unesdoc.unesco.org/ark:/48223/pf0000367416.

56 Noam, Cohen. 2019. "Why Siri and Alexa Weren't Built to Smack Down Harassment." *Wired.* https://www.wired.com/story/why-siri-and-alexa-werent-built-to-smack-down-harassment/.

57 Mark, West, Kraut Rebecca, and Chew Han Ei. 2019. "I'd blush if I could: closing gender divides in digital skills through education." *Unesco.* https://unesdoc.unesco.org/ark:/48223/pf0000367416.

58 Creutzig, Felix et al. 2022. "Digitalization and the Anthropocene." *https://doi.org/10.1146/annurev-environ-120920-100056.* https://www.annualreviews.org/doi/10.1146/annurev-environ-120920-100056.

59 Isabel, Vander Molen. 2022. "Bolivia: Pursuing Sustainable Lithium Mining." *Centre for Strategic & International Studies*. https://www.csis.org/blogs/development-dispatches/bolivia-pursuing-sustainable-lithium-mining.

60 Oberhaus, Daniel. 2020.AI Is Throwing Battery Development Into Overdrive. Wired. https://www.wired.com/story/ai-is-throwing-battery-development-into-overdrive/.

61 Perrigo, Billy. 2022.Inside Facebook's African Sweatshop. TIME. https://time.com/6147458/facebook-africa-content-moderation-employee-treatment/.

62 Perrigo, Billy. 2023.Exclusive: The $2 Per Hour Workers Who Made ChatGPT Safer. TIME. https://time.com/6247678/openai-chatgpt-kenya-workers/.

63 Gadonniex, Heather. 2020.From Dreams to Reality: Our Journey to Becoming a Certified B Corporation - SAMA. Sama Ai. https://www.sama.com/blog/we-are-a-b-corp/.

64 Perrigo, Billy. 2022.Inside Facebook's African Sweatshop. TIME. https://time.com/6147458/facebook-africa-content-moderation-employee-treatment/.

65 Perrigo, Billy. 2023.Exclusive: The $2 Per Hour Workers Who Made ChatGPT Safer. TIME. https://time.com/6247678/openai-chatgpt-kenya-workers/.

66 Perrigo, Billy. 2023.150 AI Workers Vote to Unionize at Nairobi Meeting. TIME. https://time.com/6275995/chatgpt-facebook-african-workers-union/.

CHAPTER 4: THE FUTURE OF WORK

67 A.I. Artificial Intelligence. 2001. http://www.imdb.com/title/tt0212720/characters/nm0004978.

68 Jackson, Greg. 2023.AI is like going from muskets to missiles, everywhere all at once. The Times. https://www.thetimes.co.uk/article/ai-is-like-going-from-muskets-to-missiles-everywhere-all-at-once-3kx5v0kn9.

69 Schmidt, Alice, and Claudia Winkler. 2021. *The Sustainability Puzzle: How System Change, Circularity, Climate Action and Social Transformation can improve Health, Wealth and Wellbeing for All.*

70 Center for Collective Intelligence. 2023. MIT. http://catalog.mit.edu/mit/research/center-collective-intelligence/.

71 Malone, Thomas, Daniela Rus, and Robert Laubacher. 2020.ARTIFICIAL INTELLIGENCE AND THE FUTURE OF WORK. MIT. https://workofthefuture.mit.edu/wp-content/uploads/2020/12/2020-Research-Brief-Malone-Rus-Laubacher2.pdf.

72 Eloundou, Tyna, Sam Manning, Pamela Mishkin, and Daniel Rock. 2023. "GPTs are GPTs: An Early Look at the Labor Market Impact Potential of Large Language Models." https://arxiv.org/pdf/2303.10130.

73 McKinsey. 2022. "The state of AI in 2022—and a half decade in review." https://www.mckinsey.com/capabilities/quantumblack/our-insights/the-state-of-ai-in-2022-and-a-half-decade-in-review.

74 Tianjin Binhai Library. 2022. MVRDV. https://www.mvrdv.com/projects/246/tianjin-binhai-library.

75 Randall, Tom. 2015.The World's Smartest Office Building Knows How You Like Your Coffee. Bloomberg. http://www.bloomberg.com/features/2015-the-edge-the-worlds-greenest-building/.

76 Wikipedia. 2023.Creativity. https://en.wikipedia.org/wiki/Creativity.

77 Sian, Cain. 2023.'This song sucks': Nick Cave responds to ChatGPT song written in style of Nick Cave. Guardian. https://www.theguardian.com/music/2023/jan/17/this-song-sucks-nick-cave-responds-to-chatgpt-song-written-in-style-of-nick-cave.

78 Wikipedia. 2023.Creativity. https://en.wikipedia.org/wiki/Creativity.

79 Wikipedia. 2023.AlphaZero. https://de.wikipedia.org/wiki/AlphaZero#Reaktionen.

80 Connolly, Jim. 2013.Steve Jobs was right: Real Artists Ship! Creative Thinking Hub. https://www.creativethinkinghub.com/steve-jobs-was-right-real-artists-ship/.

81 Wikipedia. 2023.Midjourney. https://en.wikipedia.org/wiki/Midjourney.

82 Wikipedia. 2023.DALL-E. https://en.wikipedia.org/wiki/DALL-E.

83 Wikipedia. 2023.Stable Diffusion. https://en.wikipedia.org/wiki/Stable_Diffusion.

84 Novak, Matt. 2023. "That Viral Image Of Pope Francis Wearing A White Puffer Coat Is Totally Fake." https://www.forbes.com/sites/mattnovak/2023/03/26/that-viral-image-of-pope-francis-wearing-a-white-puffer-coat-is-totally-fake/.

85 Hyken, Shep. 2023. "How AI And ChatGPT Can Crush Customer Service." https://www.forbes.com/sites/shephyken/2023/04/16/how-ai-and-chatgpt-can-crush-customer-service/.

86 Malone, Thomas, Daniela Rus, and Robert Laubacher. 2020.ARTIFICIAL INTELLIGENCE AND THE FUTURE OF WORK. MIT. https://workofthefuture.mit.edu/wp-content/uploads/2020/12/2020-Research-Brief-Malone-Rus-Laubacher2.pdf.

87 Top Considerations Before Implementing AI. 2023. CompTIA. https://comptiacdn.azureedge.net/webcontent/docs/default-source/research-reports/08497-ai-considerations-document-online-final.pdf?sfvrsn=789806ef_0.

CHAPTER 5: TOO COOL FOR SCHOOL – AI IN EDUCATION AND SCIENCE

88 Strickland, Eliza. 2022. "Timnit Gebru Is Building a Slow AI Movement." https://spectrum.ieee.org/timnit-gebru-dair-ai-ethics

89 WU Vienna. 2023.AI and ChatGPT in teaching. WU Vienna. https://www.wu.ac.at/en/staff/information-for-teachers/chatgpt-in-der-lehre/.

90 Miao, Fengchun, Wayne Holmes, Ronghuai Huang, and Hui Zhang. 2021. *AI and education: guidance for policy-makers.* Unesco.

91 Spiewak, Martin. 2023. "Künstliche Intelligenz in der Schule : Die 8a gegen die KI." https://www.zeit.de/2023/08/kuenstliche-intelligenz-schule-unterricht.

92 Miao, Fengchun, Wayne Holmes, Ronghuai Huang, and Hui Zhang. 2021. *AI and education: guidance for policy-makers*. Unesco.

93 Holmes, Wayne, and Ilkka Tuomi. 2022. "State of the art and practice in AI in education - Holmes - 2022 - European Journal of Education - Wiley Online Library." *European Journal of Education* 57: 542 – 570. https://doi.org/10.1111/ejed.12533.

94 Ibid. and IBM. 2018.Art of the possible: IBM Watson and Pearson drive cognitive learning for college students. IBM. https://www.ibm.com/watson/education/pearson.

95 Aardman. 2023.StorySign. https://app-aardman-cms-prod.azurewebsites.net//interactive /storysign/.

96 Miao, Fengchun, Wayne Holmes, Ronghuai Huang, and Hui Zhang. 2021. *AI and education: guidance for policy-makers*. Unesco.

97 Holmes, Wayne, and Ilkka Tuomi. 2022. "State of the art and practice in AI in education - Holmes - 2022 - European Journal of Education - Wiley Online Library." *European Journal of Education* 57: 542 – 570. https://doi.org/10.1111/ejed.12533.

98 Spiewak, Martin. 2023. "Künstliche Intelligenz in der Schule : Die 8a gegen die KI." https://www.zeit.de/2023/08/kuenstliche-intelligenz-schule-unterricht.

99 Ibid.

100 Miao, Fengchun, Wayne Holmes, Ronghuai Huang, and Hui Zhang. 2021. *AI and education: guidance for policy-makers*. Unesco.

101 Ibid.

102 "How China Is Using Artificial Intelligence in Classrooms." 2019. Wall Street Journal. Embedded Video https://www.youtube.com/watch?v=JMLsHI8aV0g.

103 Holmes, Wayne, and Ilkka Tuomi. 2022. "State of the art and practice in AI in education - Holmes - 2022 - European Journal of Education - Wiley Online Library." *European Journal of Education* 57: 542 – 570. https://doi.org/10.1111/ejed.12533.

104 Moriarty-McLaughlin, Fiona. 2020.More colleges eye AI to track, monitor students. The College Fix. https://www.thecollegefix.com/more-colleges-eye-ai-to-track-monitor-students/.

105 page 21 Miao, Fengchun, Wayne Holmes, Ronghuai Huang, and Hui Zhang. 2021. *AI and education: guidance for policy-makers*. Unesco.

106 Zembylas, Michalinos. 2021. "A decolonial approach to AI in higher education teaching and learning: strategies for undoing the ethics of digital neocolonialism." *Learning, Media and Technology*: 25-37. https://www.tandfonline.com/doi/full/10.1080/17439884.2021.2010094.

107 Miao, Fengchun, Wayne Holmes, Ronghuai Huang, and Hui Zhang. 2021. *AI and education: guidance for policy-makers*. Unesco.

108 Toews, Rob. 2021.AlphaFold Is The Most Important Achievement In AI—Ever. Forbes. https://www.forbes.com/sites/robtoews/2021/10/03/alphafold-is-the-most-important-achievement-in-ai-ever/.

109 PDB. 2023.wwPDB: Worldwide Protein Data Bank. https://www.wwpdb.org/.

110 Press, Gil. 2020.12 AI Milestones: 4. MYCIN, An Expert System For Infectious Disease Therapy. Forbes. https://www.forbes.com/sites/gilpress/2020/04/27/12-ai-milestones-4-mycin-an-expert-system-for-infectious-disease-therapy/.

111 Powell, Alvin. 2020.Risks and benefits of an AI revolution in medicine. Harvard Gazette. https://news.harvard.edu/gazette/story/2020/11/risks-and-benefits-of-an-ai-revolution-in-medicine/.

112 Ibid.

113 Stieg, Cory. 2020. "How this Canadian start-up spotted coronavirus before everyone else knew about it." https://www.cnbc.com/2020/03/03/bluedot-used-artificial-intelligence-to-predict-coronavirus-spread.html.

114 IBM Research. 2020. "IBM RoboRXN." https://research.ibm.com/science/ibm-roborxn/.

115 Toniato, Alessandra, Oliver Schilter, and Teodoro Laino. 2023. "The Role of AI in Driving the Sustainability of the Chemical Industry." *Chimia* 77 (144). https://www.chimia.ch/chimia/article/view/6265.

116 AI, CO2. 2023.CO2 AI - The Leading End-To-End Carbon Management Software For Large Corporations. https://co2ai.com/.

117 Eva, Corlett. 2022. "Antarctic researchers gain insights from on high as they count seals from space." https://www.theguardian.com/world/2022/sep/19/antarctic-researchers-gain-insights-from-on-high-as-they-count-seals-from-space.

118 LaRue, Michelle, Leo Salas, Nadav Nur, David Ainley, Sharon Stammerjohn, Jean Pennycook, Melissa Dozier, Jon Saints, Kostas Stamatiou, Luke Barrington,

119 Jay Rotella. 2021. "Insights from the first global population estimate of Weddell seals in Antarctica." https://www.science.org/doi/10.1126/sciadv.abh3674.

120 Martínez-Sánchez, Álvaro, Eneko Lazpita, Adrián Corrochano, Soledad Le Clainche, Sergio Hoyas, and Ricardo Vinuesa. 2023. "Data-driven assessment of arch vortices in simplified urban flows." *International Journal of Heat and Fluid Flow* 100: 109-101. https://www.sciencedirect.com/science/article/pii/S0142727X22001692.

121 Spiewak, Martin. 2023. "Künstliche Intelligenz in der Schule : Die 8a gegen die KI." https://www.zeit.de/2023/08/kuenstliche-intelligenz-schule-unterricht.

CHAPTER 6: DO LOOK UP – AI'S COMPLICATED RELATIONSHIP WITH NATURE

122 Don't Look Up Quotes. 2021. MovieQuotes.com. https://www.moviequotes.com/s-movie/dont-look-up/.

123 Creutzig, Felix et al. 2022. "Digitalization and the Anthropocene." *https://doi.org/10.1146/annurev-environ-120920-100056*. https://www.annualreviews.org/doi/10.1146/annurev-environ-120920-100056.

124 Zimmermann, Erich W. 2023. *World resources and industries;: A functional appraisal of the availability of agricultural and industrial resources*. Harper.

125 Jevons, William Stanley. 1865. *The coal question : an unquiry concerning the progress of the national and the probable exhaustion of our coal-mines.* MacMillan.

126 Freitag, C., M. Berners-Lee, K. Widdicks, B. Knowles, G. S. Blair, and A. Friday. 2021. "The real climate and transformative impact of ICT: A critique of estimates, trends, and regulations." *Patterns (N Y)* 2 (9): 100340. https://www.ncbi.nlm.nih.gov/pubmed/34553177.

127 OECD. 2022. *MEASURING THE ENVIRONMENTAL IMPACTS OF AI COMPUTE AND APPLICATIONS: THE AI FOOTPRINT.* https://www.oecd-ilibrary.org/docserver/7babf571-en.pdf?expires=1686253344&id=id&accname=guest&checksum=E40DDE7AF0728EF3D66D4165EF4C6E4D.

128 "AI's carbon footprint and a DNA nanomotor — the week in infographics." 2022. *Nature.* https://www.nature.com/articles/d41586-022-02064-5.

129 CMS, Carbon Footprint Ltd using RADsite. 2023. "carbonfootprint.com - International Electricity Factors." https://www.carbonfootprint.com/international_electricity_factors.html. March 2022 data.

130 "AI's carbon footprint and a DNA nanomotor — the week in infographics." 2022. *Nature.* https://www.nature.com/articles/d41586-022-02064-5.

131 Mytton, David. 2023. "Influencing the carbon emissions of AI." https://www.devsustainability.com/p/influencing-carbon-emissions-of-ai.

132 Heikkilä, Melissa. 2023.We're getting a better idea of AI's true carbon footprint. MIT Technology Review. https://www.technologyreview.com/2022/11/14/1063192/were-getting-a-better-idea-of-ais-true-carbon-footprint/.

133 Patterson, David, Joseph Gonzalez, Quoc Le, Chen Liang, Lluis-Miquel Munguia, Daniel Rothchild, David So, Maud Texier, and Jeff Dean. 2021. "Carbon Emissions and Large Neural Network Training." https://arxiv.org/pdf/2104.10350.

134 Ludvigsen, Kasper Groes Albin. 2023. "The Carbon Footprint of ChatGPT." https://towardsdatascience.com/the-carbon-footprint-of-chatgpt-66932314627d.

135 *Children and digital dumpsites: e-waste exposure and child health.* 2021. WHO. 2019 data

136 Creutzig, Felix et al. 2022. "Digitalization and the Anthropocene." *https://doi.org/10.1146/annurev-environ-120920-100056.* https://www.annualreviews.org/doi/10.1146/annurev-environ-120920-100056.

137 Bender, Emily M., Timnit Gebru, Angelina McMillan-Major, and Shmargaret Shmitchell. 2021. "On the Dangers of Stochastic Parrots: Can Language Models Be Too Big? ." Proceedings of the 2021 ACM Conference on Fairness, Accountability, and Transparency, Virtual Event, Canada. https://doi.org/10.1145/3442188.3445922, Institute, The Alan Turing. "On the dangers of stochastic parrots: Can language models be too big? ." Embedded Video https://www.youtube.com/watch?v=N5c2X8vhfBE, Narayanan, Arvind. 2023.How to recognize AI snake oil. https://www.cs.princeton.edu/~arvindn/talks/MIT-STS-AI-snakeoil.pdf.

138 Institute, The Alan Turing. "On the dangers of stochastic parrots: Can language models be too big? ." Embedded Video https://www.youtube.com/watch?v=N5c2X8vhfBE

139 Narayanan, Arvind. 2023.How to recognize AI snake oil. https://www.cs.princeton.edu/~arvindn/talks/MIT-STS-AI-snakeoil.pdf.

140 Patterson, David, Joseph Gonzalez, Quoc Le, Chen Liang, Lluis-Miquel Munguia, Daniel Rothchild, David So, Maud Texier, and Jeff Dean. 2021. "Carbon Emissions and Large Neural Network Training." https://arxiv.org/pdf/2104.10350.

141 Lannelongue, Loïc. 2023. The Green Algorithms project. https://www.lannelongue.eu/research/green-algorithms/.

142 Greenberg, Chris. 2023. "Amazon rainforest fires 2022: Facts, causes, and climate impacts." https://www.greenpeace.org/international/story/55533/amazon-rainforest-fires-2022-brazil-causes-climate.

143 AI for the Planet. 2023. https://www.aifortheplanet.org/.

144 UN Environment. 2022. "How artificial intelligence is helping tackle environmental challenges." http://www.unep.org/news-and-stories/story/how-artificial-intelligence-helping-tackle-environmental-challenges. and UN Environment Program. 2023.World Environment Situation. https://data.unep.org/.

145 Thesing, Gabi. 2023.'Tech for good' had a very good year in 2022. Here are 6 companies that led the way. https://www.weforum.org/agenda/2023/01/tech-for-good-innovations/.

146 WWF. 2023. "What is the sixth mass extinction and what can we do about it? ." https://www.worldwildlife.org/stories/what-is-the-sixth-mass-extinction-and-what-can-we-do-about-it.

147 Biodiversity. 2023. National Geographic. https://education.nationalgeographic.org/resource/biodiversity.

148 Nature Metrics. 2023. https://www.naturemetrics.co.uk/. and Clavey, Molly. 2021. "BIOSTREAM - Bringing rainforest nature data to life." https://www.naturemetrics.co.uk/2021/04/14/introducing-biostream-bringing-rainforest-nature-data-to-life/.

149 Wildlife Insights. 2023. https://www.wildlifeinsights.org/.

150 RESET. 2020. "Wildlife Insights: A Google-Built AI is Taking Animal Surveillance to New Levels." https://en.reset.org/wildlife-insights-google-built-ai-taking-animal-surveillance-new-levels-05072020/.

151 "The Sound of Nature: Using AI to protect life on land and below water." 2020. https://programs.wcs.org/india-beta/Newsroom/Blog/ID/14299/The-Sound-of-Nature-Using-AI-to-protect-life-on-land-and-below-water.

152 Silvestro, Daniele, Stefano Goria, Thomas Sterner, and Alexandre Antonelli. 2022. "Improving biodiversity protection through artificial intelligence." *Nature Sustainability* 5 (5): 415-424. https://www.nature.com/articles/s41893-022-00851-6.

153 Grunwald, Sabine. 2022. "Artificial intelligence and soil carbon modeling demystified: power, potentials, and perils." https://oaepublish.com/cf/article/view/4791.

154 4 million euro grant for predicting and improving soil biodiversity. 2023. https://www.uu.nl/en/news/4-million-euro-grant-for-predicting-and-improving-soil-biodiversity.

155 Flash Forest is evening the odds in the fight against climate change. 2023. https://www.innovatebc.ca/blog/flash-forest-is-evening-the-odds-in-the-fight-against-climate-change.

156 Luthy, Quinn. 2022. "Reconsidering Reforestation and Tree Planting Projects." https://earth.org/reforestation-projects/.

157 "How to make Africa's 'Great Green Wall' a success." 2022. *Nature* 605 (7908): 8-8. https://www.nature.com/articles/d41586-022-01201-4.

158 Landsberg, Florence, Katie Reytar, Fred Stolle, Dow Maneerattana, Will Anderson, and John Brandt. 2020. "The Challenge of Tracking How a Trillion Trees Grow.", *Global forests*. https://www.wri.org/blog/2020/07/trillion-trees-tracking-challenges.

159 Miller, Matthew 2023. "Using Artificial Intelligence to Understand Solar Energy's Impact in India." *Nature Brains*. https://blog.nature.org/science-brief/using-artificial-intelligence-to-understand-solar-energys-impact-in-india/.

160 The role of digitisation in building back better. 2023. The Carbon Trust. https://www.carbontrust.com/news-and-insights/insights/the-role-of-digitisation-in-building-back-better.

161 Dashboard. 2023. The Ocean Cleanup. https://theoceancleanup.com/dashboard/.

162 Institute, International Food Policy Research. 2023. "SDG 12.3 - Food Loss and Food Waste: A Once in a Generation Opportunity." https://www.ifpri.org/event/123-event-food-loss-and-food-waste.

163 Winnow. 2023.Food Waste Management Technology. https://www.winnowsolutions.com/product/vision.

164 Ellen Macarthur Foundation. 2023.Artificial intelligence and the circular economy. https://ellenmacarthurfoundation.org/artificial-intelligence-and-the-circular-economy.

165 IEA. 2023.Fossil Fuels Consumption Subsidies 2022 – Analysis - IEA. IEA. https://www.iea.org/reports/fossil-fuels-consumption-subsidies-2022.

166 UN Biodiversity Lab. 2023. "Providing decision makers with the best available spatial data to put nature at the center of sustainable development." https://unbiodiversitylab.org/en/.

CHAPTER 7: ETHICS, FAILURE AND RESPONSIBILITY

167 This is a quote that could be attributed to many philosophers, but instead originates from a man named Alexander Nix. If his name is unfamiliar, the company he ran is not: Cambridge Analytica. Andrzejewski, Cécile. 2023."Team Jorge": In the heart of a global disinformation machine. Forbidden Stories. https://forbiddenstories.org/story-killers/team-jorge-disinformation/.

168 Wang, Yilun, and Michal Kosinski. 2023. "Deep neural networks are more accurate than humans at detecting sexual orientation from facial images." *Journal of Personality and Social Psychology* 114(2): 246–257. https://doi.org/10.1037/pspa0000098.

169 The Economist. 2023.Advances in AI are used to spot signs of sexuality. The Economist. https://www.economist.com/science-and-technology/2017/09/09/advances-in-ai-are-used-to-spot-signs-of-sexuality.

170 Wikipedia. 2023.Phrenology. https://en.wikipedia.org/wiki/Phrenology.

171 Agüera y Arcas, Blaise, Alexander Todorov, and Margaret Mitchell. 2018.Do algorithms reveal sexual orientation or just expose our stereotypes? Medium. https://medium.com/@blaisea/do-algorithms-reveal-sexual-orientation-or-just-expose-our-stereotypes-d998fafdf477.

172 Institute, The Alan Turing. "On the dangers of stochastic parrots: Can language models be too big? ." Embedded Video https://www.youtube.com/watch?v=N5c2X8vhfBE.

173 Coeckelbergh, Mark. 2023.Chatbots can kill. https://coeckelbergh.medium.com/chatbots-can-kill-d82fde5cf6ca.

174 Schmidt, Alice, and Claudia Winkler. 2021. *The Sustainability Puzzle: How System Change, Circularity, Climate Action and Social Transformation can improve Health, Wealth and Wellbeing for All.*

175 "CoastRunners 7." https://www.youtube.com/watch?v=tlOIHko8ySg.

176 Ai, Open. 2023.Faulty reward functions in the wild. OpenAI. https://openai.com/research/faulty-reward-functions.

177 Pemberton, Max. 2023.Medical myths: Spinach is full of iron. Readers Digest UK. https://www.readersdigest.co.uk/health/health-conditions/medical-myths-spinach-is-full-of-iron.

178 Wikipedia. 2023.List of scientific misconduct incidents. https://en.wikipedia.org/wiki/List_of_scientific_misconduct_incidents.

179 Wikipedia. 2023.Open source. https://en.wikipedia.org/wiki/Open_source.

180 Netcraft News. 2023.Web Server Survey. https://news.netcraft.com/archives/category/web-server-survey/.

181 Wikipedia. 2023.BLOOM (language model). https://en.wikipedia.org/wiki/BLOOM_(language_model).

182 Wikipedia. 2023.LLaMA. https://en.wikipedia.org/wiki/LLaMA.

183 AI, Meta. 2023. Introducing LLaMA: A foundational, 65-billion-parameter large language model.

184 Mori, Giancarlo. 2023.The Technical Side of XAI. Medium. https://gcmori.medium.com/the-technical-side-of-xai-fe059396d017.

185 NYU Web Communications. 2023.When a Tesla on Autopilot Kills Someone, Who Is Responsible? http://www.nyu.edu/content/nyu/en/about/news-publications/news/2022/march/when-a-tesla-on-autopilot-kills-someone—who-is-responsible—.

186 Dawson, Aimee. 2018.Facebook censors 30,000 year-old Venus of Willendorf as 'pornographic'. The Art Newspaper. https://www.theartnewspaper.com/2018/02/27/facebook-censors-30000-year-old-venus-of-willendorf-as-pornographic.

187 Darcy, Oliver. 2022.Elon Musk bans several prominent journalists from Twitter, calling into question his commitment to free speech | CNN Business. CNN Business. https://www.cnn.com/2022/12/15/media/twitter-musk-journalists-hnk-intl/index.html.

188 I, Robot. 2004. https://www.imdb.com/title/tt0343818/.

189 Mortensen, John. 2023.Can an AI Create Another AI? Tech Evaluate. https://techevaluate.com/can-an-ai-create-another-ai/.

190 New AI improves itself through Darwinian-style evolution. 2023. Big Think. https://bigthink.com/the-present/automl/.

191 Researchers Build AI That Builds AI. 2022. Quanta Magazine. https://www.quantamagazine.org/researchers-build-ai-that-builds-ai-20220125/.

192 BrandPost. 2022.4 Reasons Why Companies are Using AutoML. https://www.cio.com/article/405608/4-reasons-why-companies-are-using-automl.html.

193 Vienna Manifesto on Digital Humanism. 2019. Dighum. https://caiml.dbai.tuwien.ac.at/dighum/dighum-manifesto/.

CHAPTER 8: POLITICS, POWER, AND PEACE

194 Coldewey, Devin. 2023.Ethicists fire back at 'AI Pause' letter they say 'ignores the actual harms'. Tech Crunch. https://techcrunch.com/2023/03/31/ethicists-fire-back-at-ai-pause-letter-they-say-ignores-the-actual-harms/.

195 Connolly, Kate. 2022.KFC apologises for Kristallnacht chicken and cheese promotion. Guardian. https://www.theguardian.com/world/2022/nov/10/kfc-apologises-for-kristallnacht-chicken-and-cheese-promotion.

196 Binley, Alex. 2023.KFC apologises after German Kristallnacht promotion. BBC World. https://www.bbc.com/news/world-europe-63499057.

197 Stark , Holger, and Fritz Zimmermann 2023.Desinformationsfirma "Team Jorge": Sie manipulieren die Welt. Zeit online. https://www.zeit.de/2023/08/desinformation-team-jorge-social-media-storykillers.

198 Andrzejewski, Cécile. 2023."Team Jorge": In the heart of a global disinformation machine. Forbidden Stories. https://forbiddenstories.org/story-killers/team-jorge-disinformation/.

199 Ibid.

200 DemTech. 2023.Industrialized Disinformation: 2020 Global Inventory of Organized Social Media Manipulation. DemTech. https://demtech.oii.ox.ac.uk/research/posts/industrialized-disinformation/.

201 Hambling, David. 2023.The US Navy wants swarms of thousands of small drones. MIT Technology Review. https://www.technologyreview.com/2022/10/24/1062039/us-navy-swarms-of-thousands-of-small-drones/.

202 Moonraker. 1979. https://www.imdb.com/title/tt0079574/.

203 Wikipedia. 2023.Manned Orbiting Laboratory. https://en.wikipedia.org/wiki/Manned_Orbiting_Laboratory.

204 The Terminator. 1984. https://www.imdb.com/title/tt0088247/.

205 "I Could Solve Most of Your Problems': Eric Schmidt's Pentagon Offensive." 2020. https://www.nytimes.com/subscription/gateway/subcon/variants/variant-5.html.

206 Will, Knight. 2023.Eric Schmidt Is Building the Perfect AI War-Fighting Machine. Wired. https://www.wired.com/story/eric-schmidt-is-building-the-perfect-ai-war-fighting-machine/.

207 DoD Announces Dr. Craig Martell as Chief Digital and Artificial Intelligence Officer. 2022. U.S. Department of Defense. https://www.defense.gov/News/Releases/Release/Article/3009684/dod-announces-dr-craig-martell-as-chief-digital-and-artificial-intelligence-off/.

208 Wikipedia. 2023.Peter Thiel. https://en.wikipedia.org/wiki/Peter_Thiel.

209 Wikipedia. 2023.Palantir Technologies. https://en.wikipedia.org/wiki/Palantir_Technologies.

210 Daws, Ryan. 2023.Palantir demos how AI can be used in the military. @ai_technews. https://www.artificialintelligence-news.com/2023/04/28/palantir-demos-how-ai-can-used-military/.

211 Statista. 2022.Largest military spenders worldwide 2022. https://www.statista.com/statistics/262742/countries-with-the-highest-military-spending/.

212 Wikipedia. 2023.PRISM. Wikipedia. https://en.wikipedia.org/wiki/PRISM.

213 Wikipedia. 2023.XKeyscore. https://en.wikipedia.org/wiki/XKeyscore.

214 Wikipedia. 2023.Edward Snowden. https://en.wikipedia.org/wiki/Edward_Snowden.

215 Wikipedia. 2023.Five Eyes. https://en.wikipedia.org/wiki/Five_Eyes.

216 Largest tech companies by market cap. 2023. https://companiesmarketcap.com/tech/largest-tech-companies-by-market-cap/.

217 WarGames. 1983. https://www.imdb.com/title/tt0086567/.

218 Labuschagne, Hanno. 2023.ChatGPT passes Google's coding job test. My broad band. https://mybroadband.co.za/news/software/479059-chatgpt-passes-googles-coding-job-test.html.

219 ChatGPT outperforms 85% of the 4 million programmers assessed on Python on LinkedIn. 2023. https://courses.cfte.education/chatgpt-outperforms-4m-programmers/.

220 The Circle. 2017. https://www.imdb.com/title/tt4287320/.

221 AI Index Report. 2023. Stanford University. https://aiindex.stanford.edu/report/.

222 Rockwell, Anyoha. 2017. "The History of Artificial Intelligence - Can Machines Think?", *Harvard University*. https://sitn.hms.harvard.edu/flash/2017/history-artificial-intelligence/. and Wikipedia. 2023.Timeline of artificial intelligence. https://en.wikipedia.org/wiki/Timeline_of_artificial_intelligence.

223 Wallach, Omri. 2021.The World's Tech Giants, Compared to the Size of Economies. Visual Cap. https://www.visualcapitalist.com/the-tech-giants-worth-compared-economies-countries/.

224 Ramos, Gabriela, and Mariana Mazzucato. 2022.AI in the Common Interest. Project Syndicate. https://www.project-syndicate.org/commentary/ethical-ai-requires-state-regulatory-frameworks-capacity-building-by-gabriela-ramos-and-mariana-mazzucato-2022-12.

225 Ibid.

226 Leslie, David. 2019.Understanding artificial intelligence ethics and safety: A guide for the responsible design and implementation of AI systems in the public sector. https://doi.org/10.5281/zenodo.3240529.

227 Pause Giant AI Experiments: An Open Letter. 2023. Future of Life Institute. https://futureoflife.org/open-letter/pause-giant-ai-experiments/.

228 Statement on AI Risk. 2023. Center for AI Safety. https://www.safe.ai/statement-on-ai-risk#open-letter, Vallance, Chris. 2023. "Artificial intelligence could lead to extinction, experts warn." https://www.bbc.com/news/uk-65746524.

229 Munn, Luke. 2023. "The five tests: designing and evaluating AI according to indigenous Māori principles." *AI & SOCIETY*: 1-9. https://link.springer.com/article/10.1007/s00146-023-01636-x.

230 Feingold, Spencer. 2023.The EU's Artificial Intelligence Act, explained. WEF. https://www.weforum.org/agenda/2023/03/the-european-union-s-ai-act-explained/. and Regulatory framework proposal on artificial intelligence. 2023. European Commision. https://digital-strategy.ec.europa.eu/en/policies/regulatory-framework-ai.

231 Bender, Emily. 2023.Policy makers: Please don't fall for the distractions of #AIhype. Medium. https://medium.com/@emilymenonbender/policy-makers-please-dont-fall-for-the-distractions-of-aihype-e03fa80ddbf1.

CHAPTER 9: SHAPING A MEANINGFUL FUTURE

232 Hawking, Stephen. 2016. ""The best or worst thing to happen to humanity"." 2016-10-19, University of Cambridge. https://www.cam.ac.uk/research/news/the-best-or-worst-thing-to-happen-to-humanity-stephen-hawking-launches-centre-for-the-future-of.

233 Creutzig, Felix et al. 2022. "Digitalization and the Anthropocene." *https://doi.org/10.1146/annurev-environ-120920-100056*. https://www.annualreviews.org/doi/10.1146/annurev-environ-120920-100056.

234 Clifford, Catherine. 2018.Google CEO: A.I. is more important than fire or electricity. CNBC. https://www.cnbc.com/2018/02/01/google-ceo-sundar-pichai-ai-is-more-important-than-fire-electricity.html.

235 Creutzig, Felix et al. 2022. "Digitalization and the Anthropocene." *https://doi.org/10.1146/annurev-environ-120920-100056*. https://www.annualreviews.org/doi/10.1146/annurev-environ-120920-100056.

236 DAIR (Distributed AI Research Institute). 2023. DAIR Institute. https://www.dair-institute.org/.

237 Partnership on AI. 2023. https://partnershiponai.org/.

238 AI for Good. 2023. ITU AI For Good. https://aiforgood.itu.int/.

239 Werthner, Hannes, Erich Prem, Edward A. Lee, Carlo Ghezzi, and SpringerLink. 2022. *Perspectives on Digital Humanism*. 1st 2022. ed. Cham: Springer International Publishing : Imprint: Springer.

240 Wien, Stadt. 2022.Digitaler Humanismus in Wien. https://www.wien.gv.at/forschung/wissenschaft/digitaler-humanismus-broschuere.html.

241 Mukherjee, Supantha, and Giselda Vagnoni. 2023.Italy restores ChatGPT after OpenAI responds to regulator. Reuters. https://www.reuters.com/technology/chatgpt-is-available-again-users-italy-spokesperson-says-2023-04-28/.

242 Lomas, Natasha. 2023. "EU and US lawmakers move to draft AI Code of Conduct fast." https://techcrunch.com/2023/05/31/ai-code-of-conduct-us-eu-ttc/.

243 Delcker, Janosch. 2019. "Finland's grand AI experiment." https://www.politico.eu/article/finland-one-percent-ai-artificial-intelligence-courses-learning-training/.

Printed in Great Britain
by Amazon

29724922R00131